# Local government today

MANCHESTER
1824

Manchester University Press

# Politics Today

Series editor: Bill Jones

# Local government today

### Fourth edition

## J.A. Chandler

## Manchester University Press
### Manchester and New York

distributed exclusively in the USA by Palgrave

The right of J.A. Chandler to be identified as the author of this work has been assserted by him in accordance with the Copyright, Designs and Patents Act 1988.

*Published by* Manchester University Press
Oxford Road, Manchester M13 9NR, UK
*and* Room 400, 175 Fifth Avenue, New York, NY 10010, USA
www.manchesteruniversitypress.co.uk

*Distributed in the United States exclusively by*
Palgrave, 175 Fifth Avenue, New York,
NY 10010, USA

*Distributed in Canada exclusively by*
UBC Press, University of British Columbia, 2029 West Mall,
Vancouver, BC, Canada V6T 1Z2

*British Library Cataloguing-in-Publication Data*
A catalogue record for this book is available from the British Library

*Library of Congress Cataloging-in-Publication Data applied for*

ISBN   978 0 7190 7695 4   *paperback*

First published 2009

18  17  16  15  14  13  12  11  10  09      10  9  8  7  6  5  4  3  2  1

Typeset in Monotype Photina
by Servis Filmsetting Ltd, Stockport, Cheshire
Printed by the MPG Books Group in the UK

# Contents

# List of maps, figures and tables

## Maps

## Figures

## Tables

# Preface and acknowledgements

Local government ought to be seen as a far more important institution than is often suggested by the popular press. Local government is important not only because of the many services it provides to the citizens of Britain, but also its far from realised capacity to contribute to a more democratic, free and humane society. This study develops a challenging critique and interpretation of the role of local government in Britain today and how the system evolved into its present state. Thus the study aims to provide an understanding of the value and potential of the system of local government in Britain.

This book is intended to explain the structure and processes of local government in Britain for degree level, BTEC and 'A' and 'AS' students of politics, public sector studies, business studies and economics. It should also be of more general interest to anyone working in or with local government or more generally concerned with how the system is changing.

There have been many changes to the system of local government in Britain since the third edition was published in 2001. Structurally the 2000 Local Government Act has revolutionised the way in which local authorities make decisions and ushered in the probability of directly elected mayors as significant political figures in Britain. Managerially the implementation of Best Value will also have major repercussions on the process of local management. Perhaps the most significant change in the operation of local government that is considered in this book is the emergence of local authorities as agents facilitating in partnership with other public, voluntary and private sector organisations the governance of communities.

The British local government system should not, however, be viewed as particularly typical of the local government structures of other major liberal democracies. When considered in a comparative perspective British local government has some rather strange features, most of all illustrated in the size of its units, its lack of smaller community based structures and the centralisation of the system. This study places the system in comparative perspective through a series of inserted highlighted paragraphs which, if read separately, will also

ix

provide a basic introduction to the structure of local government in the larger countries of the European Union and the United States.

Acknowledgement and thanks are due to the many organisations and individuals who have helped me with this edition. Among my many academic colleagues particular thanks go to John and Ann Kingdom, Ralph Spence and Roger Ottewill. Outside Sheffield Hallam University this book has been greatly helped over the years through conversations with Michael Cole, Colin Copus, Professor Howard Elcock, John Fenwick, Chris Game, Josie Kelly, Professor Steve Leach, Professor Rod Rhodes, Mike Smith and Professor David Wilson, to name but a few. I have also received valuable help from local councillors and officers including Sir Robert Kerslake.

The diagrams in the book have been much improved by Daniel Smith.

Last but not least my wife Krys has as usual facilitated the completion of the edition by allowing me space and time to write and research.

# List of abbreviations

| | |
|---|---|
| AMICUS | is not an acronym but the Union's name |
| BBC | British Broadcasting Corporation |
| CCT | compulsory competitive tendering |
| CIPFA | Chartered Institute for Public Finance and Accountancy |
| CLP | Central Local Partnership |
| CND | Campaign for Nuclear Disarmament |
| COSHE | Confederation of Health Service Employees |
| CoSLA | Confederation of Scottish Local Authorities |
| CPA | Comprehensive Performance Assessment |
| CSO | Central Statistical Office (now Office of National Statistics) |
| DCLG | Department of Communities and Local Government |
| DETR | Department of the Environment, Transport and the Regions |
| ERA | Education Reform Act (of 1988) |
| ESRC | Economic and Social Research Council |
| FSS | Formula Spending Share |
| GCSE | General Certificate of Secondary Education |
| GLA | Greater London Authority |
| GLC | Greater London Council |
| GMB | General Municipal and Boilermakers Union |
| HMSO | Her Majesty's Stationary Office |
| IDeA | Improvement and Development Agency for Local Government |
| JP | justice of the peace |
| LAA | Local Area Agreement |
| LEA | Local Education Authority |
| LG | Local government |
| LGA | Local Government Association |
| LPSA | Local Public Service Agreement |
| LSP | Local Strategic Partnership |
| MDC | Metropolitan District Council |
| MHLG | Ministry of Housing and Local Government |

| MIND | National Association for Mental Health |
|------|---------------------------------------|
| MP | Member of Parliament |
| NALGO | National Association of Local Government Officers |
| NHS | National Health Service |
| NPM | New Public Management |
| NSPCC | National Society for the Protection of Cruelty to Children |
| NUPE | National Union of Public Employees |
| NVQ | National Vocational Qualification |
| OFSTED | Office for Standards in Education |
| PFI | Private Finance Initiative |
| QUANGO | Quasi autonomous national government organisation |
| RDA | Regional Development Agency |
| SNP | Scottish National Party |
| SOLACE | Society for Local Authority Chief Executives and senior managers |
| SRB | single regeneration budget |
| SSA | Standard Spending Assessment |
| STV | single transferable vote |
| TAS | Total Assumed Spending |
| TUC | Trades Union Congress |
| UCATT | Union of Construction and Allied Trades and Technicians |
| UDC | Urban Development Corporation |
| UNISON | is not an acronym but the Union's name |
| UNITE | is not an acronym but the Union's name |

# 1

# The local government system: an introduction

Local government is a unique and valuable institution. It is the only organisation subject to election by all registered voters of Britain other than the national and regional legislatures. As such it should have an authority in the governance of the Nation second only to Parliament.

### What is local government?

In Britain, 'local government' refers to the elected authorities and dependent agencies that are established by Parliament to provide a range of specified services and represent the general interests of a specific area. The web of public and private agencies that supply the needs of communities is, however, far wider than just the local authority. In recent years many authors have observed that Britain is subject to local governance, rather than simply local government (Rhodes 1999: xiii). This is to emphasise that local authorities do not have a unique role in supplying the needs of their communities. The government of a locality involves many non-elected agencies such as health trusts, regional development authorities, colleges of further and higher education, and housing associations. Private as well as public agencies are also involved in the provision of collective services through the supply of essential services such as water, gas and electricity.

Local government should, nevertheless, be valued in a democracy more highly than the numerous other bodies that also shape aspects of urban and rural life. It differs from other agencies that supply local services in two important respects:

1 Local authorities are the only agencies representing communities in Britain whose councillors are chosen by elections open to all adult citizens of that community. Thus, local authorities not only provide many services, they can also claim to represent the views and aspirations of their communities.

2  Local authorities supply a large range of services rather than, as in the case of many *ad-hoc* agencies or quangos, a small number of specific tasks. They are, therefore, capable of co-ordinating many separate functions and determining a strategy for the well-being and development of a community as a whole.

## The constitutional status of local government

Local government can trace its origins to Anglo-Saxon times before England, let alone Britain, had coalesced into a unified nation. Nevertheless, throughout this century governments have operated on the principle that local government only exists by grace and favour of the state. A Government Enquiry into political parties and local government in 1986, typically, states that

> It would be wrong to assume that constitutional convention amounts to or derives from any natural right for local government to exist. It is a convention based on, and subject to, the contribution that local government can bring to good government. It follows from this that there is no validity in the assertion that local authorities have a 'local mandate' by which they derive their authority from their electorate placing them above the law. (Widdicombe 1986: 46, para. 3.6)

Local government in Britain exists by virtue of Acts of Parliament. The structures, functions, funding and many of the processes of local authorities are determined by law. If a local authority operates outside this framework, it may be held by the courts to be acting *ultra vires* and obliged to stop its unlawful action. However, legislation by the Blair Governments has widened the discretion local authorities may have to undertake actions which they feel are beneficial to their community, albeit within rather tight restrictions. In Scotland the power to determine how local government is structured and what it can do has been devolved from the Westminster Parliament to the Scottish Assembly whilst in Wales the Assembly can, within limits set by the British Government, also determine the shape of its local government structures.

> In most Western liberal democracies local, as opposed to federal government, is organised through ordinary legislation rather than constitutional arrangements. In some federal systems, such as the United States, it is the states and not the national government that determine the structure and powers of local authorities.

## The range and functions of local government

All areas of Britain are divided into local authorities and there are in total over 10,000 local governments. The great majority are, however, legally classified as 'minor authorities'. These are the parish, town and community councils, which can provide only a few services and have very restricted funding. The number of principal authorities, that is, those with major responsibilities in England, Wales and Scotland in 2008 was but 442, but by 2009 this will be reduced by at least a further 27 English districts to 415. The design for the principal structures of local government is based on single tier and two tier structures. Where a single tier authority is established there is but one principal local authority covering that particular area. If a two tier system is present the tasks administered by local government are divided between a smaller district authority and a larger county in which there will be several districts. The two tiers are not, however, in an organisational hierarchy so that the smaller 'lower' tier of government is not subject to control by the larger 'upper' tier as both are given a separate range of functions.

In Britain there has been an increasing enthusiasm for a simple structure of a single tier of local government. Such a structure, at least as far as principal authorities are concerned, has been secured in Wales, which has 22 unitary authorities, as shown in Map 1.1, and in Scotland, which is structured into 32 districts as illustrated in Map 1.2.

Two tier structures are only present in England and, apart from London, cover predominantly rural areas. Unitary local governments in England exist in large conurbations that came into existence in 1974 as metropolitan areas. Although they initially had a two tier structure, the 6 metropolitan counties were abolished in 1985, leaving local government in these areas under the control of 36 single tier metropolitan districts. In the first half of the 1990s a further restructuring of the system established in some larger towns and a few counties 46 single tier, unitary local governments. In England the 2007 Local Government Act invites local authorities to put forward proposals for establishing themselves as a unitary authority by themselves or by combining with other authorities. There are 34 counties and 238 districts associated with this system. Following the Greater London Authority Act of 1999 that came into force in July 2000, London is governed for certain purposes by the London Authority and for others by 32 London boroughs plus the separate City of London. These arrangements for England and Wales are illustrated in Map 1.1.

The distribution of functions in two tier authorities outside London, which will be discussed later on, is shown in Table 1.1. Some services, it should be noted, are shared. A district for example may repair minor roads in its area leaving maintenance of more important roads to the county or the national Highways Agency. Where there is but one tier of government then all of these functions become the responsibility of the single local authority.

*Joint boards for police, fire and transport services*

During the first half of the twentieth century police and fire services were the responsibility of county councils and county boroughs. However, the merger of

| | |
|---|---|
| 1 NEWCASTLE UPON TYNE | 11 BLACKPOOL |
| 2 NORTH TYNESIDE | 12 SEFTON |
| 3 SOUTH TYNESIDE | 13 WIRRAL |
| 4 SUNDERLAND | 14 LIVERPOOL |
| 5 GATESHEAD | 15 HALTON |
| 6 HARTLEPOOL | 16 KNOWSLEY |
| 7 REDCAR & CLEVELAND | 17 ST HELENS |
| 8 MIDDLESBROUGH | 18 WARRINGTON |
| 9 STOCKTON-ON-TEES | 19 WIGAN |
| 10 DARLINGTON | 20 TRAFFORD |

| | |
|---|---|
| 21 SALFORD | 31 KIRKLEES |
| 22 BOLTON | 32 BARNSLEY |
| 23 BLACKBURN WITH | 33 SHEFFIELD |
| DARWEN | 34 ROTHERHAM |
| 24 BURY | 35 DONCASTER |
| 25 MANCHESTER | 36 WAKEFIELD |
| 26 STOCKPORT | 37 BRADFORD |
| 27 TAMESIDE | 38 CITY OF KINGSTON |
| 28 OLDHAM | UPON HULL |
| 29 ROCHDALE | 39 NORTH EAST LINCOLNSHIRE |
| 30 CALDERDALE | 40 TELFORD AND WREKIN |
| | 41 CITY OF STOKE-ON-TRENT |

| |
|---|
| 72 DENBIGHSHIRE |
| 73 FLINTSHIRE |
| 74 WREXHAM |
| 75 SWANSEA |
| 76 NEATH PORT TALBOT |
| 77 BRIDGEND |
| 78 RHONDDA CYNON, TAFF |
| 79 THE VALE OF GLAMORGAN |
| 80 MERTHYR TYDFIL |
| 81 CAERPHILLY |
| 82 CARDIFF |
| 83 TORFAEN |
| 84 NEWPORT |
| 85 MONMOUTHSHIRE |

| | | |
|---|---|---|
| 42 CITY OF DERBY | 52 COVENTRY | 62 SLOUGH |
| 43 CITY OF NOTTINGHAM | 53 LUTON | 63 THURROCK |
| 44 CITY OF LEICESTER | 54 NORTH SOMERSET | 64 SOUTHEND-ON-SEA |
| 45 CITY OF PETERBOROUGH | 55 CITY OF BRISTOL | 65 MEDWAY |
| 46 CITY OF WOLVERHAMPTON | 56 SOUTH GLOUCESTERSHIRE | 66 CITY OF PLYMOUTH |
| 47 WALSALL | 57 BATH & NE SOMERSET | 67 POOLE |
| 48 DUDLEY | 58 READING | 68 BOURNEMOUTH |
| 49 SANDWELL | 59 WOKINGHAM | 69 CITY OF SOUTHAMPTON |
| 50 BIRMINGHAM | 60 BRACKNELL FOREST | 70 CITY OF PORTSMOUTH |
| 51 SOLIHULL | 61 WINDSOR & MAIDENHEAD | 71 CITY OF BRIGHTON & HOVE |

Map 1.1  *English and Welsh local authorities*

smaller police services and the abolition of the metropolitan county councils
have resulted in many police and some fire services being shared between a
number of county or unitary authorities through joint boards or authorities.
There are currently 43 police authorities in England and Wales but some recent
home secretaries have put forward plans to reduce this number. The committees for police administration also include magistrates and other personnel
appointed by the secretary of state for justice and are, therefore, not wholly
under local government jurisdiction. In London the police and fire services are

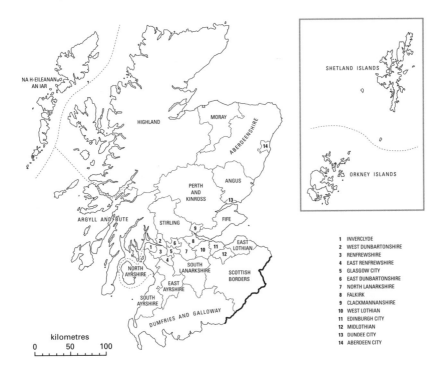

Map 1.2  *Scottish district authorities*

Table 1.1 *Function of local authorities*

| Function | County | District | Unitary |
|---|---|---|---|
| Education | * | | * |
| Housing | | * | * |
| Social services | * | | * |
| Highways | * | * | * |
| Transport | * | | |
| Museums and art galleries | * | * | * |
| Libraries | * | | * |
| Planning | | * | * |
| Strategic planning | * | | * |
| Economic development | * | * | * |
| Recreation, parks, sports facilities | * | * | * |
| Weights and measures | * | | * |
| Food and health inspection | * | | * |
| Cemeteries | | * | * |
| Markets | | * | * |

Table 1.2 *Minor authorities*

| Area | Minor authorities |
|------|-------------------|
| London | No parishes |
| Metropolitan districts | A few parishes or town councils in more rural areas |
| English unitary authorities | Parish and town councils in more rural areas |
| Two tier areas | Predominantly parish or town councils |
| Scotland and Wales | Community councils in rural areas |

administered by the Greater London Authority although prior to its creation they were directly under the authority of central government, which assigned them to Home Office supervision. Scotland has 8 police forces whose members are drawn from councillors nominated by the districts within a police board's area. There are 48 fire services in England and Wales and 8 in Scotland, some of which are governed by a single county council or, in Scotland, a district council, whilst others are merged under joint boards formed by councillors nominated by member authorities. Joint boards to operate local bus services were also established in metropolitan areas with the abolition of the metropolitan county councils. Following deregulation and privatisation of most bus services these boards now have a largely planning function.

### *Minor authorities*

The many minor authorities in England are parish or town councils and in Scotland and Wales are community councils. The evolution of local government in Britain has led to a peculiarly disjointed distribution of minor authorities in Britain. They cover predominantly rural areas and small towns and are only occasionally present in cities. A parish or community council in England can apply to the Department for Communities and Local Government (DCLG) to become a town council. This status allows its chair to be dignified as mayor of the community but conveys no other significant duties. This structure is summarised in Table 1.2.

The functions of parishes are discretionary and many are but forums for the discussion of local problems. Parishes can, however, provide for the recreation and cultural and economic development of their communities. A few parishes, generally larger town councils, have taken up these duties and provide sports facilities, parks, museums and arts festivals or have installed closed circuit surveillance cameras in town centres. Parishes also have the right to be consulted on planning issues affecting their areas and may be involved in street lighting. In general, most parish and community councils wish simply to raise local issues with larger more powerful local authorities but, potentially, they have a greater capacity to affect their areas than is often realised.

Table 1.3 *Population of lower tier authorities*

|  | Average population of lower tier |
| --- | --- |
| Britain: metropolitan, non-metropolitan districts and unitary authorities | 139,300 |
| Belgium: municipalities | 17,000 |
| Denmark: municipalities | 19,000 |
| Ireland: cities and boroughs | 93,000 |
| France: communes | 1,500 |
| Germany: gemeinden | 9,000 |
| Italy: communes | 7,120 |
| Netherlands: municipalities | 49,000 |
| Portugal: municipalities | 32,349 |
| Spain: municipalities | 4,877 |
| USA New York State: cities and towns | 19,389 |

*Source:* National Population from International Institute for Democracy and Electoral Assistance (IDeA) at www.idea.int and number of authorities from www.carlbro/library/subnat/RLGinEU. For New York State www.infoplease.com/ina/A0108252.

### British local government: an odd case among liberal democracies

As shown in Table 1.3, very few larger countries follow the British trend towards establishing local government with executive powers in single tier communities encompassing large populations.

> In the larger countries of Western Europe, such as France, Italy and Spain, local government is built up from a base of relatively small community governments, with a second larger tier covering areas equivalent to the British county and a third regional tier which in Italy and France deals with economic planning and in Spain has a wide range of powers devolved from central government. In the United States the regional tier, the States, have the power to structure their local government systems. Almost all States have small community governments, often called cities despite their size, alongside larger city governments such as Chicago with a larger county-wide government above these. Despite many cities being only the size of an English parish, they have substantive powers to determine how refuse is collected or local roads are maintained. Usually these tasks are contracted out to private companies or may be provided by voluntary co-operative arrangements between these communities. Small communities may even provide a police force and fire service.

### Why local government?

There have been numerous government enquiries into local government and its functions during the twentieth century and also much academic and political writing on this vital institution. It is possible to identify from this literature a muddled but generally consistent set of arguments that are used to justify the role of local government within the British administrative system. The most influential British theorist on the role of local government is the nineteenth century Utilitarian John Stuart Mill, who set within his wider vision for democratic government and liberty a role for local government that has been instrumental in shaping the system in Britain for the last 150 years. Mill accepted the well established point that central government bureaucrats, however wise and learned, cannot be as knowledgeable on, for example, the best site for a school in Inverness or Chorlton-cum-Hardy as the elected representatives of the people who live in those areas. 'It is but a small portion of the public business of a country that can be well done, or safely attended to by the central authorities' (Mill 1975: 361). Similarly a modern report on local government finance observes that

> If all public services were provided directly by the government and ministers were formally accountable to Parliament for all local decisions, the machinery of government would become even more overloaded. (Layfield 1976: 53, para. 15)

and, as stated more recently, local government can ensure

> economy in resource utilisation in a society which cannot afford the waste of national standards unrelated to local perceptions of need. (Jones and Stewart 1983: 10)

Justifications for local government based solely on the institution's capacity to deliver efficient services or take some of the administrative load from central government, do not, however, in themselves require elected, as opposed to appointed, councils to achieve these tasks. Service delivery can be secured by unelected quangos such as the health trusts or privatised businesses such as water companies. Local government as the only other institution of the state elected by all citizens must be justified by additional arguments. It was argued by J.S. Mill (1975: 365) that participation in local government can be an important means of ensuring that citizens and politicians gain a mature education in the values required to establish a stable democracy. Jones and Stewart consider that an essential value of local government is its capacity for enhancing 'democracy and self government in a society which cannot afford to entrust control over bureaucracy to twenty-one ministers and 650 MPs' (1983: 10).

Government reports have all endorsed the importance of local government for securing democracy in Britain. Widdicombe divides this contribution into the areas of participation, responsiveness and pluralism (1986: 47, para. 3.11). An effective democracy requires that many of its citizens participate in the political system. Local government ensures that there is a much greater opportunity for people to be involved as councillors in making the decisions that affect their communities and also greater opportunities to affect the decisions of councillors through activity in local parties and interest groups. A democracy must also respond to the many requirements of its members. It is more likely that different needs expressed by geographical communities can be satisfied by locally democratic governments that are subject to influence by these varying demands. The pluralist theory of democracy developed by theorists such as R.A. Dahl (1961, 1971) maintains that power should be spread throughout society and no single organisation can be completely dominant. Where power is concentrated in governments, the principle of election can ensure that those who lead governments must respond to the demands of the many interests in society if they are to win elections and remain in office. Local governments are, therefore, important for spreading power and also establishing authoritative organisations concerned with local issues whose leaders will be sensitive to the wishes of local groups.

### Inconsistencies and omissions

Whilst these justifications for local government are rarely subject to criticism, it must be questioned whether they are sufficiently robust as a defence of local institutions in Britain. The arguments favouring local government tend to be instrumental. The institution is valued as it lightens the load of central government, improves and co-ordinates service delivery, and enhances democracy. What is omitted from such justifications are arguments that value local government as important *in itself* rather than because it enhances the well being of the Nation as a whole. Liberal theory maintains that individuals should be free to conduct any activity provided it does not harm others. J.S. Mill argued that

> the liberty of the individual, in things wherein the individual is alone concerned, implies a corresponding liberty in any number of individuals to regulate by mutual agreement such things as regard them jointly, and regard no persons but themselves. (Mill 1975: 125)

This implies that if an elected government of a community wishes to act in its own interest without harming others external to that community it should be allowed to do so. In many countries communities are seen to have a right to express their views and to retain their integrity. Britain only adhered to the European Charter of Local Self Government under the Blair Government in 1997. This document establishes a right for local authorities 'to regulate and manage a substantial share of public affairs under their own responsibility and in the interests of the local population'. (Article 3.1) The European Union values the concept of 'subsidiarity', which is the principle that power ought to be passed down to the smallest political unit within a society that is capable of undertaking a required public function. British political culture pays little regard to this value. The subsidiarity principle entails that if district authorities can, for example, manage the housing issues of a community they should be empowered to undertake that function rather than national or regional governments.

In Britain the now rather neglected nineteenth century campaigner against centralisation, Joshua Toulmin Smith, argued that local self-government was the basis for ensuring freedom of the individual. His theory followed liberal ideals that individuals should have as much freedom as possible but accepted that people must on occasion provide services collectively for themselves. If each individual could participate directly in the policy process necessary for securing these collective services, they would have greater freedom to shape that policy. The larger the community devising a policy the greater the number of opinions that must be weighed in the decision making process and, as a consequence, each individual will have, potentially, less power and freedom to influence decisions. Thus, individual freedom is enhanced where decisions are made by direct participation in the smallest governments capable of efficiently providing a necessary communal service.

> Alexis de Tocqueville, the early nineteenth century French theorist who analysed the politics of the United States, provided a powerful liberal justification for this principle. De Tocqueville found such a bastion of liberty in the small townships of New England where, as in some towns today, all the citizens of a town met regularly to decide their local policies. Whilst direct democracy exists in only a few local authorities in the United States, there remains a strong ethos in the Nation that local communities are an expression of local independence and hence, compared with Britain, local people are very resistant to changing local government boundaries.

The failure in Britain to establish clear ethical grounds for the existence of local government in its own right rather than expedientially as a means of enhancing administrative efficiency and democratic stability of the government of the Nation has laid the grounds for the constant stream of changes in the structure and powers of local government and the erosion of its capacity to allow local communities to determine policies that affect themselves alone. A prevailing attitude as expressed by the Widdicombe Report's assertion that local government in Britain has no right to exist except by permission of Parliament allows the state to legislate so as to interfere in local actions when the government of the day feels that this is in the interests of its party leaders. Since competing political parties are increasingly seeking to show they are better able than their rivals to deliver efficient but effective public services at little cost to the taxpayer, they cannot afford to leave decisions on local services such as public housing or social services solely to the choices of local electors but must constantly set targets and monitor the provision of these services to satisfy national rather than local opinion. In the absence in Britain of a clear understanding of the differing ethical tasks that should be assigned to local and national government, the inevitable consequences of electoral competition increasingly undermine the autonomy of local government.

## Further reading

A considerable number of general textbooks on local government in Britain that gave an overview of the system were published in the 1990s. Byrne (1992), Elcock (1991) and Kingdom (1991) could be recommended and provide a sound analysis of the system at that time. Care must, however, be taken to refer to books that have editions later than 2000 as change to the system has been so extensive since then that any earlier study will describe aspects of the system that are no longer in force. General overviews, in addition to this volume, that are sufficiently up to date and can be widely recommended are Wilson and Game (2006) and Leach and Percy-Smith (2001). Local government in Scotland is detailed in McConnell (2004). Putting local government in a wider context of the British administrative system, Greenwood, Pyper and Wilson (2002) is a valuable text and for British politics as a whole, Kingdom (2003) is highly readable.

Introductory textbooks need to be descriptive in order to help those unfamiliar with the system, and can often provide little interpretation of how local government has developed or relate the system to wider political theories. There are texts that assume more prior knowledge and have more space for greater depth but give an interpretation of recent developments of the system. Important studies include Stoker (2000) and Stewart (2000, 2003).

Justifications for local government became a concern among writers in the mid-1980s and there are a number of studies that touch on this area. Widdicombe (1986) is a good example of the 'official' view but a more expansive position is provided by Jones and Stewart (1983) and in material produced by the Commission for Local Democracy and especially studies by Phillips (1994) and Stoker (1994). The Commission's material is re-edited in Pratchett and Wilson (1996) and there are also valuable essays in King and Stoker (1996). Chandler (2008) provides a succinct discussion on the development of political theory relating to local government since the eighteenth century.

The unusual nature of the British local government system cannot be fully appreciated without some familiarity with the local government systems of other countries. Recommended comparative studies include Chandler (1993), Batley and Stoker (1991), Page and Goldsmith (1987) and Bowman and Hampton (1983). A clear but detailed analysis of local government in the United States is provided by Dye (2000) whilst the French and British systems are iconoclastically compared by Ashford (1982) but, given that this is not a quick read, Lagroye and Wright (1979) is an approachable source. Wollmann and Schroter (2000) have edited a useful comparative study of local government reform in Germany and Britain.

*Web sites*

Accessing material on local government through the internet is an important means of ensuring that you can obtain the most recent information on legislative changes to the system. The most useful entry is through the government's web pages on www.direct.gov.uk. From this site you can find through the index material published by individual government departments. The Communities and Local Government web pages at www.communities.gov.uk are most relevant for local government. You can also access from the web pages of individual local authorities. These differ greatly in quality but generally the larger metropolitan districts and the London Authority have extensive details on their activities.

Considerable information can also be obtained from the Local Government Association's web site www.lga.gov.uk and IDeA, the organisation established by the local authorities with Government support, to improve the efficiency of the system, at www.IDeA.gov.uk. The local government sections in the Audit Commission's web site are also a useful source at www.audit-commission.gov.uk.

Information on the Scottish system of local government can be obtained from the web site for the Scottish Executive, www.scotland.gov.uk and on Wales through www.wales.gov.uk.

# 2

# The structure of the system

Until the nineteenth century local government in Britain had a broadly similar structure to the systems of France or the States of America. In rural areas small community governments, the parish in Britain, the commune in France or the city or township in the USA dealt with most local government matters. Their boundaries emerged through a gradual process of land settlement that reflected local, rather than central, needs. In England counties, boroughs and parishes began to emerge under Anglo-Saxon Kings. In an age where religion and politics were closely intertwined the parish was as much a subdivision of church territory as an area of governance. Parishes often formed the focus for the loyalties and consciousness of place and belonging for their inhabitants. Many parishes, initially, were governed as democracies. Residents of the community would meet at regular intervals, often in the church vestry, and reach decisions through consensus or majority vote. They appointed officers who usually served the parish on a voluntary basis. By the sixteenth century the most important role of the parish was to administer the poor law to provide a measure of social security but also it ensured, if it could, law and order in the community, and maintained roads and bridges and community property.

In most of Europe the lowest tier communities have, superimposed above them, larger administrative areas created and sustained by central government. In Britain, from Anglo-Saxon times, these took the form of the counties, which were often divided into smaller areas such as ridings or hundreds. The county was intended to consolidate the power of the monarch, who subdivided territory into areas to be managed on their behalf by a trusted lieutenant, who was often designated the sheriff, an office much despised in the legend of Robin Hood. By the reign of Elizabeth I most of the powers of the sheriff had been transferred to a lord lieutenant, who was normally an aristocrat with large estates in the county.

The lord lieutenant was responsible for keeping the peace in the county on behalf of central government and usually had a seat in Parliament and could, therefore, influence legislation and national policy. One of the lord lieutenant's most important functions was to keep the home secretary informed of political dissent from the lower classes by marshalling networks of spies in the pay of government. The lord lieutenant appointed within his county justices of the peace (JPs). These worthies, who were usually gentlemen farmers or Anglican parsons, presided over local courts and the county court of quarter sessions. From this lofty position they dealt summary justice to the agrarian felon and poacher. The quarter sessions were the means by which central government could ensure parishes respected the values of the landed classes and, in effect, governed the counties. The parish councils had to report each year to the quarter sessions on their financial stewardship so that their many activities could be checked by their betters. Under this system many once-democratic parish governments had by the eighteenth century decayed into oligarchic systems dominated by wealthy families and particularly by the local landowner, the squire, and that other local luminary, the parson or rector of the parish.

Outside the structure of county and parish, a number of larger towns, which had at some time in their history commercial or military importance, enjoyed independent status through the award of a Royal Charter that established them as a borough council. This power often included the right to send one or two worthies to the House of Commons. Although these towns were self-governing, and not directly subject to supervision by JPs, they were by the eighteenth century rarely free islands of democratic radicalism. For the most part their councils were selected, as opposed to elected, by a coterie of self-perpetuating councillors. Some towns, such as Liverpool, were governed well as enterprising centres of commerce but in many their unelected councillors did little but embezzle local funds for their own enjoyment. The system by 1800 was however subject to incremental change as many industrialising parishes created by private acts of Parliament more modern elected councils, often called Improvement Commissions, to raise a rate and undertake tasks such as street cleansing, lighting and policing.

> The structure of local government in France or the United States in 1800 was not radically different from that of Britain. Both systems had many, usually very small, local councils covering village areas with a larger county-sized unit superimposed above them. Larger towns were often in practice less subject to pressure from a higher tier of government.

### The growth of towns and decline of the parish

During the nineteenth century British local government diverged in its structure from its European neighbours through a process that marginalised the parish. Behind this change was the philosophy of liberalism that supported the growth of free enterprise against the concern of many smaller landowners to restrict industrial growth. In 1832 the Electoral Reform Act secured the breakthrough of liberal values and opened the path for the capitalists to participate in the government of the industrialising cities that they had largely created and sustained. The subsequent Municipal Corporations Act of 1835 required larger boroughs to be governed by councils elected by rate payers, in effect property owners, to manage the environmental concerns of the community and police its lawless streets. Parishes or Improvement Commissions encompassing a substantial population could petition to be designated boroughs and so create elected councils in many communities that had, due to industrialisation, expanded into towns. Not all towns immediately leapt at the opportunity afforded by the 1835 Act. New local authorities cost money if they were to effectively improve living conditions. Rate payers then, as now, were initially reluctant to participate. However, by the 1850s most large towns had a borough council and by the 1870s many local businessmen saw that local control could be developed so as to greatly benefit their commercial interests. Through the zeal and genuine local sentiment of local industrialists, city governments reached a zenith of power and influence in the late nineteenth century and built as their cathedrals the neo-gothic town halls that are among the largest public constructions of that age.

## The demise of the parish

Whilst municipal government flourished, the liberal values that had created the Victorian town hall moved like an inexorable juggernaut to roll over the parish as a unit of government in rural areas. The rural parish was seen by Liberals as a bastion of Tory influence. Its most costly function, the administration of poor relief, was becoming increasingly costly to manage and, as it required those without work to seek support in the parish of their birth, was a barrier to social mobility. Many wealthy Tories as well as Liberals who paid for the system through the rates were easily convinced that such welfare fostered idleness. Conservative landowners, however, could not accept the idea of elected county governments to parallel the new boroughs and hence administrative change in rural areas emerged through the growth of *ad-hoc* agencies for specific functions. The 1834 Poor Law Amendment Act established a system for alleviating poverty which was to be administered by new single-purpose authorities, the poor law unions. The members of the unions were elected by local taxpayers but were subject to tight, centrally determined, controls and inspection by poor law commissioners. The system effectively bypassed parishes by removing their most important function and set a precedent to be followed by later governments caught up in the process of coming to terms with the growth in population and the social demands of industrialisation. In 1848 an *ad-hoc* network of health authorities was established to eradicate the scourge of deadly epidemic disease through water purification and sewage systems. In 1862 parishes were grouped together to form highways boards and in 1870 the introduction of compulsory education led to the formation of *ad-hoc* school boards. By the 1880s local government consisted of a complex amalgam of structures that included some 300 multi-purpose urban governments and in other areas a bewildering patchwork of agencies operating alongside the older parish and county governments. Local government structures were nowhere more complex than in London. A fiercely independent City of London occupied but a small fraction of the conurbation. The remainder was divided into numerous parish vestries, boards for specific purposes and improvement commissions, although by 1855 a Metropolitan Board of Works had been created to secure a measure of clean water and drainage for the whole area.

Rationalisation of this complex system began with the democratisation of county government in the wake of electoral reform at the national level. The 1888 Local Government Act established elected county councils, including a London County Council (LCC) and thus removed the powers of JPs and lord lieutenants over most aspects of local administration. The Act also gave some of the larger cities the accolade of a county borough, confirming their status as unitary authorities. The 1894 Local Government Act created multi-purpose rural and urban district councils based on the boundaries of the health boards. Finally, in 1899 parishes and boroughs within the LCC boundaries were consolidated into London boroughs. Once the new framework was in place many of the *ad-hoc* agencies created to bypass the parish and county were merged with the new structures, although the poor law unions remained until 1929 as a separate entity. The parish remained as a vestigial unit of government with few significant powers. Local government was the responsibility of much larger territorial units and much of the ethos of communal government that still exists in much of Europe had evaporated. The structure of the system is outlined in Table 2.1. Similar restructuring into counties, boroughs and districts was also put in place in Scotland and Wales.

In many European states and in the United States the second tier of local government, equivalent to the county in Britain, was traditionally viewed as the unit that supervised and co-ordinated the smaller community-based first tier units. Thus, in France, the department, which was until the 1980s controlled by an appointed civil servant, the prefect, supervised the activities of the communes and could suspend their mayor or council if he or she was thought to be acting improperly. Similar arrangements existed in Spain and Italy although reforms in these Mediterranean countries have now decreased the powers of the prefect or provincial governor and created elected councils which select a president to run the activities of department or province, leaving the prefect to take a more managerial than policy making role. In the United States the county, although always subject to an elected council, was seen as a body representing State rather than local interests.

### From large to huge authorities

Few politicians or local government activists were happy with the compromises that created the system of the early twentieth century. Politically influential

Table 2.1 *Local government in Britain, 1899–1974*

| Area | First tier | Second tier |
|------|-----------|-------------|
| Cities | County borough | N/A |
| Larger towns | County | Borough |
| Smaller towns | County | Urban districts |
| Rural areas | County | Rural district |

Fabian thinkers such as the Webbs (1920) and G.D.H. Cole (1947) argued that the structure was outdated. W.A. Robson, one of the most distinguished authorities on local government in the 1940s and 1950s, observed that-:

> For more than thirty years the organisation of local government has been growing obsolete and is now hopelessly out of date. Far larger units of administration than those afforded by counties and county boroughs are needed for such services as town and country planning, technical education, sewerage disposal, electricity and gas supply. (1954: 35)

Cities had burst out of their nineteenth century boundaries to create urban conurbations governed by several independent local authorities. In such circumstances, argued the reformers, it was impossible to plan for cities as a whole without involving the agreement and co-ordination of several councils. Small local authorities were also argued to be inefficient as they could not employ economies of scale or serve special minority needs. The system could not, moreover, attract and retain well-qualified specialist officers or interest the most competent people of the community to become councillors. These problems were fuelled by internecine strife between the counties and the county boroughs. Expanding cities with serious housing problems could only buy cheap land on which to build new estates in neighbouring rural local authorities that had no wish to give up land to meet urban over-spill. Several larger boroughs were petitioning for county borough status which would provide them with new powers at the expense of the counties. Attempts to restructure London in the 1920s and, in the 1940s local government as a whole, met fierce resistance, particularly from the county councils. The local authorities were, however, themselves concerned about conflict over boundaries and came to an agreement with the Government in 1956 that an independent boundaries commission should be established with powers to recommend changes to the shape but not functions of local authorities.

It was not until 1957 when Henry Brooke, who had formerly been an opposition leader on London County Council, became Minister of Housing and Local Government that root and branch structural change was found to be possible. Brooke's special interest in London led him to establish a Royal Commission in the light of the repeated requests from a number of London boroughs for county borough status. The recommendations of the Herbert Report (1960) were, apart from a few details, accepted by the Government. The subsequent Act of 1963 abolished the county councils of London and Middlesex and drastically reduced the number of lower tier authorities from over 100 to 32 London boroughs. The City of London that covers approximately a square mile of Britain's financial centre was, however, not included in the reform and allowed to retain its separate identity and traditional practices. London as a whole was represented by a unique strategic authority, the Greater London Council (GLC), which had some powers, such as the provision of housing, not normally assigned to county councils but, unlike other counties, did not control police and education. The prestige of the education department of the abolished LCC prompted the Government to retain this body as the separate Inner London Education Authority.

The restructuring of London government was soon followed by restructuring of local government throughout Britain. Richard Crossman, Minister for Housing and Local Government in the Labour Government elected in 1964, was a man not disinclined to father constitutional reforms. He was also being pressured to turn down proposals for restructuring the boundaries of local authorities in Lancashire that had been proposed by the Boundaries Commission set up by the Conservative Government in 1956. The issue affected more than just local government since parliamentary constituency boundaries were usually altered to fit within, rather than across, local government boundaries and in Lancashire this could mean a loss of Labour seats. Crossman realised he could stave off this unpleasant difficulty by postponing boundary changes through an enquiry into the structure and functions of local government as a whole (Crossman 1975: 331). The Prime Minister, Harold Wilson, readily perceived the electoral value of such a plan. A Royal Commission to review the structure of English local government was established in 1966, chaired by a former civil servant and academic, Lord Redcliffe-Maud. A separate Royal Commission for Scotland was chaired by a lawyer, Lord Wheatley. The newly created Welsh Office jealously guarded for itself the right to undertake a review of local government in its Principality.

The membership of the Redcliffe-Maud Commission was carefully balanced to represent the interests of the counties and larger county boroughs and the Conservative and Labour Parties. No thought was given to the interests of smaller communities so that the Commission was stacked against any solution other than the creation of fewer and larger local authorities. In conformity with orthodox academic and political thought, the Commission argued that 'the movement of opinion in favour of large authorities is impressive' (1969:, 33, para.110). It proposed that most of England should be divided into 59 single tier districts, based as much as possible around a major urban centre, which would have populations ranging from just over a million to 200,000 inhabitants. Three conurbations, the West Midlands, Merseyside and Greater Manchester, were to have a different arrangement built around a two tier metropolitan county and district structure. The Wheatley Commission on Scottish local government agreed with Redcliffe-Maud on the need for larger authorities but adopted a two tier region/ district format. The Welsh Office similarly advocated a two tier structure for the Principality of enlarged counties and districts. The findings of the Commissions were accepted by the Labour Government, with a few modifications, but legislation to adopt the structure was shelved when the Government fell in 1970. The Conservative Administration of Edward Heath picked up the principle of reform but not the single tier structure proposed for England due to pressure from Conservative 'knights of the shire'. The Government decided on a two tier system of counties and districts and also increased the number of metropolitan areas to six, with the addition of South and West Yorkshire and Tyne and Wear. The proposals for Scotland and Wales were more to the taste of the Conservatives and were adopted with few changes.

> Few other liberal democracies have engaged in such root and branch restructuring of their local government systems but have relied on occasional piecemeal change. During this period West Germany and Sweden reduced the number of lower tier authorities but not to the extent of Britain. In France there have been but a few mergers of communes and in Italy small communes are increasingly tending to co-operate and effectively merge on a voluntary basis. In the United States it is generally the practice that the citizens of any area subject to proposals that change their local government area are asked to approve the idea through a local referendum. In most cases citizens reject the changes.

### Drawing the new political map

Although the arrangement of local government boundaries established by the 1972 Local Government Acts was not as radical as the Redcliffe-Maud proposals, changes were considerable. The small counties of Rutland, Westmorland and the divisions of Lincolnshire were removed and Herefordshire and Worcestershire merged into a single county. New counties, such as Avon and Cleveland, were created and smaller adjustments made to county boundaries such as, to the horror of traditional cricketing rivals, apportioning some areas of Yorkshire into Lancashire (Bradford 1988). In Wales the 13 counties were merged into 8 larger units which had little cultural identity that were further divided to form 37 district authorities. Predominantly English speaking Pembroke was, for example, joined with the more Welsh speaking counties of Cardigan and Carmarthen to create Dyfed, a wholly new name to most Welsh people let alone the English. Glamorgan was split into three separate counties in a desperate struggle to ensure, irrespective of geographical size and cultural diversity, that each Welsh county had roughly similar populations. In Scotland, the traditional counties were swept away altogether to be replaced by nine large regions divided into a total of 53 districts.

Although the county structure was severely mauled, the community element of the local government structure, in as much as this was represented by the boroughs and urban and rural districts, was wholly destroyed. In England the district map was almost entirely a new creation drawn up largely by Whitehall on the advice of a Boundary Commission established by the 1972 Act which kept firmly to Government guidelines that districts should generally have a population range between 75,000 and 100,000 with no area of less than 40,000 inhabitants (Wood 1976: 162). For the most part, they adopted the Redcliffe-Maud procedure of joining together existing local government units and only in relatively few cases split existing authorities. Consultation took place with the local authority associations on matters of principle but there was little attempt to stimulate grassroots discussion on boundaries. Not surprisingly, their findings initiated numerous local protests from offended councils who were about to lose their identity. The Commission received 28,000, largely adverse, written comments (Wood 1976: 164). Despite a few concessions, the new districts had little rationale in terms of community. In Wales and Scotland a sense of tradition could be said to have been preserved by making many of the old redundant counties into districts. However, such action has little bearing on the values of community life. In England many of the districts were assigned names that were anonymous new creations which did not convey any geographical meaning let alone sense of place.

Dissatisfaction with the new districts was widespread but localised. The local press in some areas showed signs of parochial resentment and, on occasion, spectacular protest reached the smaller columns of the national press. A number of councillors representing Morecambe Bay publicly established themselves as a group seeking the division of the seaside town from Lancaster City Council; inhabitants of Newmarket petitioned to be included in Cambridgeshire rather than Suffolk; Penistone Town Council passed a symbolic declaration of independence from Barnsley Metropolitan District. Such protest may underlie even greater popular concern.

After 1974 British local government was radically different from most other developed states. France has some 36,000 communes, many of which have populations of less than a thousand. Sweden, which has comparatively large units, has but 3 municipalities with populations of over 200,000 and 66 with fewer than 10,000 inhabitants (Gustafsson 1988: 32). Despite a considerable reduction in its lower tier authorities Germany still has nearly 9,000 such structures. In the United States there is considerable variation in the number and size of city and county governments. Illinois at one extreme has 6,500 units of local government compared with less than 20 for Hawaii. In most States many cities have less than 1,000 inhabitants but the largest cities such as New York and Los Angeles administer populations of several million.

### Restructuring once again

The Thatcher Government had no immediate thoughts of again changing local government boundaries but soon came to regret the creation of the GLC and the metropolitan counties. Official criticisms rested largely on the cost of their administration and the belief that their removal would save money. In reality their abolition was largely due to the fact that they were predominantly Labour controlled and some were highly critical of Mrs Thatcher's Government. The GLC in particular exhausted Tory patience. Abolition of these troublesome authorities had been considered but rejected by a cabinet committee in 1981 but when the Government failed to find a popular alternative to the existing method for collecting local taxation in time for inclusion in the manifesto for the 1983 election, a sudden inspiration from Thatcher led to the re-earthing of the abolition policy. The decision was, therefore, as much borne out of the need to be seen to be actively restructuring local government than from any well considered desire for reform (Chandler 1988). Once the policy was enshrined in the manifesto a bandwagon was on the roll. Despite popular feeling, parties normally manage to honour their commitments however misconceived they may be. The Bill proved to be the most troublesome of the 1983–1987 Government but, despite widespread opposition, promoted, in part, by skilled public relations led by Ken Livingstone, it became law in 1985. The GLC and metropolitan counties ceased to exist on 1 April 1986. Although the metropolitan counties disappeared as multi-functional units of elected government, they still exist in an attenuated form since the abolition legislation set up *ad-hoc* authorities in each metropolitan county to deal with police services, fire and civil defence, and public transport.

Less than five years later Michael Heseltine returned in the Major Government as Secretary of State for the Environment, with unfinished reform on his mind. He began preparing White Papers to redesign both the external and internal structures of local government. Whilst his proposed reforms to the management of local government made little progress, the White Paper on the structure of local government published in 1991 suggested that a unitary structure was probably the best system for organising local government and that a Local Government Commission should be established to make recommendations on a new pattern for local government based on this idea. A Local Government Commission for England was established in 1992 under the chairmanship of Sir John Banham, previously Secretary General of the Confederation of British Industry and a former Director of the Audit Commission. Parallel studies of local government structure in Wales and Scotland were also undertaken by the Welsh and Scottish Offices. The Banham Commission was given the task of reviewing the boundaries of local authorities in the non-metropolitan authorities of England and recommending how these could be changed into a more efficient and yet also popularly acceptable pattern. The Commission decided that the task of redrawing local government boundaries in England was to be determined pragmatically through studies conducted by commissioners on the needs of particular areas of the country and the views of local interests. The views of commissioners diverged sharply and some teams favoured the Heseltine suggestion of unitary authorities whilst others recommended a two tier structure.

The structure of local government in England that emerged from the Enquiry appears to have little overall guiding rationale but the principal addition to the system was the formation of single tier 'unitary' authorities that were not dissimilar to the metropolitan districts. Several former county boroughs such as Derby, Nottingham, Peterborough and Leicester became unitary authorities and effectively regained the single tier status they enjoyed before 1974. In some sectors there was, however, little or no coherence in the Commission's recommendations, which removed, for example, the county of Berkshire by dividing it into four unitary authorities whilst retaining two tier status in many similar areas such as Surrey and Hertfordshire. Counties such as Avon, Humberside and Cleveland, created following the Redcliffe-Maud Report, were also abolished and divided into unitary authorities.

The reorganisation of local government in Scotland and Wales was subject to a much more rapid and less controversial process. The Secretary of State for Wales, following consultations with local authorities in the Principality, drew up proposals to abolish the county councils set up by the 1972 Local Government Act and transformed the majority of districts into unitary authorities. In effect, this has led to many areas that were county councils prior to 1974 receiving, once again, their former powers as a county whilst retaining their district authority powers which they gained from the abolition of these smaller areas in 1974. In Scotland the Secretary of State established a similar arrangement by abolishing the regions created in 1972 and transferring their powers to the existing districts to create a pattern of unitary authorities. The new arrangements for Scotland and Wales came into effect in April 1996.

The gradual transformation of English local government into unitary structures is given further impetus in the 2007 Local Government Act, which allows any principal local authority to request the creation of a unitary authority. This enables either a district to rid itself of the county and take over powers for education and social services or a county to propose that it becomes a unitary authority and absorbs the powers of the district authorities in its areas. The Secretary of State for the DCLG on the advice of a Boundary Committee will be final arbiter of applications. Even before the Act had been passed the Government invited local authorities to submit proposals for securing unitary status. Twenty applications were received and of these nine have been successful, creating unitary councils from 2009 for the counties of Cornwall, Durham, Northumberland, Shropshire and Wiltshire, dividing Cheshire into two unitary authorities and establishing unitary authorities around the towns of Exeter, Bedford, Ipswich and, although yet to be fully agreed, Norwich. Several of the successful proposals were accepted despite opposition from the public. In Durham local referenda in some now to be abolished districts firmly rejected

Table 2.2 *Responsibilities of the Greater London Authority*

| |
|---|
| Transport |
| Planning |
| Economic development |
| Policing |
| Fire and emergency planning |
| Culture |
| Health |

takeover by the unitary county, albeit on a low turnout. A number of applications, such as a unitary authority for the whole of Cumbria, were, however, rejected but the Act will leave open the possibility of new unitary arrangements being developed within these areas. The DCLG also announced a pathfinder scheme that invited remaining areas with two tier government to find ways of ensuring closer working between the county and its districts. A number of authorities such as Lincolnshire and Buckinghamshire have forwarded proposals as to how the rather vague remit could be managed but at the time of writing no clear model of streamlining the two tier system has emerged.

In addition to this potential change there is strong pressure within the Government to establish city regions in which large metropolitan authorities may be able to take control of the wider area in which they form the central urban hub. The White Paper *Strong and Prosperous Communities* that set out the last Blair Government's strategy for local government made much use of the term 'city–region' as an engine for economic growth. In reality, however, city regions currently remain more as an aspiration as areas larger than the boundaries of metropolitan districts such as Birmingham or Manchester. For example, whilst Sheffield regards itself as a potential city region, its development arm, Sheffield Enterprise, does not take within itself the economic development of the conjoined Metropolitan District of Rotherham. There is in the future the possibility that the politicians favouring city regions may gain sufficient ascendancy to forge new governing arrangements in the metropolitan areas but this has yet to emerge.

### The London Authority

In opposition, the Labour Party had continued to argue for an elected London wide authority following the abolition of the GLC and evolved policies to tie such a structure in with its ideas on regional government. The London Act of 1999 created a Greater London Authority (GLA) covering the area of the former GLC without exactly replicating its functions and duties. The powers of the GLA which are listed in Table 2.2 are predominantly concerned with strategic issues such as transport and economic development that require integration between the various London boroughs.

Although the London Authority does not, like the former GLC, have detailed powers for service implementation over, for example, housing, its powers are substantial. An important change was to give oversight of the Metropolitan Police to the GLA, which was a rare example of central government transferring detailed oversight to an elected local authority. Powers over transport, which include the underground services, are also significant and have facilitated the pioneering introduction of congestion charges to reduce traffic in the city centre.

All large liberal democracies establish a strategic authority to govern their capital city. In some cases, as in Sweden, this is a local authority constituted little differently from other local governments in the country but in many regimes special arrangements apply to the capital. Washington, for example, is not within any State but has a special federal district status that makes it a unique institution within the United States.

## The regions

New Labour came to power with a promise to establish regional government to Scotland, regional administration to Wales, planning regions for England and a strategic authority for the London conurbation. The development of regions within Britain was not, of course, a new idea and the Blair Government responded to a long history of unification and separatist pressure that has marked England's relationship with the United Kingdom as a whole. Scotland became a part of Britain subject to government from Westminster in 1707 through the Act of Union, an arrangement in which the Scottish aristocracy was accepted into the House of Lords and effectively became part of the establishment that governed Britain as a whole. The system of devolved government to the landed elite in England enabled the Scottish nobility to control their territories with the freedom given to their English peers and this also ensured Scotland retained separate systems of public administration that included the legal system, education and local government structures. Opposition to Scottish integration into Britain emerged in the early nineteenth century, stimulated by Irish separatism and also the growth of a partly invented Scottish nationalist culture by romantic educated Scots such as the novelist Sir Walter Scott. This movement led in 1885 to recognition of the identity of Scotland through the creation of a separate department of state, the Scottish Office, to deal with Scottish issues and a Scottish Grand Committee in Parliament where Scottish MPs could review legislation that affected the Province (Kellas 1968: 120–37). Wales, in contrast to Scotland, had never established a strong landowning class to rival the English aristocracy and by the sixteenth century had become under the Tudors subject to the same administrative system as

Table 2.3 *Activities devolved to Scottish and Welsh Assemblies and Executives*

Local government
Health
Education
Transport
Housing
Planning
Policing (not Wales)
Economic development
Environment
Agriculture
Arts and sport

England in return for having Welsh representatives in the English Parliament. Welsh nationalism emerged as a substantial political force in the 1960s, prompting the Labour Government of Harold Wilson to create a Welsh Office mirroring the Scottish Office but with rather fewer powers.

Fears in the Labour Party that the growth of nationalist parties in Scotland and Wales would be electorally damaging to their parliamentary strength minded the Wilson and Callaghan Governments to propose devolution to these regions. In 1979 referenda were held on devolution in both Provinces. In Scotland a majority of those voting supported devolution but legislation required an absolute majority of all Scottish electors to put devolution into effect and this was not achieved. A majority in Wales opposed the measure. The Thatcher and Major Governments had no interest in devolution, a stance that partly ensured the virtual disappearance of the Conservative Party as a political force in these areas. The Labour Party retained support for devolution in its manifestos throughout the Thatcher and Major years and following its election in 1997 the Blair Government immediately began the process of devolving power to Scotland and Wales. Referenda to agree a Parliament and Executive for Scotland and an Assembly and Executive for Wales received majority support allowing the new structures to operate after elections in May 1999. The formation of the Scottish Parliament and the Welsh Assembly marks an important change in the political structure of Britain. Their powers, outlined in Table 2.3, are determined by the Acts of 1998 that established the devolved governments.

The Scottish Parliament and Executive have, unlike any British local authority, the power to put forward legislation on a range of issues which substitutes any laws relating to England and Wales. Among these powers is the capacity to make arrangements for the local government system in Scotland. Thus, the Scottish Parliament, led by its Executive and First Minister, is capable of restructuring its system of local government without reference to Whitehall and Westminster. The Scottish Parliament also has discretion on how local government in the Province should be funded and structured and, within the limits of the Assembly's powers, it has the ability to determine exactly what the Scottish authorities should do. So far, however, the Scottish Parliament seems relatively content with the structure of the system bequeathed to it by the Scottish Office and retains the pattern of 32 single tier districts that came into being in 1996 and has not as will be shown later, followed the reform route outlined by Blair in the 1998 White Paper as wholeheartedly as the rest of Britain.

The Welsh Authority has fewer powers than the Scottish Parliament, with only the capacity to make secondary legislation which is, in effect, a power to modify broad framework laws made by the British Parliament in a process analogous to the development of statutory instruments. The Welsh Assembly is not capable of establishing legislation that is incompatible with law made in Westminster. The Assembly and Welsh Executive is, nevertheless, delegated considerable powers to implement policy on a wide range of domestic issues and also to propose policy changes within the framework of existing legislation. In practice, local government in Wales was structured through the Welsh Office and, in the new devolved arrangement, effectively authority to structure the Welsh system of local government lies with the Welsh Assembly and Executive. However, issues such as funding may still rest heavily with London. As in Scotland, the Welsh Executive has not thought it necessary to substantially restructure its system for local government.

> The Constitutions of the United States can only be amended to affect the powers of the 50 States with the consent of the majority of State governments, whilst in Germany the federal system, based on 16 Land governments, can only be restructured by the agreement of the upper house of the German legislature, which is composed of representatives of the Länder. Several European countries such as Spain and Italy have, however, developed regional governments that are being given increasing numbers of powers and would, politically, be very difficult for the central government to abolish given local political support for such structures.

### English regionalism

Pressure to develop regions in England derives far more than in Scotland and Wales from considerations on good local government practice as opposed to resolving nationalist pressures. The view that there should be a further regional tier of local government in England was suggested in the 1940s by G.D.H. Cole (1947), who saw regions as a means for decentralising power concerning major public enterprises such as gas and electricity distribution or higher education to units of government large enough to handle these services efficiently but still responsive to a local population rather than the national government. Further impetus was given to regionalism through the growth of economic planning as a means of resurrecting declining economies. By the 1960s these pressures had led to the emergence of numerous *ad-hoc* single-purpose regional administrations in England dealing with utilities such as gas and electricity, the collection of statistics and economic planning (Hogwood and Lindley 1982). None of the many regional bodies that were created had consistent boundaries. The Redcliffe-Maud Commission advocated non-elected planning regions for Britain. This proposal was ignored by the Heath Government but accession to the Common Market added further pressures to develop regional government since the European Union directs development aid to the more economically deprived regions of Europe rather than a member country as a whole. A further boost to regionalism was set in train by John Major by grouping regional offices for most central government departments into single integrated regional government offices that would, among other roles, liaise with local government on issues such as housing, transport, planning and economic development.

> Most larger European states including France, Italy, Germany and Spain let alone the USA with its federal structure have elected regional tiers for local government. Britain is again the exception in this context.

New Labour has always been divided on the issue of English regions. A faction led by John Prescott advocated the idea but received little enthusiasm from other Cabinet colleagues. As a compromise, the Cabinet agreed to create regional structures that would, at least in the first five years of the Government, fall short of elected assemblies. The 1998 Regional Development Agencies Act created Regional Development Agencies (RDAs) which mapped on to the areas, as shown in Map 2.1, covered by the Regional Government Offices created by John Major in 1994. The RDAs are broadly responsible for promoting the economic development of their areas and this also includes promotion of business efficiency, employment, skill enhancement and sustainable development.

The agencies, appointed by the Government, include four representatives from local authorities but have a majority of business members. In addition to the agencies, the Act created regional assemblies with greater local authority and voluntary group representation which were to be consulted on the strategies of the RDAs. Following the 2001 Election legislation was passed to allow any region to form an elected assembly subject to a referendum and on condition that, if a region were created, all two tier systems in the area would have to be reorganised on a unitary basis. Three regions proposed elections and the first was held for the North East in 2004 but the proposal was soundly rejected by the electorate and the remaining two hopeful regions, Yorkshire and the North West, shelved their plans for a referendum. After the failed referendum, following a review of local economic development, the Government in 2007 proposed the abolition of regional assemblies and that the RDAs would be more directly accountable to the leaders of larger authorities. The Government envisages an

REGIONAL DEVELOPMENT AGENCY

SCOTLAND

ONE
NORTH
EAST

YORKSHIRE
FORWARD

NORTH
WEST
DEVELOPMENT
AGENCY

EAST
MIDLANDS
DEVELOPMENT
AGENCY

ADVANTAGE
WEST MIDLANDS

WALES

EAST OF
ENGLAND
DEVELOPMENT
AGENCY

LONDON

SOUTH EAST
OF ENGLAND
DEVELOPMENT
AGENCY

SOUTH WEST
OF ENGLAND
DEVELOPMENT
AGENCY

*Regional Development Agencies: England (MSU 07/99)*

Map 2.1 *Regional Development Agencies in England*

arrangement in which powerful leaders of large sub-regional local authority units will work with businesses and the voluntary sector through the RDAs to economically and socially reshape their communities.

### Further reading

The history of local government in Britain has most recently been analysed in Chandler (2007), which analyses their development since 1800. A useful older text is Keith-Lucas and Richards (1978) and much is also covered in the misleadingly titled study by Sheldrake (1992). The post-Second World War developments up to the Blair Governments have been chronicled by Young and Rao (1997) and from Thatcher to Blair by Atkinson and Wilks-Heeg (2000). The socio-economic development of the modern system is skilfully analysed by Redlich and Hirst (1970) in an extensive study first published in 1903. Bulpitt (1983), whilst not a history, nevertheless provides a valuable insight into the development of sub-national government in Britain.

Studies of the geography, boundaries and community basis of local government in Britain are, for reasons that should be evident from the chapter, rather thin. There are, however, a reasonable number of studies on the concept of community such as Plant (1974) and Bell and Newby (1971). Among writers who apply the question of community to local government Hampton (1970) provides a thoughtful analysis and the Redcliffe-Maud Report (1969), especially the research volume material on community and parish councils, repays further study. A study of the changes in structure in the 1990s is provided by Leach (1998).

Devolution to Scotland and Wales is considered by Bogdanor (1999) and Pilkington (2002), and for Scotland in Lynch (2001) and McConnell (2004). Cole (2006) has written an interesting comparative study of devolution in Wales and Brittany. Recent developments in English regionalism are provided in Sandford (2005) and Hardill (2006). The growth and development of the GLA are dealt with in detail by Travers (2004).

# 3

# The functions of local authorities

The Local Government Act 2000 substantially refocused the role of local authorities. They are charged with powers to promote the 'well being' of their area in respect to economic, social and environmental concerns. The modern local authority is, therefore, seen to have a wider remit than providing a range of services largely concerned with social welfare but is to be the lead agency in the overall economic and social development of its area. However, it is not expected that the local authority is itself to supply the means to achieve this goal. To use a phrase popularised in the United States, local government should be 'steering, not rowing' (Osborne and Gaebler 1992). The modern local authority needs to lead the community by drawing other public and private sector organisations into partnerships that ensure that local organisations co-ordinate their activities and ensure that the most efficient agencies, whether they be public or private, capable of undertaking a necessary service, are entrusted with supplying appropriate services. It can, however, be questioned whether this vision of the Blair Government was fully formed or even possible. Many of the traditional social service values of local government remain entrenched within the system and remain supported firmly by the rigid legal framework in which local authorities must operate.

## The legal framework

Britain has no single legislative document that determines the role and functions of local authorities. The allocation of responsibility for particular services is assigned by individual Acts of Parliament which collectively compose a huge body of legislation. A few Acts such as the 2000 Local Government Act and the 1972 Local Government Act are, however, crucial in defining the powers and organisation of local authorities and will be referred to frequently in this book. The Acts themselves do not exactly define what local governments can do since they are further refined through the use of statutory instruments. Law relating to local government is further complicated by legal rulings made by judges as to the interpretation of the law which set a precedent that must be followed by the courts.

Any actions of a local authority must, however, be justified by reference to law. A local authority that pursues an activity that has no legislative justification may be instructed by the courts to stop its behaviour through a court order ruling the activity to be *ultra vires*, that is, outside the law. Some statutes impose a duty on a local authority to undertake a specific activity. For example, the 1944 Education Act requires that a local education authority must provide education for any child of school age within its boundaries. If the local authority fails to comply with this Act it may be sued in the courts under a writ of *mandamus*, an order requiring conformity with a statutory duty. In many cases, however, statutes give local authorities discretion as to whether they perform a particular task. There is, for example, no compulsion on any local authority that it should provide parks, swimming baths or promote the arts, since these activities are permissible but not mandatory under the 1972 Local Government Act.

### Statutory instruments

Most public acts relating to local government provide only a broad outline of powers or restraints and, indeed, it would often be impractical to do otherwise. To solve this problem legislation often delegates to government ministers powers to set and amend more detailed regulations relevant to the principles of an act. Delegated legislation is enacted as regulations termed statutory instruments. For example, Statutory Instrument Number 194 laid before Parliament on 29 January 2007 regulates procedures for Local Education Authorities (LEAs) to inform schools and parents about applications they receive to particular schools in their area. It can be appreciated by the number of this Order laid in January how many are created each year. A full list of all statutory instruments can be found at www.opsi.gov.uk/stat.htm. An act will stipulate whether any related statutory instrument requires the approval of Parliament. In some cases no prior consent is needed. A few acts require Parliament to approve statutory instruments such as the grant settlement to local authorities. Most statutory instruments have, however, only to be notified to Parliament and, if no objection is made by MPs, they become legally binding. Objections to these orders are not uncommon but are usually ineffective. An MP concerned at the maximum charge for student fees may try to object to a statutory instrument fixing their level but, unless he or she has the support of a considerable number of government backbenchers or the issue is taken up by opposition leaders, little will be made of the complaint. The loyalty of backbenchers to their government ensures that it is extremely rare for a statutory instrument not to be approved. A careful check on delegated legislation is, however, provided by a select committee of the House of Commons which reviews the orders tabled by the government and reports to Parliament on their validity within the framework of existing legislation. As many acts and statutory instruments can be interpreted in a variety of ways the government also clarifies how it expects them to be interpreted through circulars. These documents are issued with some regularity by government departments and are made publicly available although sent specifically to those organisations, such as local authorities, that are affected by an act.

Few powers are given to local authorities without qualification. Legislation usually stipulates many conditions regulating services and these rules may often be varied through the application of statutory instruments. The extent to which controls apply to each particular service will vary considerably. In some cases, such as local responsibility for distributing housing benefit, councils can do little but administer a task following a set of rigid rules closely monitored by central government and subject to frequent amendment. Local authorities may, on the other hand, have wide discretion over certain services. For example, there are very few restraints on local promotion of the arts.

*Powers of general competence*

In some of the States of the USA and in Scandinavian countries local governments are given powers of general competence that effectively reverse the principle of *ultra vires* by allowing a local authority to undertake any activity that is not specifically prohibited to it by law. This arrangement may not always be as liberating as it appears, as in the USA there may be an extensive body of prohibitive legislation.

In the past, powers granted to United Kingdom local authorities tended to be specific to particular services rather than general responsibilities that enabled them to undertake a wide range of innovatory activities. Section 137 of the 1972 Local Government Act was a gesture in allowing local authorities a measure of freedom to incur expenditure, strictly limited to a few pence for each council tax payer, 'which in their opinion is in the interests of their area or any part of it or all or some of their inhabitants'. The wider powers granted by the 2000 Local Government Act to incur expenditure to promote the improvement of the economic, social and environmental well being of their communities provide a much more effective basis for local authorities to develop more original strategies for supporting their communities. The powers granted through this legislation cannot, however, override existing legislative restrictions on how local authorities can act nor can it be used to find new ways of raising revenue for the authority. The legislation encourages local authorities to work in partnership with private and voluntary agencies within or outside their area to fulfil the broad objectives set out in the Act. During the next few years it will be interesting to evaluate how skilfully local authorities use these more general powers and the extent to which the government will avoid the temptation to restrain their use when an authority seeks to act in ways not wholly approved by Whitehall.

### Local acts

Most laws defining local government functions are the product of general acts of Parliament that apply to all authorities within a specified category. It is, however, possible to frame laws that give a unique power to a particular local authority through a private bill to secure a local act of Parliament. In the late nineteenth century many county boroughs gained lucrative trading powers through such means, including the right to generate and supply electricity and gas, and develop tram and bus services. Many of these powers have subsequently been repealed or consolidated in general legislation through nationalisation and then privatisation of such services. It is now impossible to forward any controversial measure through this means. Demands on parliamentary time ensure that these acts are only subject to formal debate on the floor of the House of Commons, which in practice means that the proposed act is simply announced at each stage of its procedure, apart from the committee stage where it may be considered in greater detail by a small group of MPs dealing with such legislation. If any MP objects to the content of a private bill he or she need only indicate their dissent on the floor of the House of Commons to effectively kill the bill since time will then have to be found to debate the issue and this is never allocated. Thus, in practice, all private acts must have the consent, or at least acquiescence, of all MPs and also, therefore, the government. Local acts are, nevertheless, still promoted by local authorities but usually for relatively uncontroversial tasks or issues relating to local development. A renewed interest in rapid urban transport has, for example, prompted some large authorities to seek powers to build tramways in their streets. Maidstone secured a Local Act in 2006 to regulate street trading in the town. Details of local acts can be found at www.opsi.gov.uk/acts.

### In-house provision and contracting out

Over the last 20 years local government has done less and less directly, and has become increasingly an agency for ensuring that a wide range of services and developmental initiatives are undertaken on behalf of their communities rather than the organisation that actually delivers the services. This is a relatively recent development. For most of the twentieth century larger local authorities conducted most of their functions 'in house'. They devised the policies on how they would undertake an activity within the framework of existing legislation, employed the staff who delivered the service and at times manufactured the raw materials that might be used in its delivery. Thus, a borough not only decided how many houses to build for rent but ensured its own architects designed the building, its own direct labour department built and maintained the properties, and its own officials collected rents and calculated how much, if any, housing benefit was due to the tenant.

The Thatcher and Major Governments undermined this view through legislation that compelled local authorities to become what was termed 'enabling' authorities by putting many of their services out to tender so that private companies could compete with the local authorities to run the service. Under this system of compulsory competitive tendering (CCT) the local authority drew up a contract which stated what standard of service it required and the organisation offering the cheapest price to run the services was awarded the contract. As a consequence many local authorities lost the capacity to implement some services directly and in the longer term the strategy has obliged increasing numbers of local authorities to voluntarily award contracts to private sector companies to manage some of their services as a means of saving costs. The Blair Government has through its policy of Best Value, which is discussed in more detail in Chapter 10, provided a framework in which local authorities do not have to allow private contractors to bid to run their services but must show if they manage their services 'in house' that they are providing as effective and cost efficient a service as could be supplied by the private sector. The practice of the 1970s when most local authorities implemented almost all their services is, however, now at an end.

The Blair Government has followed the enabling philosophy by emphasising that local authorities must develop a community strategy as to how they will promote the economic, social and environmental well being of their communities in consultation with other appropriate local agencies. The emphasis of the Blair Government is upon the idea of partnerships rather than single agencies securing development and service delivery, which links with the Government's aim to secure 'joined up' government as a means of resolving intractable social problems. High unemployment and rates of crime, poor schools, bad housing and ill health are often characteristic of socially deprived areas where each individual problem feeds off and reinforces the others. The solution to these difficulties cannot lie in tackling but one of a series of inter-linked issues but

---

The ethos that local authorities should provide all their functions in house is arguably a very limited view that is practised by few local authorities in other nations. Small French communes or American townships regularly co-operate with one another to provide joint services when a larger scale of operation is economically necessary. They will often use private contractors to fulfil many of their functions. Even large cities in Europe will expect private companies to undertake many of their functions. The streets of Barcelona, a city of strong left wing credentials, are cleaned by private firms working to the orders of the city governments.

Table 3.1 *Service delivery for Sheffield Metropolitan District Council*

| | |
|---|---|
| Education and libraries | Operated directly 'in house' by Sheffield City Council |
| Highways | Controlled in house with maintenance undertaken by 'street force' which operates in partnership with private agencies |
| Housing | Arm's length company Sheffield Homes |
| Housing and building repairs | Contracted to Kier plc as Kier Sheffield |
| Housing benefits/computing | Contracted to Liberata plc |
| Legal services | Some in house but excess workload contracted to DLA Solicitors |
| Museums/art galleries | Operated by Charitable Trusts set up in 1998 |
| Refuse collection | Contracted out to ONYX, a French owned multi-national company on a 20 year contract |
| Regeneration | Inner city development steered by a limited company partnership, Creative Sheffield |
| Social services | Some services such as care of the elderly contracted to a number of private companies such as Care UK |

requires co-ordinated working from a variety of public and private agencies. Local government is, therefore, a lead agency in promoting task forces and partnerships to bring together all the agencies required to resolve issues of social deprivation. Table 3.1 demonstrates some of the different systems of service delivery for the not untypical Sheffield City Council.

### The status of major services

The preceding chapter showed that local authorities progressed from being in the late nineteenth century concerned substantially with developing and supplying infrastructure for the local economy to becoming, by the mid-twentieth century, organisations largely supplying welfare services. The pattern of local authority functions is again changing to more of a regulatory and develop-

There are a range of tasks that are normally assigned to local authorities within liberal democracies across the globe. These include responsibility for refuse collection, pavements and minor roads, street lighting, and parks and recreation. There are wider differences concerning more expensive tasks. Education, rented housing provision, social services, hospitals and health care or control of police are not universally local tasks although many countries assign these tasks to local governments. There are also significant differences in the capacity of local authorities to run utilities, with some systems, such as in Germany and the United States, providing gas and electricity whilst in other countries such as Britain this is generally a matter of private supply and public regulation.

mental role. Rather than being direct suppliers of local welfare services, local governments are increasingly organisations that regulate the private and voluntary sectors' activities in these areas or co-ordinate other public agencies in these fields. However, under the regulatory and partnership framework, the local authority is also becoming more of a lead player in economic as well as social service provision. The change is, however, one of transition, as is shown in the following discussion of specific services. The newer economic, social and regulatory roles can often be found uneasily combined in the tasks currently undertaken by local governments.

## *Education*

Local councils with responsibility for education are the county councils, unitary authorities and metropolitan districts and were designated LEAs. The 2006 Education and Inspections Act, however, formally removed the LEA status to stress that local authority educational responsibilities are an integral part of local governments' functions. Local authorities took control of education through the 1902 Education Act when *ad-hoc* school boards formed in 1870 were incorporated into local authorities. The task was and still is much the most costly service operated by local government, although most of the expense is taken up by teachers' wages, which are not subject to local determination. Until the 1988 Education Reform Act the LEAs had considerable day to day controls over schools by constructing and maintaining school buildings, setting in detail their budgets, approving their curriculum and employing and appointing their staff. Before 1992 local authorities also had responsibility for further education, which is now under the supervision of the national Learning and Skills Council.

The extent of discretion over schools policy is now much more limited. The 1944 Education Act stated that compulsory education should be provided 'by local authorities under his [the Minister's] control and direction' (Regan 1977: 31) and this position was confirmed in the 1988 Education Reform Act (ERA), which was brought in by the Thatcher Government, in part to significantly decrease local authority control over schools administration. The exact inter-

Education is in many liberal democracies seen as a national rather than a local responsibility. The structure of the French education system and the curriculum is determined by national government although local governments have some responsibility for school buildings. In Germany education is a national and state responsibility. In the USA, school education is normally assigned to single purpose school boards that are separately elected from city and county governments but States operate publicly funded Universities and colleges and even some cities can and still do run their own Universities.

pretation of this power is far from clear but it has sufficient authority to permit the Department for Children, Schools and Families (DCSF) to suggest whatever it thinks necessary in educational development and to fund local education authorities accordingly. The DCSF retains powers to approve or reject local authority plans concerning the types of school they establish for children of particular age groups.

Under the 1988 ERA the Government established a national curriculum. It also required each LEA to devise a formula that must be approved by the government that determined how it will distribute funds to individual schools in its area. The governors of each school, with executive advice from the head teacher, were given responsibility for deciding how exactly the money is spent rather than the LEA. The Thatcher Government further restricted the LEAs' role by allowing schools following a referendum of parents to opt out of local authority control altogether. In 1992 the Major Government changed the rather benign Schools Inspectorate into the more adversarial Office for Standards in Education (OFSTED) and in 1997 gave OFSTED powers to inspect LEAs and recommend that those with inefficient services be suspended and some or all of their tasks transferred to external managers. The London Borough of Hackney had one of the first LEAs to be subjected to this indignity.

The Blair Governments reinstated a more hands on role for LEAs by ending the capacity of schools to opt out, and by affirming the power of LEAs to determine school catchment areas and plan the structure of pre-16 years education in their areas. Early strategies of the Blair Government to improve failing schools led to the creation of Education Action Zones in which the LEA would work in partnership with the private sector and the Government to improve schools in areas in which examination achievement is poor. Nevertheless, after 1997, many of the 1988 reforms remained intact, such as the schools' power to determine their own spending. Blair was also never comfortable with the 'one size fits all' comprehensive school and ordained that most would specialise in a particular subject area. Failed schools are to be restructured as city academies operating with some private sector support largely outside LEA control. The 2006 Education and Inspections Act further reinforced this trend and allows schools to apply for trust status which enables them to act outside any LEA influence. Under this Act, local authorities are given the task of facilitating a wide range of different types of secondary school and helping parents to be able to choose which is the best for their children. The educational role of local authorities is becoming increasingly concerned with strategic planning of the service rather than the day to day functioning of state schools.

*Housing*

Local authorities received powers in the nineteenth century to remove what were termed 'nuisances', disease ridden insanitary buildings and their attendant middens and cesspools. In 1868 the Artisan and Labourers' Dwelling Act permitted house building. Powers were, therefore, available to clear slums but it was not possible to re-house slum dwellers on an extensive basis since insufficient funds were given to construct large residential estates. The great breakthrough in housing provision came in 1919 when Lloyd George began building 'homes fit for heroes' for the returning servicemen of the First World War. Local authorities were able not only to build and maintain property but received substantial government grants to enable them to develop this service. Powers to borrow large sums for house building promoted over the next 50 years a dramatic transformation of cities as slums were replaced by new council estates, some to become in their turn slums.

In the Thatcherite heaven most property is privately owned by its occupants with a smaller housing stock rented from private owners or housing associations. In order to increase home ownership the 1980 Housing Act gave council tenants the right to buy their own houses at generous discount prices. Initially, the legislation was only partially successful in transferring public housing to private hands. As a further means of promoting the mandatory sale of houses the Conservative Governments ended the power of local authorities to subsidise council house rents from the general rate fund. This policy has forced local authorities to dramatically increase rents to council houses, making it financially more expedient for all but the poorest tenants to buy their own homes. They also drastically cut the amount of capital local authorities were permitted to borrow in order to build new properties, so that most district councils ceased to build houses and could only raise sufficient resources to undertake repairs or refurbishment of their properties. The Conservative Governments also tried, initially with little success, to get local authorities to transfer their estates to housing corporations or tenants' organisations but, with the appropriate financial incentives, by the mid-1990s increasing numbers of housing estates were being moved out of direct local authority control.

> Between 1989 and 1998 the stock of dwellings owned by housing associations in England doubled from 519,000 to 1,048,500 . . . and from 1991 associations overtook local authorities as providers of new homes. (Malpass 2000: 219)

The Blair Government did not reverse this trend but continued to shift the responsibility for providing low cost rented housing to housing associations, which are voluntary agencies that are regulated and funded by the centrally established Housing Corporation. Rented public housing began to be termed

---

Many European local authorities build and maintain housing for renting at low cost to those who would otherwise find it difficult to live in property maintained on the open market. In the USA, whilst some larger cities provide public housing, this has never been developed on the scale it has in Britain.

not council housing but social housing. Many housing associations work in partnership with local authorities, often building and owning the houses whilst the local authority provides tenants from their waiting lists. In 2004 the Government announced a new approach for housing that required local authorities to provide a strategy for 'fit for purpose' housing and encouraged all local authorities to place the care of their remaining housing stock in a separate arm's length housing agency with the promise that far more funding would be given to help modernise estates following the transfer. The Brown Government is, however, proposing to reverse the trend and allow local authorities to lead initiatives to build more houses in order to deal with the shortage of affordable new homes, in association with a New Homes Agency, a successor to the Housing Corporation.

### Social services

Social service powers have been gradually allocated to local government from a variety of sources, including children's acts that were passed in the first half of the twentieth century. By the 1960s it was recognised that, whilst local authorities had major responsibilities in the area of welfare, these were given to them in a haphazard form. Different committees often dealt with care for the elderly, protection of children and general social work practice. To remedy the situation a Government Enquiry published in 1968 as the Seebohm Report led to the creation, by statute, of social services departments in counties and county boroughs which would be managed by professional social workers and take responsibility for general social work practice and the care of children and the elderly.

Many aspects of the work of social services departments have been subject to the market pressures favoured by the Thatcher Governments. A major review of social care provision by Sir Roy Griffiths in 1993 led to the 'Care in the Community' approach. Local government is regarded as the lead agency for securing social welfare but this must be achieved as far as is possible by ensuring that those in need of assistance such as the elderly, the mentally ill or drug addicts and alcoholics are able to remain within the community in 'homely' surroundings. True to the enabling philosophy, local authorities should not be the principal providers of care to those in need but should plan and facilitate the necessary arrangements that should be undertaken primarily by private sector or voluntary agencies. The 1990 National Health Service and Community Care Act required local government social services departments to spend 85 per cent of their community care budget on provision by non-governmental bodies. This led to a mushrooming of private homes for the elderly and housing association accommodation for the mentally ill, which may be subject to inspection by the local authority but is not under its direct control (Parrott 1999: 79–83). The New Labour Governments have done little to change this trend towards contracting out care but have lent increasingly on support, provided usually by private contractors following assessment by social workers, to enable people to remain in their own homes. However, where this is not possible support is provided within private residential homes at considerable cost to the patient or their families.

Other aspects of social services seem less exposed to the enabling philosophy. The routine of social work is not a task that can easily be transferred to the private sector unless the government artificially created competing social work agencies. This sector has, nevertheless, been under serious pressure, especially in the area of child abuse following dramatic publicity in cases where social security departments have been over-zealous in taking children into care or allowed abuse to occur within children's homes. Solutions to such problems are not helped by under-funding, an increased case load on social workers and uncertainty over the exact responsibilities of different services. To resolve this latter problem the Government in the 2004 Children Act required local authorities to merge their social services sections relating to care of children with education departments in a service led by a children's director and by 2008 they are to form local children's trusts with health authority and voluntary agencies working in this field that will ensure strategic planning for child care. In the context of social services local authorities may work in partnership with other agencies but will lose much of their strategic oversight of this sector to the more clinically minded health services (Churchill 2007). The policy following the Seebohm Enquiry of placing all personal social services into a single local authority committee is now being reversed.

### Recreation, libraries and the arts

Local governments' powers over recreation and the arts are less subject to central government regulation than many other of their major tasks. Permission to maintain libraries was firmly established in 1919 when the Public Libraries Act established a county service and abolished restrictions on spending in this field. The 1972 Local Government Act reaffirmed a number of powers conferred on local authorities from parish to county level to maintain parks and sports facilities, and sponsor the arts. Larger authorities, especially big city governments, have sufficient resources to support museums, art galleries and sports stadiums, and help sponsor symphony orchestras. Even some parish councils pursue their recreational powers as far as maintaining a village hall or a small park and a few are sufficiently enterprising to maintain recreation facilities including museums, sports centres and swimming baths.

Local authority management of the arts is a testimony to the diversity and richness of provision that can be developed if communities have unfettered powers over a particular service. Large authorities have staged cultural events of international importance and most major cities heavily subsidise their repertory theatres. The Edinburgh Festival, for example, is underwritten by Edinburgh District Council whilst the Halle Orchestra would not survive without the support of Manchester City Council. Not only are the arts beholden to local government for financial support, they require the innovatory and organisational capacity of local authorities to initiate and sustain these ventures. The arts departments of local authorities often provide the organisational framework from which administrators may seek sponsorship. Such diversity is now extending into the area of sport. Manchester City Council hosted the Commonwealth Games of 2001 and the GLA has a lead role in organising the 2012 Olympic Games. At a less exalted level many a lowly league football team is beholden to local authority help to sustain its activities and many a sporting hero began training in local authority sports stadia and centres. Increasingly, however, local authorities are being urged to share the cost and administration of arts and sport with other private or voluntary partners. Many museums and sports complexes are, therefore, run by arm's length organisations as trusts in which the local authority has a share but not overall responsibility for their operation.

### Public health

The discovery that filth causes disease promoted a major growth in public services in the nineteenth century. The health boards established in 1848 formed the basis for water supply, sewage services, and regular refuse collection and disposal. The task of supplying clean water and sewage facilities was one of the greatest achievements of nineteenth-century public enterprise, requiring costly and impressive, though now largely unseen, feats of engineering.

Since 1945 the sanitation services have been taken for granted and once important posts in local government such as the medical officer of health and the borough surveyor have declined in importance. Gradually water and sewage services slipped from direct democratic control under the impact of demands for integrated systems of drainage and water catchment. The Water Act of 1945 merged many municipally controlled departments into larger jointly controlled drainage boards and water authorities that were subject to the authority of boards nominated by participating councils. In 1973 a Water Act established nine huge regional water authorities in England and a further authority to cover Wales that would undertake all sewage and water supply services. In 1983 a further Water Act recast the membership of the authorities to remove any automatic local representation on their boards and in 1988 the authorities were privatised, transferring what had been one of the greatest achievements of municipal enterprise out of democratic control. The relative autonomy of Scotland has, however, been asserted at least in the area of water supply. Following recommendations by the Wheatley Commission, water and sewage powers were returned from joint authorities to the control of the regional councils and, following their abolition, to three large but still publicly owned water companies.

Local authorities in England and Wales are now left with the residual task of refuse collection and disposal but even in this sector privatisation is taking a severe toll of local responsibility. Refuse collection, a staple routine of district and unitary authorities, is one of the principal areas which were subjected to competitive tendering by the 1988 Local Government Act. It has also proved to be the service most vulnerable to take-over by private firms and, in particular, subsidiaries of large French and Spanish owned companies. In both these countries communes do not share the British penchant for undertaking every service in house and have for many years contracted out refuse collection and street cleaning. Firms dealing with this service have now merged into a few large, highly automated organisations that are able to provide an effective service at a cost to rival that provided by British local authorities. Most authorities have now ceded their refuse collection operations to subsidiaries of the continental giants.

*Police services*

One of the most transparent myths of British political practice is that the police are not a national force but under local control. Maintaining public order was an important function of eighteenth century parish and town government although co-ordination of this function was secured by the Home Office through the work of JPs and the lord lieutenants. It is rather inaccurately maintained that the first modern police force was established in London in 1829 by Sir Robert Peel. This force, the Metropolitan Police, remained under Home Office direction until responsibility transferred to the London Authority in 2000. In the apparently strategically less important provinces, the Municipal Corporations Act of 1835 allowed the new boroughs powers to set up police services, although by 1839 the appointment of a chief constable required Home Office approval. Legislation in 1856 decreed that all counties and boroughs had a duty to establish a police force that would be partly funded by central government and subject to Home Office inspection.

In 1888 it was not thought prudent to hand police powers directly to the newly elected county councils. The influence of magistrates was maintained by the establishment of police committees jointly composed of councillors and JPs. The Police Act of 1919 gave the Home Secretary powers to regulate the control and management of police through statutory instruments. This facility is used to ensure that local police committees have little capacity for interfering in the operations of the police. Not only has there been an increase in central controls over the police, there has also been a steady decrease in the number of authorities with police powers. Before 1945 there were 181 police forces in England and Wales but, in 1946, borough council police were transferred to county council control. Further amalgamations reduced their number to only 51 forces in Britain by 1990 and the Blair Government put forward but then withdrew proposals to further reduce this number. The 1994 Police and Magistrates Courts Act further reduced the proportion of councillors and magistrates on police committees by adding a number of co-opted members from lists approved by the Home Office. Most police committees now have 17 members, of which 9 are county or unitary authority councillors, 3 are magistrates and the remainder co-opted members. They administer provision of buildings and equipment for their force and monitor their performance. Attempts to interfere in the use of the police in respect to their operations have met with strong rebuffs from chief constables and the Home Office.

There are wide variations in liberal democracies on local control of police. Some countries such as France have a national police force but in others, Spain for example, there may be local police dealing with minor issues such as traffic regulation, provincial police dealing with most crimes and a national force of militarised police dealing with civil unrest and political subversion. In the United States most levels of government employ their own police. Cities, even the smallest, employ their local police force; county law enforcement covering largely rural areas is in the hands of a sheriff and his or her deputies whilst States provide police services to aid the smaller police forces in counties and towns. At the national level the Federal Bureau of Investigation (FBI) deals with offences against federal law.

In Britain, although emphasis is still placed on the local accountability of the police, it is difficult to escape the conclusion that the Country has an increasingly nationalised force. In 1985, for example, the co-ordination of police forces throughout the United Kingdom to help break the miners' strike against the views of many members of police authorities further suggests that control of the service lies predominantly with central government.

### Transport and highways

Local authorities gained powers to operate tram and, later, bus services largely through their own initiative by sponsoring private acts of Parliament. By 1900 many cities were, in competition with the private sector, running their own public transport companies, usually on a profitable basis, and in some cities such as London and Sheffield the municipal authority even constructed its own buses and trams. As with many local tasks, central government has at times promoted and then dashed this activity. Transport acts in the 1930s attempted to remove wasteful competition between bus companies by assigning routes to a specific licensed operator. In many cities the municipal services came to have a monopoly over the transport system which, with the help of government grants, operated on a break-even basis. These established relationships were put into question firstly by South Yorkshire County Council's policy in the 1970s of subsidising bus and rail fares from the rates. This decision, practised widely in Europe, was not welcomed by the Labour Government and then outlawed by the Conservatives, who firstly tried to declare the policy illegal, and, when this failed in all areas outside London, passed the 1985 Transport Act which removed route monopolies and decreed that bus services could not be subsidised from the rates. Municipal bus companies now operate as if they were private companies in competition with the private sector. There remain, however, in the six former metropolitan county councils and the Scottish Region of Strathclyde joint local authority Passenger Transport Executives with some powers to regulate and subsidise transport services in their areas.

> In most European countries, and in particular Germany, public transport receives much greater subsidies from the national government than in Britain. This has led to the development of far more extensive networks of modern tramways and underground rail systems than in Britain.

Road building has, similarly, passed through its phase of growth and then decline as a consequence of centralisation. Responsibility for the maintenance of most roads and highways was transferred, on their creation, to the district authorities from *ad-hoc* road boards. The county councils were later given the task of looking after major highways. As road transport increased the government took the lead in classifying roads and providing funds for the development of major national routes in accord with specifications determined by the Ministry of Transport. In 1936 legislation permitted the Ministry to take direct control of major highways, which were designated as trunk roads. Since the 1960s the major road network has been further enhanced by the creation of motorways, which are now built and maintained under government direction by a Highways Agency. Local authorities today still maintain minor roads but the most important elements of the network are a central government responsibility although the Highways Agency may ask local authorities to undertake road repairs for it on an agency basis.

### Planning

Local authorities received powers to give planning permission as soon as it dawned on central government that control of building was necessary. The first planning Act arrived in 1909 and was strengthened in the inter-war years. Powers were greatly enhanced through Acts passed in 1947 and 1952 that

> Planning is a local government responsibility in most liberal democracies although the extent to which detailed plans can be resisted by local authorities varies widely. In the United States planning powers are referred to as 'zoning' and allow city or county governments to designate how particular areas of the community should be developed but generally there is rather less close inspection of designs for specific buildings over and above issues of safety.

ensured that any new building had to be approved by the district authority both in terms of its impact on the environment and the safety of its construction. These powers appear to be substantial and, if subject to no other authority than a local council, would permit councillors to determine the future physical environment and economy of their area within the possibilities allowed by market forces. However, these powers are not sovereign and any planning consent is subject to appeal to the government, effectively the secretary of state for communities and local government.

The secretary of state will often support local authority arguments opposing the granting of planning permission and the Department has no wish to use the power to indulge in inspection of every minor building project. However, local authorities are aware that they have little chance of halting schemes. Nationally controversial developments such as nuclear power stations or construction of motorways in scenic parkland, although subject to local authority planning procedures, are analysed, at the government's discretion, in quasi-judicial planning enquiries, chaired by a government appointee.

Serious delays through appeals against major planning decisions, with the building of a new runway for Heathrow airport as a *cause celebre*, prompted the Blair Government after 2005 to review planning procedures. A White Paper published in 2007 proposes the development of more streamlined national procedures to agree or refuse plans for major infrastructure projects by a streamlined system of national enquiries that would effectively by-pass the attentions of local authorities unless they wish to act as one of many supporters or complainants against a proposal.

Since the Labour Governments of Harold Wilson there have been sporadic attempts at more ambitious structural planning that required local authorities to set out longer term visions of how and where housing, industry, agriculture and recreational areas should be located. Incorporated in these ideas is the designation of green belt areas that cannot be subject to further development. The Blair Government has moved much of this planning framework to the regional tier in co-operation with local authorities but the Government retains a veto power of proposals.

### Economic development

During much of the twentieth century there was a continuous movement within local government towards low level social welfare provision and away from activities that directly affected the local economy. Apart from ritual demands from local businessmen that they should pay less in rates, commerce and local government seemed to pass each other by like ships in the night. However, in the 1980s a number of radical Labour controlled authorities such as Sheffield and the GLC, concerned with loss of traditional industries, spearheaded attempts to generate new co-operative business opportunities for the unemployed casualties of Thatcher's Governments. Initially, the Conservative

Governments did not look kindly on what they saw as socialist experiments and the efforts of the local authorities could not be sufficiently well funded to make a huge impact on declining local economies. Much of the Thatcher Governments' regeneration schemes were channelled into Urban Development Corporations (UDCs) which were managed largely by private sector interests and were established outside the local authority with planning powers.

The aims, if not the methods, of the radical authorities in the 1980s could not, however, be ignored by Conservative Governments facing serious economic change in many industrial areas such as the coal fields of Yorkshire and South Wales. The 1989 Local Government and Housing Act recognised economic development as a permissible function of local authorities but also gave the government wide powers to regulate this function through the use of statutory instruments. The Blair Government strongly reinforced local leadership of economic development in the 2000 Local Government Act, which gives local authorities the power to promote and improve the economic well being of their area and also allows the secretary of state to remove legislative restraints that are thought to detract from local economic initiatives. In effect, therefore, local authorities may apply to the government to be given greater powers to develop economic initiatives than are currently open to them.

The Major Governments, followed by the Blair Administrations, were, however, concerned that local authorities should not go it alone in securing economic redevelopment but channel their efforts into supporting capitalist industrial growth by working in partnership with the private or voluntary sectors or with the European Union. In 1994 Government schemes to further economic regeneration were simplified and brought together within a single regeneration budget (SRB). Public, voluntary and even private sector bodies were able to bid for funds although they had to adhere to criteria which included the need to match funding from the government. The last round of SRB awards in 2000 allocated over £5.5 billion to be spent over 7 years on some 900 schemes (DETR 2000a). In reality most larger successful bids are spearheaded by local authorities or are even pushed forward by central government for adoption by a local authority as the lead agency (Chandler 1998). They include, for example, schemes for major redevelopment of city centres or facilitating better training and child care schemes within an area of high unemployment.

Although a relatively new interest in Britain, economic development has been and remains a central concern of United States city governments whose populations look to the town hall as a major focus for ensuring the infrastructure to retain existing businesses within a city and attracting new sources of employment. Many cities develop strong links with business interests, so that the formation of public–private partnership to secure redevelopment of rundown areas is regular practice.

Regeneration under the Blair Governments gradually became less of a competition and more a process of developing partnerships between local government and the private and voluntary sectors mediated by the Regional Government Offices through the creation of Local Area Agreements that can be funded by a number of government sponsored schemes. Schemes are funded through a number of programmes, dependent on the regeneration problem, such as Neighbourhood Renewal or Community Development. Many projects are steered by Local Strategic Partnerships (LSPs) that are in many cases initiated by the local authority but run by partnerships that include representatives from the community, requiring support elected from outside the local authority. In addition the Blair Governments encouraged local authorities with regional agencies and a national body, English Partnerships, to establish arm's length regeneration companies, not too dissimilar from the earlier UDCs, to undertake major redevelopment within cities. These companies operate under differing titles. A scheme for the regeneration of Sheffield city centre is, for example, steered by a partnership called Creative Sheffield.

## *Other functions*

The preceding paragraphs do not provide a comprehensive review of local government services. There are many other functions of importance. Central governments have always found local authorities a useful agent to administer nationally necessary services. Thus, local governments through their education departments, handled the administration of the student grant system and currently deal with housing benefit subsidies. Local government is responsible for protecting the citizen through the fire service and developing emergency planning systems in the event of natural disasters such as floods or major accidents such as a rail crash. There has been a long tradition of local government protecting the consumer through advice and complaints bureaus, weights and measures inspectorates, and public health inspectorates. In 2003 licensing of pubs and clubs transferred from magistrates to local authorities. County councils have important powers concerning agricultural regulation and inspection and are involved in the prevention and spread of disease in farm animals. Local authorities are empowered to run markets and are, therefore, in the business of licensing stalls and street traders. They also provide permits through which they can regulate a wide variety of trading practices that range from charitable street collections to licensing taxi firms. The list of minor tasks assigned at some time to local authorities is lengthy.

## The future for local government services

Local governments in Britain have moved from being highly active in delivering productive and profitable services in the late nineteenth century, such as gas, water and electricity supply, to being more of an adjunct to the welfare state (Dunleavy 1984). Under the impact of the post-1979 Conservative Governments many of these welfare functions were moved from direct control by local government to a situation in which local authorities appointed private contractors to supply services or regulate private services providers. Since 1997 the New Labour Governments have not dramatically reversed this trend and stress the need for local authorities to act as organisations that facilitate the economic and social welfare of their areas in partnership with the private and voluntary sectors under central government regulation.

> Although in some policy areas such as education British local authorities seem to have greater importance than their equivalent structures in most other liberal democracies, local government in other nations often retains the capacity to operate productive and potentially highly profitable services. In Germany and the USA many city councils supply and distribute gas, electricity and water.

The formal assignment of a function to a particular level of government is, therefore, often misleading. As is indicated elsewhere in this chapter, local control over the police in Britain is largely illusory and the same may be true for education and housing where there have been strong arguments for removing these services from local control. Although British local authorities may exercise some powers not always enjoyed by their continental counterparts, they do not have control of some functions that are, in other countries, assigned to local authorities or the resources to finance their development.


### Further reading

Theoretical explanations of functional arrangements of local authorities are best approached through Dunleavy (1984), Hampton (1987) and Stoker (1991). These studies should lead the able student to radical interpretations of local politics in Saunders (1984, 1981), Duncan and Goodwin (1988) and then Castells (1977), though the neo-Marxist phraseology requires some prior learning, or the much more easily assimilated Cockburn (1977). Public choice texts relate primarily to national rather than local government. King (1987) presents a good introduction. Dunleavy (1991) provides an important analysis of the concept and a critique through his bureau shaping model.

The concept of an enabling authority as an organisation devoted to providing services requested and needed by citizens is developed in Stewart (1986) and succinctly described in Clarke and Stewart (1990). Walsh (1995) is the best text for analysing how these ideas operate in practice. The popularised new-right version can be found in Ridley (1988) and Beresford (1987) and an 'official' view with tendencies to the right is found in publications of the Audit Commission, especially that of 1988. Stoker (2000) contains the findings of recent ESRC sponsored studies on the functions of local authorities.

There are many studies that consider the development of each individual service but a useful discussion of the status of several of the major services is provided in contributions to Stoker and Wilson's (2004) edited study of recent change under New Labour. Developments up to 2000 in education policy are described clearly in Jones (2003).

# 4

# Finance and its control

Money does not buy happiness but it certainly helps. Neither does money necessarily buy power but it is a crucial factor in determining the effectiveness and independence of local government from central control. Given the wide range of local services and the sheer size of local governments in terms of employees they cannot function effectively without huge financial resources. Given the adage 'he who pays the piper calls the tune' the independence of local authorities to determine the quality of their services is greatly affected by their capacity to raise money on their own initiative. As will be shown in this chapter, whilst local citizens contribute about a quarter of local governments' resources, it is central government that is their major paymaster.

## The local authority budget

Each year a local authority will prepare a budget which is, in effect, a plan that details how much money is to be spent on each of its activities. The budget will be broken down into statements of the proposed spending within individual departments and on specific services. There are numerous restraints on the budgeting process so that the proportion of spending on particular services usually differs very little from one year to the next. The legal obligations on a county council to operate an effective education service will, for example, require the appointment of a sufficient number of teachers whose salaries are determined by national, rather than local, negotiations. Wide discretion in

> The budgets of British local authorities are comparatively large but this is hardly surprising given the relatively large scale of British local authorities. A small United States city of a few thousand inhabitants or a rural French commune require few resources and will have very simple budgetary procedures.

Table 4.1 *Revenue and capital spending for English local authorities, 2005/06 (£ million)*

|  | Revenue | Capital |
|---|---|---|
| Education | 40,568 | 3,492 |
| Social services | 21,602 | 468 |
| Housing | 15,084 | 4,534 |
| Police | 11,718 | 606 |
| Fire and civil defence | 2,191 | 96 |
| Transport and highways | 7,200 | 3,461 |
| Libraries, culture, recreation | 4,227 | 1,053 |
| Environmental | 5,650 | – |
| Planning and development | 3,068 | 3,447 |
| Central services | 10,925 | – |
| Other services | 6,147 | 3,502 |
| Total | 123,048 | 16,641 |

*Source:* DCLG (2007) *Local Government Financial Statistics*, London, HMSO, Tables 3.2a, 3.7b.

spending is, therefore, more pronounced in the generally less important services over which local authorities have greater control. In the relatively innovatory area of economic development some self-satisfied counties and districts choose to spend nothing at all. There may also be wide variations in the resources given to the arts or sports facilities.

Local authority accounts, like those of most large enterprises, cover two separate financial processes. Firstly, a revenue budget catalogues spending on items such as wages and goods and services that are consumed almost as soon as they are bought. A second set of accounts deals with capital spending on items such as buildings, computers and refuse trucks that are designed to remain for some years as an asset of the local authority. These two sets of accounts are connected since capital is acquired largely through borrowing money on which interest must be paid and charged to the revenue account. Table 4.1 outlines the revenue and capital spending by local authorities in England and Wales for the 2005/06 financial year.

## Revenue and the budgetary process

The annual budget of a local authority operates for a financial year that begins on 1 April and ends on the last day of March in the following year. The budget is finalised usually in February or March but is determined by detailed consultation among officers and councillors throughout the year. Officers will calculate how much they will need to spend in the forthcoming year in view of expansion or contraction in their services and the effect of price inflation on their spending. Budgeting officers will also estimate the income that the authority could receive from the Government during the following year in grants and commercial rates and also make estimates of how much they may be able to raise in charges and the council tax. Although most of a local authority budget consists of statements on the amount of revenue that will be made available to departments and sections of departments throughout the year, it will also have to determine how much of its funds will be kept in reserve to deal with any unexpected emergencies or to cope with unforeseen overspending. A local authority may build up substantial reserves and can budget to use some of this largesse in the forthcoming financial year. Some councils dip into the reserves in an election year to avoid making high council tax demands. It is, however, illegal to set a deficit budget in which the authority spends more than it has in reserve. Expenditure calculations for particular services and the projected local authority income are brought together and presented as a balanced budget to the authority's cabinet. Since the income to be received is determined largely by central government and may be unclear until late in the budgetary planning process, many local authorities develop two or three budget plans during the year which are based on different assumptions concerning revenue. When it becomes clear how much income will be received a final budget proposal is put before the full council. At the beginning of the financial year a local government officer is, therefore, aware of the amount of money he or she is entitled to spend during the year on behalf of the authority. If the officer does not spend everything budgeted to a department, she or he will normally be unable to roll that money into the next financial year but begins with an entirely new spending allowance so that unspent money transfers to its reserves.

### Local authority income

Local authorities receive funding from a wide range of sources. At the beginning of the twentieth century taxes on property, the rates, and charges for services were the most important components of income. Grants from central government have now become a crucial element of revenue and charges make up a much lower proportion of income. The source of revenue for local government as a whole in England is shown in Figure 4.1 and Table 4.2.

The system for determining local government revenue stems principally from the Local Government Finance Act of 1992 but has subsequently been subject to piecemeal change, especially in relation to terminology. In England central government after consultation with the local authority associations announces in July the Total Assumed Spending (TAS), which is the amount of money the government thinks local authorities should spend for the following financial year. It will also announce how much of this sum it will provide local authorities as grant or through the centrally collected business rate. This is approximately 80 per cent of what the Government thinks local authorities need. Thus local taxation through the rates or money raised by local charges constitutes only 20 per cent of what an authority needs to spend.

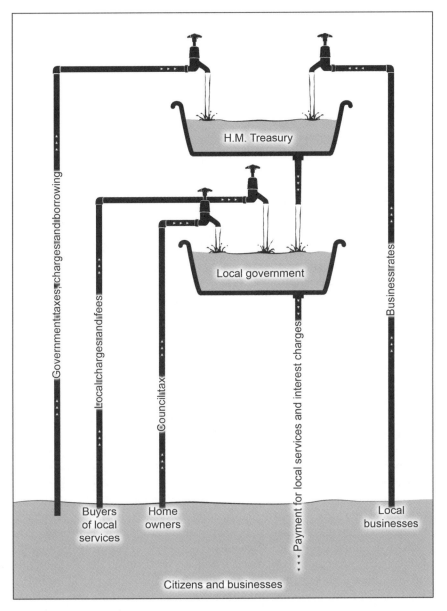

Figure 4.1 *Flow of revenue to local government*

Following the announcement of the TAS the government then determines by November how much each local authority should spend and announces in November the proposed allocation, called its Formula Spending Share (FSS), which is calculated with reference to seven programme areas: education, social

Table 4.2 *Local authority income by source for England, 2005/06*

|  | £ million | % |
|---|---|---|
| *Funded by government* | | |
| Revenue support grant | 26,663 | 19 |
| National non-domestic rates (business rate) | 18,004 | 13 |
| Grants to specific services | 34,581 | 25 |
| Capital grants to specific services | 5,298 | 4 |
| Sub-total | 84,546 | 61 |
| *Local authority funded* | | |
| Council tax | 21,315 | 15 |
| Interest receipts | 1,215 | 1 |
| Capital receipts (e.g. sales of land) | 3,777 | 3 |
| Sales, fees and charges | 11,420 | 8 |
| Council house rents | 6,208 | 5 |
| Sub-total | 43,935 | 32 |
| *Income from other sources* | | |
| European Union, lottery, private developers | 9,454 | 7 |
| Total | 137,936 | |

*Source:* DCLG (2007) *Local Government Financial Statistics,* London, HMSO, Table 2.1a.

services, police, fire and civil defence, highways maintenance, capital financing and all other services. The formula for distribution takes into account the demographic and social factors relevant to each particular service within a local authority. A local authority with a high proportion of its citizens over 65 years of age will, for example, be given more funds for social service support for the elderly than an authority with a younger age profile. If, following the calculation for a programme area, an authority would receive little or no increase or a very high increase in grant revenue, the government will set a floor and ceiling as to the increase in funding the authority can receive. The basic formulae which make up the complex calculations are discussed in regular meetings between the government and local authority representatives and accounting professionals.

The government's calculation as to how much grant a local authority is to receive will subtract from the FSS calculated for the local authority the amount of money the government calculates it will receive through the business rate and also the amount of money the government calculates a local authority ought to raise from the domestic council tax. A local authority can challenge the FSS assigned to it and, after dealing with submissions from disgruntled councils, a firm announcement on the FSS is made in January.

Once an authority knows what its FSS will be, it can determine its budget for the following year with some clarity and will be able to make a reasonably firm estimate about what it will need to raise in council tax and in charges. Local authorities must set their budget for the financial year that begins each April early in March and send details of their proposals to the DCLG. The practice of the preceding Conservative Governments which announced how much each local authority could raise in council tax, termed 'crude rate capping' by the Blair Government, has been replaced by a system in which local authorities are not given a clear limit to their council tax demands and are free to suggest the level of taxation they feel is appropriate. However, the government retains reserve powers to limit council tax increases. If the local authority submits a budget that will spend a higher sum than the FSS it will need to raise more in taxes than is acceptable to the secretary of state at the DCLG, who may use powers to cap the suggested rate of council tax. In Scotland and Wales the provincial governments follow a broadly similar system for determining local government revenue.

## Rates and taxes

Until the nineteenth century local authorities raised their own funds from their community. In parishes this was predominantly through the rates, a tax on property. Each house, shop, office, factory and area of land was assigned a rateable value that was determined largely by the rent that could be charged for the property. Local authorities each year decided how much they wished to receive from this tax and then set a rate in the pound to raise the required sum. Originally, landowners bore the brunt of this tax but, in the nineteenth century, land was progressively exempted and since 1929 rates have not had to be paid for agricultural land. The system was replaced in 1988 by Mrs Thatcher's poll tax that required every adult in Britain to pay a flat rate charge to their local authority. Hostility to this inequitable means of taxation led to its repeal in 1992 and the return of the rates in the form of the council tax.

Local authorities throughout Europe and in the United States do not subsist exclusively on the funds they raise from local taxes but require, in varying degrees, substantive levels of support from national or state governments. In a few countries such as Italy and Ireland the removal of locally collected property taxes has ensured local governments receive over 90 per cent of their income through grants. In contrast, in the United States most cities raise over half their revenue from local property taxes and municipal trading.

### *The council tax*

The council tax is like the rates calculated with reference to the market value of each house. The task of valuing property is assigned to a branch of the Inland Revenue which subcontracts the work largely to local estate agents. Each property is placed currently in one of eight bands, from band A that includes the least expensive properties through to band H for the most expensive. The Lyons Report has argued for more bands to cover the most expensive houses. The assignment of houses to each band differs between England, Scotland and Wales, with the two Provinces assigning lower values to each band than in England. Only one tax bill is levied for each house, although any person living on their own is entitled to a 25 per cent reduction. Councils fix the tax to be paid by setting an amount payable for a B and D property and then the payments for other bands are calculated on set ratios. The individual responsible for paying the tax is the legal owner of the dwelling and, therefore, most tenants do not pay the tax directly but will usually find that the charge is passed on to them by their landlord. Some people are exempt from the tax and, many readers will be pleased to learn, these include students who are living in a property not also occupied by someone who is directly or indirectly liable for payment. There has, as with the rates, been much controversy over the fairness of the council tax. It is shown to particularly disadvantage older people on pensions living in larger homes and it has long been suggested that the charge is replaced by a local income tax. This idea has been on the policy agenda since at least the 1950s but has always been opposed by civil servants as difficult to calculate and implement (Chandler 2007: 186).

> Most local government systems in liberal democracies raise at least part of their income through a tax on property similar to the rates. The system is suited to local authorities as it is relatively easy to calculate and collect and if those individuals owning larger houses pay most money it is crudely progressive in character in that the rich will tend to pay more than the poor.

### *The uniform business rate*

The council tax only applies to domestic property. The 1988 Local Government Finance Act which established the 'poll tax' retained a rating system for industrial and commercial property but removed the right of local authorities to set this rate, which is now determined for England and Wales by the government. A rateable value is set for all shops, offices and factories and each year the DCLG announces the rate in the pound which will determine the overall rates bill from a particular business. The sums paid by individual large industries are huge compared with payments made by domestic rate payers but, in comparison with the overall turnover of a business, as a fixed charge on the business that cannot be easily varied by its directors, its impact on the fortunes of a company will vary depending on whether a firm is financially successful or whether it is in serious difficulties. Although local authorities collect the tax, it is paid into a centrally controlled government account and then redistributed to local authorities in proportion to their population size. This system in effect provides a subsidy to rural areas from more industrialised local authorities. Local authorities with the agreement of representatives of local businesses can set a higher business rate with the proceeds going straight to the authority but this power is in practice rarely used.

## Grants

From the 1930s grant aid to local authorities gradually increased as an element of their income, until the Conservatives under Mrs Thatcher reversed this trend. However, as shown in Table 4.3, the New Labour Governments have returned to the former pattern.

The most important source of grant income is the revenue support grant, which is distributed throughout the year and may be used by local authorities to fund their revenue payments as they deem appropriate. Calculation of the grant is determined through the FSS calculations that are described earlier in this chapter. In addition to the revenue support grant, local authorities may be allocated specific grants directed towards aiding a particular service. A substantial specific grant is also given to local authorities for administering housing benefit which is, in effect, a national payment administered by local authorities. Several smaller grants are awarded to maintain government programmes covering, for example, inner city development, stemming the AIDS epidemic or community support for the mentally ill. In addition to specific grants, local authorities may also receive special grants which are one off payments to cover the costs of expensive and unexpected payments such as restoring coastal defences after serious storm damage.

Table 4.3 *Grants to local government as a percentage of its total revenue*

| Year | % |
|---|---|
| 1933–34 | 31 |
| 1943–44 | 31 |
| 1953–54 | 37 |
| 1963–64 | 36 |
| 1973–74 | 40 |
| 1983–84 | 40 |
| 1988–89 | 34 |
| 1991–92 | 38 |
| 1997–98 | 46 |
| 2001–02 | 59 |
| 2005–06 | 61 |

*Source:* DCLG (2007) *Local Government Financial Statistics for England and Wales*, London, HMSO.

## Charges

Local government is widely regarded as a public service which requires direct or indirect subsidies from taxpayers to maintain its activities whilst private trading organisations make profits from charging customers for their services. This has not always been the case. Local governments were much more reliant on charges in the late nineteenth and early twentieth centuries, receiving a substantial portion of their income from trading in energy supplies and transport services. Charges became a relatively minor source of revenue only after the Attlee Government had removed trading services from local authorities and replaced the lost income by grants. Substantive income was still generated through rents from council houses and bus fares but these charges generally did not meet the full cost of the service. Charges also remained as part payment for activities such as the use of sports facilities, cultural events and applications for planning permission. The most substantial charge in many authorities came in the form of rent from council house tenants, although until the Housing Acts of the 1980s this could be heavily subsidised from other sources of local authority income. Local authority housing must now balance expenditure with income from rent but, as discussed in the previous chapter, many authorities have now, following pressure from the Blair Government, handed over their housing responsibilities to arm's length companies. Policy changes in the 1980s have also obliged local authorities to charge for many of their social services such as home helps for the elderly, either directly or by employing contractors.

Local authorities still, however, have discretion on whether to subsidise many of their leisure services, to operate on a breakeven basis or use the service to make a profit. Decisions as to the pricing of sports facilities, museums or art galleries fall into this category even though none of these services can usually generate sufficient income to make a major difference to local authority income. These largely non-essential services are subject to market forces and in many cases higher charges will quickly deter members of the public from using them. Only a few authorities with popular tourist attractions such as the City of Bath are able to make a considerable impact on their finances through profits from entrepreneurial pricing of attractions (Chandler and Turner 1997). Tourist towns and big cities are also able to make substantial contributions to their funds through car parking fees, and in London, which may be followed by other big cities, the introduction of congestion charges for motorists promises a further significant source of revenue.

### Raising capital

Local authorities have since the nineteenth century been expected to raise capital by borrowing money and paying back interest through the revenue account. Most local authority equipment and property has been acquired through such means. Historically governments were more worried about local authorities borrowing more than they could afford than raising too much revenue from the rates. The annual public spending estimates announced by the government included a statement on capital spending by local authorities that was followed up by more detailed information to each individual local authority on what it could spend on capital projects for the following financial year. The Blair Government to its credit has significantly loosened the restraints on borrowing by local authorities to give them greater discretion to invest in projects they feel will in the long run bring in financially viable improvements for their communities. Following a Green Paper (DETR 2000b), the 2003 Local Government Act allowed local governments to borrow without direct government approval provided they adhere to a 'Prudential Code' established by the Chartered Institute for Public Finance and Accountancy (CIPFA). This sets criteria that ensure that for at least the next three years the overall cost of borrowing can be sustained within the financial capacity of an authority. Local authorities raise capital through a number of channels. They may borrow money on the open market from banks, from the public by issuing interest bearing bonds at a rate set by the city or county treasurer, or borrow from a QUANGO, the Public Works Loan Board. This latter source of funding is usually preferred since it will charge a slightly lower rate of interest than commercial banks. The Treasury, however, sets limits to the amount that may be obtained from the Board as a further means of regulating capital spending.

In addition to direct borrowing by a local authority the Treasury is concerned to promote some major public sector capital developments through the Private Finance Initiative (PFI). The scheme establishes a partnership between a public agency and a group of private contractors to build infrastructure such as schools or hospitals in which the private sector finances the construction of the project to plans specified by the commissioning public agency. The building is then rented back under the agreement to the public body for a specified number of years. The arrangement is not specific to local authorities and is used extensively by the National Health Service (NHS). Local authorities use the scheme most extensively to fund new school buildings but developments such as housing schemes and council offices have also been funded through this process. Over time the private construction companies expect a profitable return on their investment at the local authority's expense but the government favours a scheme that allows them to support capital funding that is not an immediate cost to the public sector. Much controversy surrounds whether in the long term repayments for PFI projects will be a serious burden on public sector budgets.

Capital can also be acquired through the sale or leasing of existing local government assets. The Conservative Governments placed considerable restrictions on the use of the sums that flow from, for example, the sale of council houses and, until 2004, at least half the money raised from this source has had to be used to pay back money already borrowed in order to reduce the authority's debts. The Blair Government then relaxed this restraint but only at the cost of requiring local authorities to repay a proportion of any capital gains from sales to the Treasury. Capital may be raised through funds received from the council tax but, given the capping arrangements that are tied to the projected revenue expenditure of a local authority, this source cannot be used to fund major projects. It is also possible to raise small capital sums for recreational and social welfare purposes through local lotteries. This power, acquired in 1976, led to a flurry of local raffles but it was soon clear that the cost of administrating such schemes was not worth the funds raised.

## Auditing the accounts

Auditing local government accounts was one of the earliest checks on local government formally imposed by central government and is now the responsibility of the Audit Commission. Local authorities like any major business organisation must keep a meticulous record of their finances in accounts kept for their departments and sections of departments. Using double entry book keeping, they record the costs and revenue of their services and show the surplus or deficits that they generate. They must keep separate accounts for revenue activities and capital expenditure, ensure that interest on capital is credited to the relevant revenue accounts and also provide an analysis of their assets and liabilities. The accounts for each financial year, along with connected information such as details of staff employed, are published for public scrutiny although the time taken to compile the final complex report may take over a year. The work of calculating and reporting the accounts of a local authority was traditionally undertaken by its treasurer's department. Located within this section was a group of internal auditors who monitored the spending and financial procedures of the various services of the authority in order to ensure that their conduct would pass external scrutiny. This task was subject to CCT and is now subject to Best Value so that local authorities must clearly demonstrate that their internal audit can be most efficiently conducted by their own staff rather than external businesses. The accounts compiled and audited within the authority are then subject to external scrutiny.

The Audit Commission was established in 1982 to monitor the financial and managerial competence and probity of local government and a number of specified QUANGOs, including the health service. The Commission is divided into districts, with considerable authority delegated to the chief auditor for each area. The annual accounts of every local authority must be passed by the Audit Commission, which will publicly report on areas of irregularity that a council needs to rectify and, as will be discussed in Chapter 10, forms part of the process through which the government assesses the performance of the local authority. If the authority is thought to be acting unlawfully the Commission may start an immediate investigation and if it finds cases of improper action it can initiate legal proceedings against offending officers and councillors. The Audit Commission is also responsible for ascertaining whether local authorities are providing value for money and this has enabled the Commission to comment extensively on the management of local government. Reports on local authorities published by the Commission are not simply an account of the financial competence of the authority but of its all-round effectiveness. Since its creation

Table 4.4 *Revenue spending by local authorities as a percentage of GDP*

|      | Local government | Central government |
|------|------------------|--------------------|
| 1968 | 6.6              | 10.9               |
| 1970 | 6.8              | 10.5               |
| 1975 | 9.1              | 12.7               |
| 1980 | 8.2              | 12.9               |
| 1985 | 8.9              | 12.9               |
| 1990 | 7.9              | 11.9               |
| 1995 | 7.5              | 12.0               |
| 2000 | 7.4              | 11.6               |
| 2006 | 8.6              | 13.5               |

*Source: National Statistics: United Kingdom National Accounts* (Blue Book) 1990, 2001, 2007; Table 2.1 UK Domestic Product and National Income.

the Commission has been an enthusiastic supporter of new management values and has published frequent reports outlining strategies for competitive enabling authorities. The Commission is not, however, a simple agent of central government and, whilst criticising some local authority practices, has also raised questions about the government's management of local finances.

### Financial restraints and local democracy

Accusations that local authorities waste money and are inefficient are as old as local government itself and were certainly a major theme for opponents of municipal city governments in the nineteenth century (Fraser 1979). There is no evidence that, historically, local government is any more prodigal than Whitehall, as is shown in Table 4.4. More to the point, since the onset of rate capping in 1984, local authorities have had progressively little autonomy in relation to how much they are able to spend. Complaints by aggrieved pensioners concerning their council tax are better addressed to central government, which in reality effectively determines what the local authority can raise in rates and how it is to be raised.

Concern over the equity of local taxes and the increasing restraint on local authority discretion led the Blair Government to appoint Sir Michael Lyons, a former Chief Executive of Birmingham City Council, to report on the framework of local government finance. The Lyons Report published in March 2007 argued that local authority finance was too tightly constrained by central government and that councils should have a wider range of sources from which to raise income and also have the incentive to improve the prosperity of their areas so as to increase their income. However, Lyons was cautious in proposing radical or immediate reforms to change the patterns of local government finance. As with many preceding studies on this subject he found a tax on property was easy to collect and difficult to evade and linked revenue with community. Whilst poorer people in large houses lost out, inequity could be assuaged by a better system of council tax benefits to decrease the burden for the worst off. The business tax could, he argued, eventually be set more at the discretion of local rather than central government but there would still be a need to transfer money from this source from urban to rural areas. A local income tax, which is currently established policy for the Liberal Democrats, was feasible, perhaps as a supplement to the rates in the longer term, but would take at least seven years to put in place. The Report has much of value to say about the need for greater local discretion over policy making but points, in practice, to the difficulties in reaching immediate solutions to the current problems in connection with the system of local finance.

### Further reading

The problem with any study of local government finance is that it may become factually dated almost as soon as it is written. A succinct official summary is provided in recent editions of the Department of the Environment's *Local Government Statistics* and guides are also published by the Local Government Information Unit and by CIPFA. The Lyons Report on local government finance also has clear descriptions of the funding system and is usefully illustrated with practical examples. It is accessible via the DCLG web pages.

There are a number of well crafted but ageing analytical studies in this area. The standard authority was Hepworth (1984), which received frequent updating in new editions but none has appeared recently. The political issues underlying financial change in the Thatcher years are well considered by Travers (1986) with some updating in Travers (1995). Valuable material on trends in expenditure is also provided by Newton and Karran (1985) and Bailey and Paddison (1988). There have been a number of studies on the poll tax and its consequences. John (1989) and Hollis et al. (1990) are useful studies and, in more detail, Butler, Adonis and Travers (1995) provide an illuminating analysis of how and why policies fail. Local government finance in Scotland prior to devolution was analysed by Midwinter (1984).

A study of local budgeting sponsored by the Joint Universities Council for Public Administration has produced Elcock, Jordan and Midwinter (1989) and Elcock and Jordan (1987), which provide much valuable empirical information. A more recent financial management study is Rawlinson and Tanner (1990). A general study of local government economics is Bailey (1999) and techniques of local government financial management are considered in Jones (1995).

# 5

# Local government and the state

It is impossible to seriously consider local government as an entity autonomous from the centre. Both central and local governments have evolved a complex network of structures and procedures for dealing with their mutual interests. Despite their labyrinthine qualities these structures are generally capable of successfully co-ordinating policy towards local authorities and sufficiently flexible to insert central guidance wherever Whitehall considers necessary. This chapter describes the structures and processes through which central government attempts to shape the structure and policies of local governments.

### The organisation of central government for local government

The British Constitution ordains that sovereignty is vested in the Queen in Parliament but the realities of cohesive and disciplined parliamentary party politics ensure that effective power lies in the executive. At the apex of the British political system the prime minister and cabinet have the power, subject to ratification by Parliament or judicial review, to make the final authoritative decisions on matters that they feel unable to delegate to subordinate levels of policy making. Thus, any major issues concerning local authorities will be considered in cabinet. This will include final agreement on proposed legislation affecting local authorities or important policies such as the size of their grant settlement.

As in all cabinet discussions, the prime minister will be able to exert a powerful influence on an issue, should he or she take an interest in the matter. Richard Crossman, when Minister for Housing and Local Government, observed in his *Diary* that

> Certainly it is true that the Cabinet is now part of the 'dignified' element of the constitution, in the sense that the real decisions are rarely taken there, unless the Prime Minister deliberately chooses to give the appearance of letting the Cabinet

decide a matter. I was also right to recognise the importance of Cabinet Committees. (Crossman 1975: 198)

Cabinet will debate only the most controversial issues. Many decisions are, effectively, made in cabinet committees composed of cabinet and more junior ministers selected by the prime minister to develop policies relating to a particular issue or policy area. Since the Governments of Mrs Thatcher there has been an established cabinet committee to consider local government matters. Gordon Brown in 2007 formed a Cabinet sub-committee for Local Government and the Regions comprising 16 ministers chaired by the Leader of the House of Commons, Harriet Harman.

### The role of government departments

In the late nineteenth century it became apparent that control of the network of multi-purpose and *ad-hoc* agencies that made up the local government system required a government department that could ensure that these agencies were better co-ordinated. To meet this need the Liberal Government of Gladstone created the Local Government Board in 1871. The Board was merged with other departments into the Ministry of Health in the 1920s. With the creation of the NHS, health became less associated with local government, which was hived off to a separate Ministry that by 1952 had a settled title of the Ministry of Housing and Local Government (MHLG). In 1970 the MHLG became a central element in a newly created larger body, the Department of the Environment, which also included responsibility for transport and public buildings. After some changes of name and functions the core of this Department was assigned in 2002 to an Office of the Deputy Prime Minister before the local government function was assigned four years later to Communities and Local Government, which is a Government Department that prefers, for as yet unfathomed reasons, to drop the 'department' soubriquet. DCLG takes the lead in establishing and reviewing policy towards the local government system as a whole and, in particular, issues relating to the structure, general powers and methods of financing the system.

Only a relatively small section of DCLG is devoted to making policy for the local government system as whole. The Department was given responsibility for community cohesion and equality and hence deals with issues relating to women and to minority groups. It also takes responsibility for housing, regeneration and planning issues. DCLG is led by its secretary of state, who is a cabinet member heading a team of junior ministers of whom one is designated the minister for local government. Reporting to the secretary of state is the permanent secretary, the senior civil servant in charge of the management of the Department, who advises ministers about the appropriate action they should take and is the manager for all civil servants in the Department. In certain circumstances a strong civil servant may be able to influence policy more effectively than a weak and hesitant politician whilst on other occasions the secretary of state may be the dominant figure. In practice, due to pressure of work ministers will often leave much detailed policy making to their civil servants but will usually dominate on matters of major importance. The permanent secretary chairs a Board which is officially the central co-ordinating body of DCLG that advises the ministers and ensures ministerial decisions are implemented and monitored. The Board includes not only seven directors general who head specific sections of the Department but also four non-executive members from outside the civil service who work in agencies that come under the remit of DCLG and help advise the civil servants on the wider perspective of policy. They include, at the time of writing, Sir Robert Kerslake, Chief Executive of Sheffield City Council.

Although DCLG has responsibility for the organisation and finance of local government, individual ministries have oversight of the functions that are implemented by local authorities. Thus, the Department for Children, Schools and Families deals with all matters relating to local authority schools, and the Home Office with the police, even though, for these functions, the final allocation of funds to particular local authorities rests, in theory, with DCLG. This complex distribution of tasks ensures specialist supervision of specialist tasks but also creates serious problems of co-ordination.

> Most European countries assign responsibility for oversight of local government to a ministry of the interior, which in Britain is most equivalent to the Home Office as it also has a lead role on policing. In France, the Ministry of the Interior has oversight over all matters relating to local government and, in theory, co-ordinates the demands of other Ministries which oversee services to be implemented by local government. In the United States, where federal government has no constitutional powers over local government, the States deal with the structure of local governments in their areas and rarely assign this to a lead department.

In addition to its Whitehall staff, the government has nine regional offices for England which were established by merging a number of separate departmental offices scattered throughout the country. The offices are delegated decision making powers concerning housing, planning, economic development and inner city responsibilities which can all influence local authorities in their region. They do not have any specific powers concerning local government finance and structures but they can act as an informal channel through which information and advice on such issues may be channelled between the government and local authorities. Each region is under the direction of an under secretary who reports to the permanent secretary of DCLG. The regional directors have a measure of autonomy which may, for example, result in some local authorities getting permission to modernise a council housing estate that would not be granted by another director in a different region.

*Local government oversight for Scotland and Wales*

Responsibility for the structure of local government in Scotland has since the nineteenth century always been assigned to the Scottish Office and regarded as a matter to be determined by Scottish rather than English interests. In Wales a similar shift of responsibility for determining local government structure did not take place until the 1960s with the formation of the Welsh Office. Under the Acts establishing devolved government in Scotland and Wales, responsibility for local government structure and powers is placed even more clearly in these Regions. In Scotland, the Assembly has the power to legislate for the structure, funding and functions of local government, provided the function is not an area reserved for the United Kingdom Government. The Scottish Executive can thus determine, subject to Assembly approval, the structure of local government in the Province and has allocated the overall responsibility for the system to a minister for communities who is assisted by a deputy minister with specific local government responsibilities. Responsibility for many functions administered by local authorities such as education and social services is assigned to other departments. The Welsh Assembly cannot, as in Scotland, pass legislation without approval of the British Government but is in practice expected to determine the organisation and financing of local government in the Province. Responsibility for this function in the Welsh Executive is currently given to the minister for finance, local government and public services.

*Co-ordination of the system of oversight*

The many central government departments with some responsibility for local authority functions need effective systems for their co-ordination. At the highest level of policy making, the cabinet and cabinet committees will draw together ministers with an interest in a particular issue. A prime minister in an entrenched position as party leader will be able to end quarrels between subordinate colleagues through pre-emptory decisions in favour of one or other of the contending factions. Policy co-ordination in Britain is also enhanced by the hierarchic civil service structure in which each department of state has one or two dominant heads, the permanent secretaries, and they in turn are expected to defer to the views of the pre-eminent civil servants, the cabinet secretary and the permanent secretaries of the Treasury. Permanent secretaries regularly meet in a committee that shadows the cabinet and serves

In some European countries, such as France and Italy, the civil service is much less co-ordinated into a hierarchy and there is no single dominant official as head of the civil servants in each ministry but rather groups of agency heads each with equal status.

to co-ordinate working practices among departments. The Treasury takes a leading role in this process since its support can be crucial for any project requiring funds. The cabinet secretary has influence as the principal official advisor to the prime minister and the cabinet and has the power to authoritatively communicate to the civil service the decisions made by cabinet.

Tony Blair even before becoming Prime Minister argued that the more traditional means of securing co-ordination within government were not operating successfully and, following suggestions by several advisory think tanks, called for more 'joined up' government both within Whitehall and between Whitehall and other decentralised agencies of government and also the private and voluntary sectors. The Government was rightly aware that many problems that beset society cannot be resolved by one organisation but require several separate organisations to work together on the many facets relating to the issue. For example, the problems of a failed school may not simply involve poor teaching or school buildings but stem from social problems such as unemployment, bad housing or drug taking. Thus, tackling problems of unemployment, law and order or educational deprivation need joined up government in which many ministries and agencies co-operate to resolve a problem. The idea that agencies must work together is far from new and was a major factor in the idea of corporate management that greatly influenced ideas on local structures in the 1970s. The formation of DCLG with a broad responsibility for community cohesion and equality demonstrates this concern. Under Blair the Cabinet Office was built up as a co-ordinating agency for functions such as alleviating deprivation in cities. Within this framework the Government established a number of task groups to try to resolve difficult problems such as social deprivation and drug dependency. The groups are required to bring multi-disciplinary working to bear on issues that cannot span the interest of one government department or even government as a whole.

Paralleling the development of task forces, the Government emphasised the need for organisations such as local government to work more in partnership with private sector, voluntary and other public bodies to secure a co-ordinated approach to resolving problems or providing services. To some degree this approach is the Blair Government's equivalent of the enabling authority in that local authorities are to be leaders of their community but leave the implementation of services to other agencies. Rather than resolving issues such as homelessness through the use of their own resources, local authorities are expected to bring together the public and private agencies at local and national level to work in partnership on the problem. This idea has influenced not only some of the operations of national government in the form of task forces but in later chapters will be seen to influence government thinking on how local authorities should be internally structured and how they should manage their responsibilities.

## Linking local and central governments

There has always been a constant stream of communications between central and local government and the local authority associations. Much of this traffic is in the form of written statements containing orders and advice or requests for information. There are also contacts between the personnel of local and central government through meetings, conferences and telephone discussions. These formal channels of communication, despite emphasis on new relationships, still form an iron grid in which more joined up co-operative working must operate.

### *Formal commands*

The most formal and compelling government communications to local authorities concern legislation. As soon as a relevant act is promulgated local authorities will receive the document and must respond to its precepts. Its content should not, of course, come as a surprise to senior policy makers since they will have monitored its progress from its origins as a ministerial statement. The meaning of an act is not, however, usually left to the comprehension of councillors but conveyed in government circulars issued by the relevant departments of state. These provide detailed instructions on how the act should be implemented as far as the government is concerned. For example, they may suggest dates for completion of Best Value public consultations or clarify membership issues concerning scrutiny committees. Usually these instructions are not binding and can be challenged or ignored, but such a reaction may well result in eventual legal confrontation between a local authority and the government over the meaning of an act. Changes to statutory orders must also be communicated to local authorities accompanied by circulars advising them on the aims and methods of implementing the new directives. The government can also issue a circular reinterpreting its powers under a long established act or provide a code of practice which informs the local authority of what it considers to be reasonable behaviour. Whilst not statutorily binding, a local authority may be sued for negligence if it ignores such codes.

### *Information and advice*

Despite their importance, only a fraction of the communications between central and local government involve commands from the government. Much information issued for the benefit of local authorities is primarily advisory in form. These may be reports relating, for example, to public health or information on better road materials or safeguards on waste disposal. There is a mass of routine communication to ensure the day to day workings of the system are kept in good working order. This activity involves as much communication from localities to the centre as information flowing from centre to periphery. There is an insatiable demand for statistical material that must be provided on a regular basis. This will include returns of data on issues as varied as levels of local authority spending, the numbers of children in schools, crime statistics and new housing starts. Such data are published in numerous central government statistical reports. The government may also require information on a more *ad-hoc* basis in order to aid policy formation or to satisfy the curiosity of a government minister. Information is also provided by arm's length QUANGOs established by the government such as the Audit Commission and IDeA, an agency established by local authorities with Government support in 2002 to replace a Local Government Management Board which advised local authorities on best practice. Potentially highly influential advisory agencies set up by John Prescott to secure economies in local authority spending are the Regional Centres of Excellence which advise local authorities on how to contract, in accordance with a National Procurement Strategy, for the essential raw materials and administrative support at as cheap a cost as possible.

## *Consultation*

Although exchange of routine information is a constant and often onerous duty for both local and central government, there is a need for more thorough consultation when policy is being reviewed with a view to legislative change. Important enquiries, such as royal commissions, solicit detailed evidence from local authorities. The development of legislation towards local authorities usually involves comprehensive consultation with the local authority associations and, on occasion, individual local governments. In recent years government departments such as DCLG have arranged meetings with senior local government officers and councillors on an *ad-hoc* basis to discuss major policy changes when in their planning stages. Most white papers and all green papers are issued by the government with a request for local authorities to send in comments by a certain date. Politicians and civil servants may also regularly seek advice from local authority representatives as a bill progresses through Parliament. If an amendment of a highly technical nature is tabled during the committee stage of a bill, ministers will require their civil servants to advise them on the consequences of the proposal and they, in turn, may seek inspiration from senior officials in the local authority associations.

## Local authority associations

Developing policy towards local government requires frequent debate, conflict and discussion between the government or the provincial governments and the local authorities in their areas. Central government does not usually care to receive a muddled jumble of ideas from the many differing local authorities and local governments themselves prefer to give a stronger unified opinion to central government than a set of conflicting views. Since the nineteenth century, local governments have, consequently, attempted to co-ordinate their approach to central government through interest groups known as local government associations. Conflict between local authorities of different types had, until recently, led in England and Wales to the development of different local authority associations for counties, cities and districts. There had since the Redcliffe-Maud Report been demands to consolidate the major association into a single group for England but this did not take place until the 1990s, when the local authorities managed to bury their differences to create in 1997 a single interest group, the Local Government Association (LGA), representing all local authorities in England and Wales above the level of the parish. Within the organisation are sub-groups for particular interests such as the Welsh Local Government Association. In Scotland the differing tiers of authority decided, following the Wheatley proposals in 1973, to develop a single association, the Convention of Scottish Local Authorities (CoSLA). Parish and town councils are not members of the associations for the larger authorities and many affiliate to a National Association for Local Councils. Membership of a local authority association is not compulsory but all local authorities regard it as an important and significant organisation for defending their interests. It is also well understood that central government will only discuss general matters affecting all local government in England with the LGA rather than with any individual local authority. In the past a few local authorities have, largely for political reasons, refused to affiliate to their appropriate organisation but they soon discovered that civil servants and ministers would not discuss proposed legislation with them.

The LGA is managed and funded by its members. Local authorities will send councillors to represent them on its General Council, which will determine the overall policy for the organisation. Since most councils are strongly partisan, the ruling party or parties within the authority will select its own councillors as delegates to the Association. The LGA is, therefore, like its member authorities, organised on party political lines and the party with the majority of representatives on the General Council of the Association will control its policy.

European liberal democracies have all developed representative bodies to co-ordinate the mutual interests of their local governments and present these to their governments. In France most influential is the Association des Maires de France (AMF). In the United States there are similar organisations representing State governors, city mayors and city managers, and county representatives. The impact of such groups is, however, variable and is much dependent on prevailing cultural attitudes towards interest groups. In France, for example, close links between mayors and national politicians ensure there are additional, more direct channels than the AMF to convey local views on the local government system.

Between meetings of the General Council its affairs are directed by an elected executive. Sub-committees deal with areas of functional responsibility, such as education and housing. The Association employs a permanent staff to advise on policy, conduct research and provide the administrative backing demanded by the Association. The permanent officers are led by a chief executive, who leads a team of senior officers who head departments responsible for overview of functions such as education or social services or tasks such as communication and public relations. Staff are usually recruited from the local government service and are often helped by advice from senior local government officers employed by member authorities.

Local authorities and their associations will seek to promote their views in both direct and indirect attempts to influence central government. The meetings of the local authority associations are an important means through which the leaders of the local governments can express their opinions. The associations issue reports, parliamentary briefings and press releases in order to forward their case. On occasion, local authorities may initiate major public relations campaigns to court public opinion. Whilst relations between local authority associations and the Thatcher Governments were stormy, since 1997 the LGA, even when it has a Conservative majority, has generally co-operated with the Labour Government and appears to be increasingly like an arm's length agency of the central state, helping to interpret central policy to its members.

### *Other associations*

In addition to the local authority associations, an important network of interests also influencing central–local relations developed from professional associations and trade unions representing the interests of local government officers. As will be discussed in Chapters 9 and 11, the influence of the local government professional associations varies substantially but some, such as CIPFA, representing chief finance officers, are powerful bodies with a high level of respect within Whitehall. The senior members and officers of such a body may exert considerable expert influence on government thinking. Outside the remit of the local authority association are bodies created by local authorities to co-ordinate their action in particular policy areas. The Centre for Local Economic Strategy develops thinking on economic intervention. Left wing local authorities along with trade unions formed a Local Government Information Unit to co-ordinate the strategy of these authorities against Conservative Government pressure. The organisation now has a more informative role.

### Partnership or new systems for control?

On taking office the Blair Government attempted to generate a much closer dialogue between government and local councillors and officers. The preceding

Conservative Governments hectored local authorities through a Consultative Council for Local Government Finance that had been formed with some initial success in 1975. This forum was replaced in November 1997 by an accord between the Government and the LGA to establish a Central Local Partnership (CLP). The CLP met three times a year with several cabinet ministers, permanent secretaries and the leaders of the LGA in attendance. The Partnership also encompassed a number of sub-groups that discuss more detailed issues concerning both the government and local authorities. Since 2006 its status has been under review and further meetings have not at the time of writing taken place. However, it may be argued that the close working between the LGA and government may make cumbersome top level meetings redundant. There has also in the last decade been a growth in informal contact between government and local authority leaders and at, a lower level, the interconnection between civil servants and local government officers through more technical working partnerships.

Partnership between central and local government reflects a wider view within the Blair and Brown Administrations that separate institutions, whether in the public, private or voluntary domain or operating at national or local level, should work together in joined up harmony rather than as divided and isolated groups. The trend followed optimistic academic and think tank reports on the value of joined up governance.

At the local level this thinking emerged, as indicated in Chapter 3, in the formation of LSPs, which brought into being groups of public, private and voluntary sector organisations to resolve, outside direct local authority control, difficult socio-economic problems in deprived areas. By the second Blair Government this policy had been widened to establish partnerships between government departments and local authorities termed Local Public Service Agreements (LPSAs). Under the scheme a local authority in consultation with, for example, the Department for Children, Schools and Families, could set itself targets for improvements in school results. Each scheme attracts grants from the Government to help the authority achieve the promised goals, and if targets are met further financial rewards will be given to the authority. Most large authorities participated in such schemes and the strategy was continued into 2005 although with greater emphasis on local setting of targets.

The success of LPSAs and the undimmed enthusiasm for partnership working prompted a new initiative following the 2005 election that brought these strands together in the form of Local Area Agreements (LAAs). The scheme seeks to involve LSPs or similar partnership organisations to work with the regional government offices to bring together a number of agencies in the field of local governance. In addition to, or even without, local government these might be agencies such as primary health care trusts or the family support QUANGO Sure Start. The LAAs set goals to achieve improved conditions initially in one of four programme areas: children and young people, safer and stronger communities, healthier communities, and economic development and enterprise. The scheme is ambitious and highly complex given the involvement of many agencies and appears to be a further example of potential side stepping of local authorities. Although local authorities are sympathetic with the overall aim to improve the social and economic well being of their communities and are glad of any financial support to facilitate this task, they may have some concern as to who is setting the agenda for what are to be the values and resultant goals for a local authority. The partnership schemes are motivation through carrots rather than sticks but they nevertheless represent some further thinning of the overall influence of local government over the development of its community.

### National politicians and councillors

Traditionally, discussions between central and local government are premised on a principle that, on general policy, ministers talk only to the leading politicians within the local authority associations whilst civil servants talk only to its officers. These barriers have, however, become less defined since the 1990s. Contacts between the government and the LGA or between the Scottish Executive and CoSLA are frequent, particularly at officer level where there may be almost daily contact between, for example, a secretary for local government finance and civil servants involved with this issue. On some minor matters, such as local authority pensions, politicians leave the detailed policy making on the issue to liaison between association officials and civil servants. Links between civil servants and the officers of individual local authorities at Whitehall level, especially on issues such as economic development or housing, will be channelled through the government's regional offices.

Until the 1990s very few senior civil servants had experience in senior posts in either the public, private or voluntary sectors. This exclusivity within the civil service is rapidly becoming superseded by a willingness among governments to recruit senior staff from the most appropriately experienced and able personnel available. In 2007 two Permanent Secretaries are former senior local government officers, including the head of DCLG, Peter Housden, who was a former

There has in the past been greater interconnectedness between the national and local bureaucracies in many other liberal democracies. In Germany, local and central government officers have a common training and may frequently move between levels of government during their career development. In France the system of prefectoral surveillance of local government ensures considerable interchange of ideas between the centrally employed prefectoral staff and local government officers.

Chief Executive for Nottinghamshire. However, for the executive members, previous experience of local government may not necessarily result in a more favourable view of the system. They may be able to understand how local governments work and think but be appointed by the government to use this understanding to ensure, when necessary, greater control of the system.

*Connecting politicians*

Councillors can often have informal connections with constituency MPs for their area and may often link up with them to put pressure for local interests on government ministers. A not untypical example of co-operation in such a context is provided by the following abstract from the news section of Birmingham City's web site in August 2006:

> Birmingham MPs, led by Gisela Stuart, are meeting with Transport Minister Dereck Twigg to urge a quick decision on funding for the Gateway Project to develop New Street Station. The move follows intensive meetings between the city council, National Rail and the MPs over recent weeks.

Close contact between councillors and politicians is, however, not so much achieved through government links as through the machinery of the political parties. All the major parties organise annual conferences for councillors to enable them to listen to the great of their national party and, if fortune smiles on them, forward their own views. Meetings between local and national party leaders may also take place in regional and national party conferences. Perhaps the most important channels of influence are the close contacts that can develop between local councillors and a leading figure in a national party through their mutual work in constituency politics. It would appear from the data in Table 5.1 that these links are increasing as more MPs have had experience as councillors.

Table 5.1 *MPs with local government experience*

| Year | 1911 | 1931 | 1951 | 1971 | 1981 | 1991 | 2003 | 2006 |
|---|---|---|---|---|---|---|---|---|
| Percentage of MPs with local Government experience | 29 | 30 | 36 | 43 | 46 | 49 | 56 | 54 |

*Note*: Number and percentage of MPs with local government experience as councillors or aldermen.
*Source:* Dod, *Parliamentary Companion*; The *Times Guide to the House of Commons* for relevant years.

However, it cannot be assumed that familiarity necessarily breeds enthusiasm rather than indifference. As councillors become MPs and even ministers, the strength of these links may weaken over time. An MP who had been a highly active local councillor observed that they were 'glad to be out of it' when asked whether they regretted losing their links with local authorities whilst a prominent former councillor, David Blunkett, as Secretary of State for Education, observed that he could only find time to concentrate on issues relating to his Department (Chandler and Kingdom 1999). It is normal practice for councillors, once elected, to drop their local office and concentrate solely on work in Westminster. Local and national party politicians argue that it would be impossible to undertake both the role of a councillor and that of an MP since the work of an MP and, even more crucially, that of a minister is so time consuming that it would be impossible to adequately fulfil the demands of either duty. Although it is assumed in Britain that national political leaders cannot be local political leaders, this is rather unusual practice in other liberal democracies.

> Britain is distinguished by the absence of any merging of central and local personnel. In France most Deputies of the National Assembly, the equivalent of MPs, also remain the leading figure in their local authorities, often retaining the executive post of mayor. Even government ministers will retain the position of mayor of their local town or city (Machin 1977: 160).

The separation of councillors from MPs is a twentieth century phenomenon. It has been observed in Chapter 2 that eighteenth century local government was linked to central government through the representation of the aristocratic lord lieutenants and gentleman JPs in the House of Lords or the Commons. These links were still strong in 1900, when many chairmen of the newly created county councils were represented in Parliament and prominent local businessmen, such as Joseph Chamberlain, had both local and national government experience. Keith-Lucas and Richards observe that in 1899 there were 101 peers and 87 MPs who were simultaneously county councillors (1978: 99), whereas in 2006 only 18 MPs were serving as councillors and but 2 of these were MPs in the previous Parliament (Dod 2006; Municipal Year Book 2006). The disappearance of local notables from national politics has had a crucial bearing on the relationship between centre and locality and will be analysed further in the next chapter.

### Further reading

There are many studies that discuss how central government generally devises policy and among those to be recommended are Kingdom (2003) and Greenwood, Pyper and Wilson (2002). A new edition of this latter study on public administration in Britain is currently being prepared. The attitudes and values of the civil service are considered by, among others, Hennessy (1989) although little is said specifically on views of local government.

Theoretical studies of central–local relations in Britain are numerous and included in the further reading for Chapter 6 but fewer studies discuss in detail the machinery of central and local government that conducts the relationship. A particular problem is the rapidity of change in the departments that manage local and regional structures and policies. Some information can be gained from web sources through the DCLG www.communities.gov.uk and the Local Government Association, www.lga.gov.uk. For Scotland, CoSLA can be accessed at www.cosla.gov.uk. IDeA can be accessed through www.idea.gov.uk. Among older studies Chandler (1988) is particularly concerned with this area and the authoritative study by Griffith (1966) is worth consulting. Crossman's *Diaries*, particularly volume 1 (1975), are a valuable source of material on the daily activity of the Minister in charge of local government. Rhodes (1986a) provides valuable material on the local authority associations of that time.

# 6

# Stewardship

Attempts to describe the relationship between local and central government have generated widely differing interpretations. The Blair Governments have been particularly keen to depict the relationship as a partnership. The 1998 White Paper *Modern Local Government*, for example, concludes with the comment that the Paper's success 'will be assured as councils everywhere join in partnership with the Government to bring about a fundamental shift in power and influence in favour of local people' (Postscript:1). In contrast, some academics have expressed fears that local government may become an agent only able to act according to rules and regulations determined by central government. W.A. Robson (1954), a doyen among academic analysts of local government, pointed out the dangers of an agency relationship and feared that such an arrangement was insidiously inserting itself into the Constitution.

Both the extremes of partnership and agency are too simplistic and, as Rhodes has shown, the relationship is a more complex arrangement based on bargaining between two sets of organisations which have differing resources; that is, means at their disposal to help them get their own way. The resources identified by Rhodes (1986a: 17; 1988: 42) can be categorised as

- the constitutional and legal position;
- political legitimacy, capacity to mobilise opinion;
- money and finance;
- organisational capacity; command of people, property and services;
- information, knowledge and access to data.

A local authority may prevent central government interference in, for example, its education plans because it is legally independent from the centre and can challenge the legality of government decisions through the courts. A local authority has resources of expertise since its officers and councillors may understand local circumstances better than more remote civil servants and may, therefore, be able to convince a government that it is financially or technically impossible to enact a particular policy. Local political support in favour of local ideas can be a valuable resource for councillors, who may convince the government that it would lose political goodwill and, more seriously, votes, were it to press forward with an issue. Local governments, finally, are not bereft of financial resources to employ public relations or technical experts, organise publicity campaigns or pay for litigation in order to pursue their interests. However, all of the resources held by local authorities are also held by central government, which has its own experts on technical issues, financial resources beyond the wildest dreams of any local authority, and the possibility of both local and national political support. Governments also have a further and crucial asset, expressed by Rhodes as the ability to change the rules of the game, through their ability to legislate, change statutory orders and restructure the finance of local government. Thus, local governments may, ultimately through the courts, successfully challenge Whitehall on the interpretation of existing law but, unlike the government, they cannot change the law to suit their own interests.

Rhodes later (1986a; 1988) wove the power dependence model into the concept of networks and policy communities. A policy network describes the framework of interactions between organisations that are influencing the determination of new policies or the retention of existing practices. A policy community develops when actors in the relationship are aware of each others' influence and form a stable pattern of interaction that often excludes outsider groups. Policy communities, for example, unite separate local authorities into a national community for local government. In general, Rhodes (Rhodes and Marsh 1992: 13–14) sees the wider central–local relationship as more extensive than a policy community and prefers the term 'inter-governmental networks'. Unlike policy communities, which are seen as developing around specific functions, there is a much greater tendency for local government organisations to relate not only to each other and central government but to a diverse range of other functional policy communities to create elaborate networks of interconnecting groups.

Even though New Labour Governments have insisted that local authorities secure policy delivery in partnership with other agencies, there can be an important difference in terms of political power between differing types of partner. Weak partners, such as neighbourhood opinions, may be involved but brushed aside if their views differ from local or central governments, whereas certain strong partners, such as business finance or central and local government, may dominate the network. In practice, as Rhodes has recognised, networks may become systems in which the interests of weaker members of the policy community are incorporated and taken over by the stronger partner and what results is corporate government in which all interests are on essential issues led and marshalled by one or two dominant players.

### The changing character of central–local relations

Prior to 1979, it was widely held, by politicians as well as academics, that local government was an established and powerful institution which it would be unwise to disturb without good cause. Central–local relations had become a quiet area of politics built predominantly on mutual understanding between representatives of local and central government. Local government and its associations bargained with the government behind closed doors in an atmosphere of mutual understanding of each others' role and spheres of interest and thus formed major elements in a policy community. Only occasionally did an issue emerge which rocked this complacent and quiet landscape, such as the hostile campaign by rural district councils against the reorganisation of local government in 1974 or in 1973 attempts by a few local authorities such as Clay Cross UDC to refuse to apply Government regulations to secure higher rents for council housing.

The era of apparently uneventful intergovernmental relations was to change with the Thatcher Governments. One of the most striking features of Mrs Thatcher's regime was her willingness to confront established organisations rather than use quiet diplomacy. The Conservatives in 1979 were determined to cut back public spending not only in central government but in all other sectors of government and that was assumed to include local authorities. This began with the 1980 Local Government Planning and Land Act, which attempted to penalise high spending local authorities but a lack of understanding of the workings of local government allowed radical left wing authorities to compensate for loss of grants by raising higher rates with the approval of the majority of voters. Radical left wing authorities also began using their powers in directions that were not welcome to the centre, such as massively subsidising public transport. The Thatcher Government managed to get its act together after the 1983 election and passed legislation that allowed the Government to cap the amount of taxes local authorities could raise through the rating system. Sixteen high spending authorities, largely metropolitan districts and London boroughs, were capped and responded by refusing to set a rate as required by the new legislation. Following three months of confrontation from March 1985 the Government forced the authorities to back down by threatening to surcharge the councillors the sums of money raised illegally and thereby oblige them to resign (Blunkett and Jackson 1987: 166–98). The crisis demonstrated that, if confrontation between centre and locality took place outside normal legal channels of negotiation, central government would be victorious unless opposed by overwhelming public opinion. After the rate capping confrontation local authorities faced a continuing onslaught of controls and rebuffs, including the abolition of the left wing metropolitan counties and the GLC, enforced privatisation of services through compulsory competitive tendering and efforts by local authorities to publicly campaign against central government. After local authorities had been put in their place, Mrs Thatcher's tenure in 10 Downing Street was ironically brought down partly by her replacement of the rating system with the poll tax. The widespread popular outrage at an inequitable tax had little to do with support for local governments, which were sufficiently cowed to be obliged to administer the system (Butler, Adonis and Travers 1994).

Battles were on occasion won by local authorities opposing the Conservatives' policies during both the Thatcher and Major Governments. The MDCs were able to thwart Conservative attempts to argue through the courts that subsidies for public transport were unlawful. However, individual victories do not necessarily win a war of independence. Despite delays in legislative time and the unpopularity of most reforms and restructuring of the local government system, the Thatcher Governments persevered in restricting the powers of local authorities. As the Government became more experienced in the methods used by local authorities to find legislative loopholes, Whitehall draughtsmen constructed laws that were increasingly difficult to evade. The Thatcher Governments used their powers to change the rules of the game to blunt many of the more potent local authority weapons that had been used against them. The 1986 Local Government Act, which prevents local authorities organising publicity campaigns critical of the elected national government, is typical of this form of legislation. Consequently, inter-governmental relations in the 1980s were characterised by a Tom and Jerry syndrome in which the government cat believed it had caught the local authority mouse through new legislation only to find that the creature had again escaped from its clutches, resulting in further central pursuit of the hapless mouse.

### Has New Labour continued the relationship of control?

Tony Blair promised in Labour's 1997 manifesto that 'Local decision making should be less constrained by central government' (p. 54) and in style, if not substance, ushered in a rather different framework for central–local relations. As described earlier, the New Labour Governments have been more willing to consult local authorities on changes to policy and have lifted some of the restraints imposed by the Conservative Governments on revenue and capital spending and restraints on local authorities' capacity to benefit their communities.

However, despite this more relaxed attitude to local authorities, many of the underlying controls established by Mrs Thatcher remain as reserved powers and some draconian restraints remain on the statute book, such as the 1986 Local Government Act that prevents elected local authorities from criticising central government. Although the government does not set rigid targets on local expenditure, it retains powers to order local authorities to decrease spending that it feels is excessive. Compulsory competitive tendering gave way to Best Value, which restored to local authorities some discretion but also established further bench marking for service standards, increased inspection to ascertain whether minimum standards are fulfilled and provides further means through which the centre can take over failing services. The 2000 Local Government Act established tighter regulations on the ethical conduct of councillors and imposed reforms to the internal structure of local authorities obliging them to accept executive government and possibly local mayors, even though there was no great enthusiasm among local authorities for the idea.

## Local government as a steward

The Blair Governments, despite a more relaxed consultative relationship, have not reversed the extent of central control. This trend has its origins long before the 1980s. In the 1920s local government suffered a major, if not, at the time, too obvious a defeat, when Parliament refused to accept any but the most innocuous private bills. During this decade a process of cat and mouse conflict arose between the Conservative Governments and the London Borough of Poplar with its associated Board of Guardians that was not dissimilar to the local socialism battles of the 1980s. Both the Labour Party councillors and guardians of Poplar on several occasions refused to accept Government regulations on wages and rates of poor relief and at one point were imprisoned for contempt of court, only to be released because of popular support (Branson 1979). In the longer term their intransigence led the Government through legislation to change the rules that ensured that councillors who were surcharged for supporting unlawful local expenditure were not sent to prison for contempt of court if they refused payment but, as a consequence of their being made bankrupt, were disbarred from holding locally elected office. This procedure was successfully used by the Thatcher Government to rid itself of troublesome councillors in Liverpool and Lambeth although it has now been replaced under the 2000 Local Government Act that allows an adjudication panel following reference to it of a case from a standards officer, to disqualify or suspend a councillor from service on an authority.

The power of the centre to determine the policies of local government is clearly evident in the restructuring of the system from the inception of the Redcliffe-Maud Commission to the Local Government Act of 1972, which was dictated by central rather than local interests and pushed through despite the strong objections of the Associations for the urban and rural districts. Despite some victories by local governments during the last hundred years, they are losing the battle for autonomy and have failed, in the long run, to successfully maintain their integrity and independence from central government. There have, of course, been many periods of co-operative working between central and local government. There are also many examples of central government taking on board ideas that were generated locally, such as the development of local initiatives to publicise the attractions of an area for footloose industry. However, this deference to local interest is a consequence of *noblesse oblige* on the part of central government. Ministers and civil servants are happy to tolerate, or even encourage, local initiatives that are consonant with central policy interests and their interpretation of the proper role of local government. Under New Labour such links have been further fortified with the innovatory trend of senior officers in local government being incorporated into senior positions in national bureaucracies. Despite these changes, where localities move into areas that seriously oppose the objectives of the centre, New Labour Governments, as have all governments since the 1920s, intervened to suppress the practice.

The essence of central–local relationships in Britain cannot be analysed simply in terms of structures and sources of power. Underlying the system are values and traditions that have been shaping the system over the last two centuries and inform the behaviour of central politicians to the periphery. This entrenched attitude may be characterised as one of stewardship. The policy makers in central government, whether party politicians or bureaucrats, use local authorities as their steward in much the same way as the aristocratic owner of a large eighteenth century estate would have employed a steward to manage his country estates. The steward is given a measure of discretion to manage his lord's estate as efficiently as possible, but this discretion is always constrained by rules determined at the whim of the aristocrat. Free from detailed managerial duties, many landed gentlemen could absent themselves from their estates in order to indulge in the pleasures of luxury, politics, war or religion. Many landowners granted their stewards a very free hand but, should they learn that the steward was acting contrary to their principles or against their instructions, they had the means to admonish the false steward or remove him from office. Some landed gentry, however, chose to interest themselves in the day to day management of their estates and constantly plagued their stewards with rules, regulations, advice and arbitrary caprice.

Similarly, within central government there is a pervasive ethos that perceives local government to be a useful but subordinate arm of a national political system that is controlled by Whitehall and Westminster. Local authorities are of value because they take from the centre the tedious and detailed task of applying general policies to fit local circumstance. Politicians and senior civil servants can concentrate on major affairs of state and leave matters of detail to their subordinate stewards. On occasion, the government will consult with local authorities and even defer to their opinions since they may also be of help in advising the government on problems of implementing policy. Good employers will always consult with their stewards to understand whether their general policies will work in practice and to ensure that they have the resources to fulfil their assigned tasks. However, the centre may often refuse to take local advice and will certainly discipline or *en extremis* remove local units that oppose central interests.

### Explaining stewardship

Stewardship is a metaphor to describe the relationship between central and local government but does not in itself explain why this relationship evolved and how it is sustained. In the eighteenth century, the century of landowner and steward, local government in the form of the parish and borough was not funded by central government and not subject to uniform legislation, and hence had the appearance of substantive independence. However, in practice, as outlined in Chapter 2, in much of rural Britain local authorities were controlled by the JPs, generally landowners or their representatives, through the courts of quarter sessions. The foremost landowners also dominated Parliament and government. It was generally accepted by this conclave of landed interests that each squire and JP would be free to determine the conduct of the towns and villages in which they had land although any developments that could occasion differences between landowners, such as the route of a turnpike road or a canal, could be settled by private acts of Parliament. Local government was not in the eighteenth century as free from parliamentary regulation as is sometimes assumed.

The arrangement of central–local relations did not change essentially from the patron–clientelism of the eighteenth century with industrialisation and the liberal breakthrough of 1832. Utilitarian writers included Bentham, who helped define liberal values and argued for the domination of local government by Parliament, as did his most distinguished successor John Stuart Mill. They differed from the eighteenth century model in regard to who should control Parliament and hence the local political system. Democracy would ensure control of Parliament and local government by the industrious intellectual rather than the spend-thrift conservative landowner. In his *Considerations on Representative Government* Mill argues that the national Parliament will have greater wisdom on the correct principles by which the Nation should be governed than any smaller locally elected body:

> local representative bodies and their officers are almost certain to be of a much lower grade of intelligence and knowledge, than Parliament and the national executive. (Mill 1975: 375)

The national assembly and government were, however, not necessarily as conversant as parochial opinion on the detailed needs of a locality and hence local government had considerable value as a means of ensuring that the principles of political and moral action determined by the sovereign Parliament were fitted efficiently and effectively to local circumstance. J.S. Mill thus advocates a central–local relationship based on the principle that

> The authority which is most conversant with principles should be supreme over principles, whilst that which is most competent in details should have details left

to it. The principle business of central authority should be to give instruction, of the local authority to apply it. (1975: 377)

This view informs much of the policy making by central government towards local authorities. The role of local government is, chiefly, to implement policies whose principles are drawn up by the centre so as to adapt the general principles to local circumstance.

Marxist theory presents a number of explanations for the arrangement. At its simplest level, local government is viewed as part of the state and, therefore, a mechanism through which wealthy capitalists sustain a political system that exploits the workers in society. Such an argument may have seemed reasonable in the nineteenth century but cannot explain the current role of central and local government in providing support and welfare for the least able in society. A more sophisticated neo-Marxist explanation of the role of urban government put forward by Castells (1977) formed the basis for an explanation of intergovernmental relations that was particularly fashionable in the early 1980s. Urban society was essential to facilitate what Marxists term the 'reproduction of labour', a need to provide education, housing, health care and recreation facilities for workers so that capitalists can rely on a continuous supply of effective workers with sufficient understanding to adapt to changes in technology in order to keep the wheels of industry and commerce turning. Urban society and urban government emerge as the most efficient device for providing the necessities to ensure the reproduction of labour through, for example, schools and cheap housing. Under this model it may be argued that in the late nineteenth century, when industrial capitalists controlled large city governments, the municipality was far more concerned with providing services necessary for direct production such as gas, electricity and transport. The growth of industry into large multi-national business rather than smaller firms owned by a family rooted in one area of the country and the emergence of the Labour Party as a governing party in large towns led central governments in Britain to take into their direct control activities that affect capital production. Local government led by local people would remain interested and capable of running those services dealing with the reproduction of labour where it had a direct affect on individual welfare and a more indirect affect on production. However, even in the provision of welfare services, central government did not trust all local authorities to use their powers of taxation to provide what was seen as essential for welfare and not use their powers to reallocate the riches of wealthy individuals and businesses to the poor.

Neo-Marxist analysis may provide some answers to the explanation of stewardship in Britain but cannot be the sole solution. Not all welfare services are provided locally and productive services are not exclusively reserved by the centre. The Health Service remains firmly outside the orbit of local authority control whilst planning policies and economic development tasks that affect business are still important local responsibilities. Whilst the relationship between labour and capital is a crucial element forging political systems, it is doubtful that that is the only factor which should be considered. There are specifically British factors that have helped shape the current relationship.

The centralisation and uniformity in the provision of local services began in the early twentieth century with the beginnings of the welfare state that were demanded by more advanced new liberals who believed everyone in society should have equal opportunity to make the most of their lives. This prompted the Liberal Governments elected after 1906 to establish policies for health and unemployment insurance and old age pension outside the control of the local poor law, which they felt stigmatised those in poverty and was implemented too inconsistently. The Labour Party supplanted the Liberals in the 1920s but many of its leaders shared the new liberal ideology. Moreover, for many Conservatives the arrival of the Labour Party, despite its generally moderate stance, awoke fears of socialism within city governments and hence the Party dominating power in the inter-war years tended to decrease local autonomy.

The growth of the welfare state also set in train for all the major parties a concern to interfere in local politics as they slowly and imperceptibly began a bidding war to secure votes in general elections through claims that they could secure better welfare for all. The first Conservative election manifestos of the late nineteenth century never mentioned welfare policies but by the 1930s the Party, like the Liberals and Labour, was seeking support through promises to improve welfare. This battle for hearts and minds continued apace after 1945 and in successive elections the leading parties have promised to improve services that in the nineteenth century were never seen as a central government responsibility. Once a party has gained power promising to secure, for example, better school results, improved housing or safer streets, it cannot sit back and allow local authorities to simply deliver these results on its behalf but must legislate and control through grants local policies that will secure these promises.

### Further reading

A useful summary of theories on inter-governmental relations is provided by Stoker (1995), which categorises theories into historical, neo-Marxist and network approaches. The study of inter-governmental relations in Britain received a major impetus in the late 1980s through the development of a research council sponsored survey of the subject. Rhodes (1981, 1986a, 1986b, 1988, 1999) developed the theoretical framework underlying a series of studies on this theme which have included Gyford and James (1983) on the role of political parties, Laffin (1986) on professional associations and Rhodes (1986a) on the local authority associations.

Neo-Marxist approaches to inter-governmental relations were importantly developed by Castells (1977), whose position is explained and critically examined in Dunleavy (1980). The development from this position of an explanation of the distribution of services to central and local government by Saunders (1981, 1984) is critically appraised by Dunleavy in Boddy and Fudge (1984).

A more historical approach is developed by Bulpitt (1983) and for a nineteenth century insight Redlich and Hirst (1970) is still of importance. To get an insight into nineteenth century liberal values Mill (1975) is very readable and also a seminal study. Chandler (1988) considers the mechanics of central–local relations from the perspective of the organisation of central government and also develops a differing interpretation of inter-governmental relations in this study and, in a comparative context, in later articles (1992, 2005). The argument in the final section of this chapter is developed more fully in Chandler (2007).

# 7

# Policy making and democracy

Local governments are democratic institutions. The electoral basis of local authorities gives them a unique and authoritative role among the plethora of sub-governmental institutions. The decisions of a local authority cannot be passed off as solely the views of an appointed elite but derive from a body representative of the local population as a whole. How far the representative and democratic framework of local government is effective is the subject of much debate and this question will be considered further in the concluding chapter. To answer such a question it is necessary to understand how local authorities arrive at decisions and how they are accountable for their actions. This chapter will begin to unravel these issues with an outline of the policy making structure of local authorities.

## The local electoral system

The policy and actions of a local authority are legally the responsibility of either its elected councillors or, in the few authorities that have adopted the system, a directly elected mayor. To be a member of a council – that is, a councillor or a mayor representative of local citizens – it is necessary to stand for election to the local authority. Councillors in Britain are normally elected for a four year term of office to represent an electoral ward, which is the local equivalent to the constituency which returns an MP to the national Parliament. The Greater London Authority, as will be explained later, is an exception. Exactly when a councillor's term of office expires depends upon the type of authority she or he represents since local authorities do not all go to the polls in the same year, nor do all members of a council necessarily stand for election at the same time. County councils, London boroughs, the GLA and most district and unitary authorities hold elections for the full council once every four years. In metropolitan districts only one councillor stands for election in any year. Thus one third of the council is elected in three out of every four years in metropolitan districts. The fourth

Table 7:1 *The timing of elections*

| | 2007 | 2008 | 2009 | 2010 | 2011 | 2012 |
|---|---|---|---|---|---|---|
| County councils | | | * | | | |
| London boroughs | | | | * | | |
| Greater London Authority | | * | | | | * |
| Metropolitan districts | ⅓ | ⅓ | | ⅓ | ⅓ | ⅓ |
| Some non-metropolitan districts | ⅓ | ⅓ | | ⅓ | ⅓ | ⅓ |
| Some non-metropolitan districts | * | | | | * | |
| Some English unitary authorities | * | | | | * | |
| Some English unitary authorities | ⅓ | ⅓ | | ⅓ | ⅓ | ⅓ |
| Scottish districts | * | | | | * | |
| Welsh districts | * | | | | * | |

*Notes:* * All council seats to be elected.
⅓ One third of council seats to be elected.

year, when there is now no contest in these areas, was the year for elections to the now defunct metropolitan county councils but can now be used, if appropriate, for the election of an executive mayor. Some unitary authorities and many non-metropolitan districts also operate an electoral system similar to that of the metropolitan districts and a few districts elect councillors every other year. In Scotland and Wales local elections are held for all members of each council on a four year cycle. Given the complexity of these arrangements some local elections are taking place each year. Table 7.1 indicates the present pattern in a four year cycle.

A significant difference between the national and local electoral system is that local elections are statutorily held on a specific date and not at the convenience of the leading councillors. The date is normally the first Thursday in May. Should a councillor resign or die between elections then a by-election to replace the departed politician must, according to the 1972 Local Government Act, normally be held within 42 working days of the notification of the vacancy. An important consequence of the fixed date for elections is that political parties in control of a council are not able to aid their chances of re-election by choosing to resign at a time most favourable to them, as does the National government. Only individual councillors can resign and there is no way in which the leader of a local party can force his or her opposition rivals to vacate their seats by dissolving the whole council.

The restrictions on eligibility to stand for election that are applied nationally also apply locally. Candidates must be at least 18 years of age, be registered voters and have no un-discharged criminal sentence or be certified as insane. Council candidates must also demonstrate to the returning officer that they are either resident in that local authority, own property there or have their main place of work within its borders. In contrast to national elections, local political parties cannot simply invite a famous or able candidate who does not have the links with that community that qualify him or her to be a candidate to stand for their local council or as an elected mayor. Candidates cannot be employed by the local authority for which they wish to stand and senior local government officers may not stand for any local authority. These restrictions can be unfair. A local dustman or a school teacher, whose salaries and conditions of service will be effectively fixed by national negotiations will, in practice, have less to personally gain by being a councillor than, for example, a local estate agent interested in property development in that community.

The method of balloting for local elections has always been similar to the procedures for national elections but concern within the Blair Government about low turnout in local elections led to clauses in the 2000 Local Government Act to allow local authorities to experiment with voting procedures. Some local authorities have consequently piloted schemes to allow voting through the internet or by telephone but increasing postal voting is the only innovation that has so far significantly increased electoral turnout.

The implementation of the electoral rules is in the hands of a returning officer, usually the mayor or the chief executive of a district council. He or she is responsible to the courts for the correct conduct of the election and could be sued or prosecuted for bad practice. The returning officer is, however, usually a figurehead and the real work of electoral organisation is undertaken by a deputy who will normally be a full time local authority officer charged with running a small office concerned with the management of elections both for the local authority and for Parliament. This officer's principal task is to compile each year the register of electors, draw up the timetable for an election, receive and check the validity of nominations for candidates, arrange for votes to be cast and counted, and receive and act on complaints about the conduct of the elections. The returning officer, rather than the deputy, nevertheless usually steals the glory of announcing the winner of a parliamentary, if not local, elections.

### *The electoral system and adversary politics*

In England and Wales most elections follow the first past the post, simple plurality voting system that is used in Westminster elections. The candidate with the highest number of votes wins the contest. This system has attracted strong criticism since, as in general elections, the system benefits the larger parties, which receive a much greater proportion of seats than their share of the popular vote would merit whilst smaller parties may win a considerable proportion of the vote but gain no seats. Smaller parties, such as the Liberal Democrats, complain that they have far fewer councillors than they feel they ought to be entitled to on the basis of their national vote. However, whilst they are sometimes under-represented on a national scale, smaller parties can reap the benefits of undisputed control of a local authority in those areas where they are a dominant political force. The system did not prevent the Liberal Democrats from securing overall control of large cities such as Liverpool. Independents may also benefit from the system since it is possible for active individuals to win local elections if they are well known in a ward but not recognised throughout the local area as a whole. There are many alternatives to the first past the post system which can elect representatives more proportionately but such systems are likely to result in the majority of local authorities becoming hung councils in which no political party has an overall majority. In Scotland a proportional system ensured in 2007 that only two authorities are controlled by a party with an overall majority. Such an outcome is welcomed by some but may not produce decisive government and can entrench in power small centrist parties that can link their support to any of their major rivals.

Most European local government systems utilise some form of proportional representation to select their councillors and multi-ballot systems to select mayors when they are directly elected. The United States, like Britain, however, remains firmly wedded to the first past the post system although many 'reformed' local governments elect councillors or commissioners to represent the city or county as a whole rather than a ward.

In response to pressure for electoral change, the Blair Government established a system of proportional representation for elections to the Scottish and Welsh and London Assemblies through a system similar to that adopted in Germany for national elections in which, in addition to representatives elected on a first past the post basis from single member constituencies, further members are selected from lists drawn up by the parties so that the final Assembly has representation from all the major parties in proportion to votes cast within the Province as a whole. For elections of executive mayors in England and Wales the Government has adopted the supplementary vote which allows voters to mark a first and second choice on the ballot paper if more than two candidates are standing. If no candidate gets over 50 per cent of the first choice votes cast, the candidate with the lowest number of first choice votes is eliminated and his or her second choice votes are then assigned to the remaining candidates. The candidate who then has the largest number of votes is selected. In Scotland, pressure from the Liberal Democrats, then in coalition with the Labour Party, resulted in 2004 in the introduction of single transferable votes (STVs) to select councillors. This method, which requires voters to number the candidates in order of preference, was first introduced for the 2007 elections. At the same election voters chose Assembly members by the different additional member method, resulting in much confusion and many a spoilt ballot paper.

### Policy structure

The central structures through which local authorities make and implement policies are determined in broad outline by the Local Government Acts of 2000 and 2007. Local authorities must adopt one of the models for executive governance permissible in these Acts. The executive is responsible for developing and implementing local authority policy. The most widely adopted choice requires the councillors to elect one of their members as their leader, who chairs a cabinet formed from among the councillors selected either by the leader or the full council. Under the 2007 Act the leader is elected for a four year term in office or for as long as she or he remains an elected councillor. The leader will, however, depend for her or his continued role in office on the support of the council and can be replaced by the council. Thus, if a Party loses overall control of a local authority following an election, the opposition parties may vote to remove the leader and replace him or her with their own favoured candidate. The cabinet, including the mayor or leader, must have no more than ten members unless permission is received from the secretary of state to have a few more members.

A second, more radical option for local authorities replaces the leader by an elected mayor voted into office by the electorate for the local authority. The elected mayor chairs the cabinet and selects its members from among the councillors. The 2007 Act has in addition allowed local authorities to choose a system in which both the mayor and the members of the cabinet are directly elected but at the time of writing no authority has taken up this option. The system requires a local referendum to come into effect that can be called either by the local authority itself or if requested in a petition signed by more than 5 per cent of its citizens. The three systems are outlined in Figures 7.1–7.3.

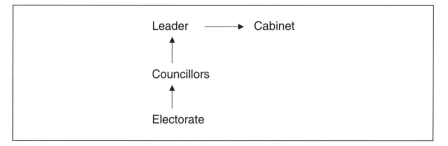

Figure 7.1 *Leader – cabinet*

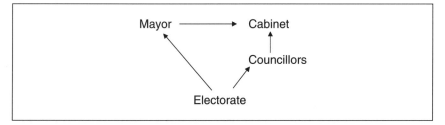

Figure 7.2 *Directly elected mayor*

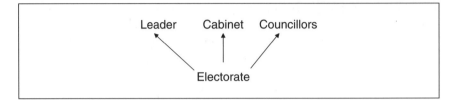

Figure 7.3 *Elected leader and cabinet*

In addition to these structures the 2000 Local Government Act allowed a local authority to adopt, following a referendum, a City Manager system in which the mayor rather than selecting a cabinet of councillors works alongside a chief executive, who would be an employee of the authority, selected by the council. The mayor would be expected to take a longer term strategic vision of the progress of the authority and the manager would be expected to put the vision into practice. Only one local authority, Stoke on Trent, adopted this system and its performance has been subject to considerable criticism from its electorate. The 2007 Act does not endorse such a system and it appears that this structure is now out of favour. It is finally possible for a local authority to request approval from the government for establishing some other form of decision making structure along mayoral, executive lines. They could, for example, develop a system in which a number of cabinet members, in addition to the mayor, are directly elected. At the time of writing no local authority seems to have shown an interest in this idea.

The structures for policy making in local authorities established by the 2000 Local Government Act replaced a system that had emerged in the nineteenth century in which all elected councillors had a role in making policy and it was not possible to enact even the most minor decision, such as repairs to council houses, without it being formally approved by the full council following advice from the appropriate specialist sub-committee of councillors dealing with a particular policy area. All councillors were members of a number of what, in larger authorities, formed a bewildering array of sub-committees and even sub-sub–committees which largely discussed advice given to them by officers attached to each committee. The result was that whilst councillors could be thoroughly immersed in policy details the decision process was bureaucratic and slow. During the twentieth century the system was gradually streamlined with the development of a policy committee which made the most important strategic policy decisions made up of sub-committee chairs, chaired by a leader of the council. The structural changes of the 2000 Act were designed to streamline the system by creating a cabinet of councillors who, like the former sub-committee chairs, were the chief spokespersons for specific services and were co-ordinated by a leader or directly elected mayor.

Remnants of the older system survive in Scotland, as will be indicated later, and in the smallest English authorities. The 2000 Local Government Act does not require local authorities with a population below 85,000 to choose an executive style system of local government although the committees of these authorities are expected to make decisions without referring every detailed issue to the full council for approval, as was the case under the preceding committee systems. These smaller local authorities are, nevertheless, required to establish a scrutiny committee. Under these arrangements many smaller district authorities have been able to involve a larger proportion of their councillors in their decision making process and usually operate through a small number of sub-committees of the council which involve a high proportion of their elected councillors. For example, Penwith District Council in Cornwall has as its central executive bodies a policy committee and a resources committee rather than a cabinet but also has a scrutiny committee for backbench members. In 2006 there were 49 such authorities in England.

Most local authorities, required by the 2000 Act to create a cabinet, preferred to adopt the system of cabinet and leader government which most closely resembles the former committee structure for making policy decisions. The structure differs greatly from the old system in that most minor policy matters can be enacted immediately rather than being referred to the full council, and hence the backbench, non-cabinet member has no direct role in enacting and implementing policy but instead, as will be described below, has the task of scrutinising the policy of the cabinet. In reality the cabinet, rather like the committee chairs of the former system, is selected as the senior councillors within the majority party on the council and their presence in the cabinet is partly determined by the leader but also pressures within the party group from influential members whose views cannot be ignored by the leader. Where there is a hung council the leader of the council will usually defer to the views of the

---

In France a council elects a mayor, and in Germany councils elect a similar political executive, the *burgermeister*, who is regarded as the political leader of the community. Italy has started to adopt a system of separately elected mayors and councils. In the United States there is a variety of local governance systems. Many cities, such as New York, have a strong mayoral system in which the mayor is separately elected from the council and serves as the head of an executive style government and appoints its members. In others, termed weak mayor systems, the council chooses the mayor or he/she may be separately elected but in either case the councillors have the power to appoint other leading executive politicians. Weak mayors can, as in Chicago, nevertheless be effective leaders of the council if the city has a disciplined dominant party of which the mayor is leader. In some mid-sized cities a smaller number of commissioners are elected to jointly run the authority. In many, although by no means all of the United States cities, the mayor, councillors or the commissioners will appoint a city manager to run the city in accord with the strategic lead established by the mayor or commissioners.

leader of other parties in a governing coalition, who will expect that they or their nominees will be given cabinet places. Thus, unlike the normal practice of the United Kingdom government, cabinets on many local authorities are not composed of a single party.

Whilst the 2000 Act applied to England and, with amendments, to Wales, it was not applied to Scotland. Following their formation, the Scottish Parliament and Executive appointed a former Chief Executive for Strathclyde, Neil McIntosh, to review the relationship between local government and the Executive and Parliament and also how local government could be more democratic. The McIntosh Report suggested that the system of committees was too often dominated by the party system to make any sense of democracy within the structure and recommended local authorities review their administrative structures. A further study by Alasdair McNish, a former Chief Executive for Lanarkshire, however, made no recommendation as to specific structures that should be adopted by Scottish local authorities but took the ethically sensible view that local authorities should develop the system most suitable for them and their electorate. Consequently, there has been no pressure as in England and Wales to form cabinet governments, let alone have directly elected mayors. Many Scottish authorities have, nevertheless, reviewed and amended their policy making structures. McConnell (2004: 86–7) identifies three types of decision making structures. A small group of six authorities, including Edinburgh, have approximated to cabinet style government, forming an executive to determine and implement policy and committees to scrutinise their behaviour. Three other authorities, Fife, the Highlands, and Argyll and Bute, the latter two covering large areas, have created decentralised area councils. The remaining 23 authorities, which include the major cities of Glasgow, Aberdeen and Dundee, have retained a more streamlined committee structure.

### Executive mayors

Many members of the Blair Government who took an interest in local authority matters expected far more local authorities to take up the option of having a directly elected mayor, and had established mechanisms that could force local authorities to hold a referendum on the issue if requested by a petition from 5 per cent of the local electorate or by the Government if it had evidence that a council was wilfully preventing public opinion having a voice on the issue. Few local authorities were however obliged to hold a referendum and of the 34 which have so far been held only 12 have resulted in a vote favouring a directly elected mayor, as shown in Table 7.2.

None of the largest cities in Britain have opted for a directly elected mayor, with the exception of London where the GLA was required to have a mayor through the separate legislation that established the Authority. Several of the electorates that have chosen the system, such as in Doncaster, seem to have reacted against reports of corruption within the old structures and several

Table 7.2 *Elected mayors and referenda*

|  | Year of referendum | Triggered by |
|---|---|---|
| *London boroughs* | | |
| Hackney | 2002 | Council |
| Lewisham | 2001 | Council |
| Newham | 2002 | Council |
| *Metropolitan districts* | | |
| Doncaster | 2001 | Council |
| North Tyneside | 2001 | Council |
| *Unitary* | | |
| Hartlepool | 2001 | Council |
| Middlesbrough | 2001 | Council |
| Stoke on Trent | 2002 | Petition |
| Torbay | 2005 | Petition |
| *Non metropolitan districts* | | |
| Bedford | 2002 | Petition |
| Mansfield | 2002 | Petition |
| Watford | 2001 | Council |

others, such as in the London Borough of Lewisham, have had an ambitious leader who favoured the system. The status of the elected mayor has also been somewhat tarnished by attracting successful independent candidates from less than conventional backgrounds. Most famously in Hartlepool the post was won by Stuart Drummond, who also acted as the football team mascot 'Hangus' the Monkey, and in neighbouring Middlesbrough Ray Mallon, a senior police officer who was at odds with his Chief Constable, was elected as an independent.

In the United States where many, but not all mayors are directly elected, there is less likely to be a total breakdown in the relationship between the mayor and councillors even if the majority of councillors are from a different party from the mayor since party loyalties are generally far weaker and politicians are rarely disciplined if they vote against the party line. In France, as the mayor is elected by the councillors, the mayor will generally be supported by a majority of councillors and can remain effective despite a more partisan political system than in the United States.

### The council

The creation of cabinets necessitated a radically different role for the full council of most local authorities and for non-executive, backbench councillors. The full council has to approve each year the broad policy plans and the budget of the authority as laid out by the cabinet. It also approves decisions which could not on any account be construed as having formed part of the broad approved policy proposals. The budget and policy plans are usually presented to the full council in February or March in time to be implemented for the next financial year. The council will also at its annual meeting ratify the membership of the cabinet and confirm membership for committees such as those concerned with planning that are outside cabinet control.

The meetings of the council are presided over by a 'chairman', elected on an annual basis by and from the members of that council. Historically, the chairman in chartered boroughs and, after 1835, municipal boroughs was accorded the title of mayor. This title is conferred on all chairs of metropolitan districts, London boroughs and many district councils who have pretensions to being urban areas. Any of the authorities created in 1972 is able to petition the Queen to confer upon it a charter giving it the status of a borough and the right to elect a mayor. Parish councils, especially those covering old urban communities that were formerly boroughs or districts, have petitioned to become town councils and dignify their chairperson with the mayoral accolade. Larger local authorities that have been granted by Royal Charter the status of a city appoint a lord mayor. Counties have always remained content with a mere chairman. In Scotland, the chair of the district council is often referred to as the provost or, in the large cities, the lord provost.

The chair is, in most cases, an active and distinguished member of a political party but should not be confused with a directly elected mayor who has executive powers. The non-executive mayor is expected to maintain, like the Speaker of the House of Commons, strict neutrality in her or his dealings with the council. Very occasionally neutrality may go out of the window since the chair has a casting vote in the case of a tied vote in council and, should party groups in council be evenly balanced, the political preferences of the mayor may be crucial in determining which party controls the local authority. Since the position of mayor is awarded through a vote of the council, it is possible for a majority party to ensure that their friends always retain the chairmanship or mayoralty within the party. Most local authorities will, however, ensure that opposition groups have a share of the honours and it is frequently the case that each party gets a turn at nominating one of its members to be the mayor, in conformity with the size of party groups within the council, under a well established principle of equity and 'buggin's turn'. It is, therefore, not infrequent for a Labour controlled authority to have, from time to time, a Conservative Party mayor and vice versa.

*Scrutiny*

A major function of councillors is to scrutinise and check the work of the executive and where necessary call the cabinet or its members to account publicly for their actions. Councils appoint one or more scrutiny committees, which can demand that cabinet members or officers appear before them to explain their policies. They are able to 'call in' cabinet decisions by requiring the cabinet to reconsider policies or actions that they consider to be unacceptable. For the most part scrutiny committees select a number of long standing problems facing the authority and study these in some depth and report their findings to the cabinet with the hope that their senior political colleagues will act on their recommendations. Reference to your local authority's web site should lead you to the minutes of scrutiny meetings. For example, Manchester City Council's economic regeneration scrutiny committee for March 2007 can be found to have discussed, among other issues, housing strategy plans with the Director of Housing and priorities for Local Area Agreement funding. The system parallels the arrangement of select committees in the House of Commons, which can, on occasion, be influential in raising difficult and embarrassing issues for the government that can be taken up by the press and become matters of public interest which help determine voters' attitudes to the government.

The effectiveness of scrutiny has yet to be fully established as the system has not as yet had time to evolve or realise in most authorities what potential may lurk within its depths. Studies so far made of scrutiny procedures in local authorities reveal a very mixed pattern of practices and enthusiasm for the system among local authorities. In practice the capacity of powerful party groups to control their members probably ensures that matters which would be highly embarrassing to the local authority are either avoided or not subject to as withering a scrutiny as possible (Leach and Copus 2004). There is also little evidence to suggest that the local press pays much attention to the findings of scrutiny boards (Chandler 2007: 292).

## Decentralisation

Many local authorities have developed systems through which they attempt to devolve a measure of decision making or consultation to local areas within their communities. This trend follows a number of local initiatives in the 1980s to break up the relatively large authority into areas which corresponded more closely to the sense of community cherished by its citizens. The most radical initiative was in the London Borough of Tower Hamlets which, for a few years under Liberal Democrat control, split itself as far as was legally possible into seven mini-local authorities. A more practical and longer lasting scheme of area committees was developed by South Somerset District Council.

These initiatives were accepted with rather muted enthusiasm by both the Thatcher and Major Governments and the New Labour Administrations. The White Paper *Modern Local Government*, despite its secondary title *In Touch with the People*, devoted but four paragraphs to the idea and damned the initiative with faint praise. Many local authorities have, nevertheless, formed area committees but the majority of these have a largely consultative role in which the local councillors for the area will make themselves available to answer questions from the public but have little or no executive powers to resolve local concerns without persuading cabinet members to take an interest in the problem.

The 2007 Local Government Act similarly permits the creation of area committees and allows unitary authorities to form urban parishes but does not make decentralisation schemes mandatory despite the proposals in the Act that facilitate the creation of even larger single tier authorities. Indeed, the Government appears to be more favourable to the creation of organisations such as Local Strategic Partnerships that act in partnership with, but remain outside, the local authority, as a means of creating greater participation. New Labour has yet to recognise that the size of a local authority may greatly contribute to lack of enthusiasm among community minded residents to participate in what for many citizens is now just another rather distant bureaucracy.

### The other roles of councillors

In addition to their probable membership of a scrutiny committee and possible membership of an area committee, the non-executive backbench councillor is likely to be almost as involved in committee work as was the case before the restructuring of policy making in 2000. Most important is the task of approving planning permission for building and construction, which is a task undertaken by a sub-committee of the council that is not subject to the cabinet and requires members to act with a high level of integrity given the possibilities for corruption in this area of policy making. A few backbenchers will also serve on the standards committee of their authority. In addition the growing numbers of partnership arrangements that require councillors to sit on the boards of arm's length public bodies or LSPs mean that backbenchers are frequently involved in work on organisations, usually in a role not of making policy but approving the decisions of others.

The 1988 White Paper *Modern Local Government* maintained that councillors who have no executive responsibilities should not waste their time sitting in endless committee meetings in the town hall but be out on the streets and footpaths of their wards talking with and working for their local electorate and reporting back to the executive their needs and demands. Whilst there has been considerable research on the role of scrutiny and elected mayors, there is as yet little evidence as to whether backbench councillors are more involved in the community than before the 2000 Local Government Act. It is difficult, however, to see how the hope can be fulfilled that, under the new arrangements, backbench councillors will be henceforth more active in the community and as a result create greater enthusiasm for local government and facilitate greater local democracy. Much of their work may still have to be within the town halls engaging in even more futile posturing on scrutiny committees or trying to gain the attention of remote cabinet members to draw their attention to issues relating to their ward. The effectiveness of the new arrangements will be considered again in Chapter 13 against the wider background of local democracy and party politics.

### Further reading

The basic internal structures of local authorities are covered in most textbooks but more detail on new management ideas can be obtained from Leach, Stewart and Walsh (1994). Walsh (1995) provides a wider theoretical view of new management thinking. Stoker (1999, 2000) includes valuable articles on the changes being pursued in the early years of New Labour Governments. The more specific issue of joined up government has been popularised by Perri 6 et al. (2002) and the emphasis by New Labour of local government working in partnership with other agencies is discussed by Goss (2001) and Sullivan and Skeltcher (2002). Copus (2006) surveys the directly elected mayoral system.

The earlier ideas on corporate management produced an extensive literature and are best approached through one of its principal advocates, Stewart (1971, 1974). Also of value are Greenwood and Stewart (1974) and R. Greenwood et al. (1980). The Bains Report (1972) is also worth reading to gain an impression of this management style. Policies concerning decentralisation are best covered by Hoggett and Hambleton (1988), by Burns, Hambleton and Hoggett (1994) and Chandler et al. (1995).

# 8

# Leaders, councillors and the party system

Throughout the twentieth century it was legally considered that the decisions of a local authority reflected the majority view of elected councillors who were supposedly representative of the citizens who voted for them. Democracy seldom operates like this in practice. Even before the 2000 Local Government Act decisions within all but a few of the principal local authorities were made, not in formal committees of the local authority, but in the informal conclaves of political parties. Representation of the electorate is also not a simple relationship between councillors and constituents but is mediated through the campaigns and programmes of local and national parties. In the late nineteenth and first half of the twentieth century many commentators on local government regretted the rise of partisanship and the decline of the independent councillor but realism about the role of political parties was established by the 1980s when the Widdicombe Enquiry concluded that

> we regard the continued presence of political organisation in local government as inevitable for the foreseeable future. Indeed we would expect to see a continuing trend towards political organisation in those authorities which at present are relatively apolitical. We do not regard this in itself either as desirable or undesirable. (Widdicombe 1986: 61, para 4.16)

The members of a particular party elected to a local authority normally formally organise themselves into what is termed the 'party group'. If the party has an overall majority in the local authority it is often, in reality, within the party group that most of the crucial policy decisions are made.

Party divisions in local government are as old as the emergence of the Tory and Whig parties but it was not until the 1920s that most cities had established more rigid discipline among the party rank and file and the decisions of the party group were expected to be binding on members (Chandler 2007: 227). Until the restructuring of local authorities in 1974 many smaller district councils fought elections on party lines but once elected councillors did not rigidly vote together in their party group as required by their leader. It is now generally assumed that, since 1974, local politics has become more partisan and that this includes a much greater tendency for party groups to vote cohesively.

There have always been fears that local political independence would be submerged by the domination of local political activity by national party machines directing the conduct of councillors who are members of their party but, as Gyford and James (1983: 3) concluded, there is little evidence that this has ever occurred in practice. The major national parties provide rules for the selection of their local candidates for positions of councillor or elected mayor and outline standing orders to guide the conduct of party group meetings and rules on maintaining disciplined support for the party. The rules are most comprehensive and binding within the Labour Party but do not, as will be indicated, entail that local Labour councillors follow policies dictated to them by their national Party leaders. In the Conservative and Liberal Democrat Parties even the standing orders are for guidance and, whilst usually respected, local differences in the organisation of their local councillors are not infrequent.

> Within most European Union countries party politics is a major feature of the political life of all larger authorities but in smaller local governments, such as rural French communes, it may have little relevance and councillors are effectively independent of party ties. In the United States the movement to reform city government in the late nineteenth century led several cities to forbid political party affiliations being part of local elections and in such cities councillors stand as independents. The consequence of this arrangement is to advantage middle class candidates, often with business affiliations, who can afford the personal cost of standing for election.

## The organisation of the party group

In most local authorities the councillors supporting a particular party will meet as a party group before any full meeting of the council and, in some authorities, even the cabinet (Copus, 2004: 231) in order to co-ordinate their strategy towards items on the agenda. They may meet at other times to discuss ideas and problems. Council groups in the Labour, Liberal and most Conservative Parties will usually make decisions on a majority basis, although this should not be taken to mean that each member has equal power. Each group of any size will have an elected inner executive committee composed of the most respected and authoritative party members which will recommend what action should be taken on important issues and initiate many of the policies to be adopted by the group. Most members of the executive will be cabinet members or, if in opposition, shadow a cabinet post. A chair, who is often an elder worthy of the party, is elected to control the group's meetings. A secretary arranges the meetings, circulates their agenda and takes the minutes. A group whip has the task, like the House of Commons equivalent, of informing members of their strategy in any debate, monitoring how colleagues vote and, in consultation with other senior party members, instituting disciplinary procedures should a member fail to follow the party line. However, the introduction of scrutiny ensures that most party standing orders allows backbench councillors to be openly critical of their local party leaders in their role as scrutineers even though it is not expected that they criticise their leaders in full council meetings (Copus 2004: 130).

The effectiveness of the group in delivering a common stance is primarily a function of its ability to discipline its membership but leaders of local parties are less vulnerable to rebellions from backbenchers than is the case of the British prime minister. In the House of Commons a rebellion that results in defeat for the party in government on an issue of importance will lead to new elections and possibly loss of power. The cabinet system within local government ensures that backbench councillors cannot easily stop an unpopular policy through a vote in the council. Discipline is, therefore, in part, secured by the fear of loss of status, promotion prospects and positions of responsibility in the party and local authority. The greatest constraint is, however, expulsion from the party group since, should the district or county party accept this decision, the errant councillors will not be re-selected as the party's candidate in the next election and have to take their chances as an independent. Expulsion from the party is not uncommon and it is even more frequent for councillors to resign from the party ahead of the threat of expulsion.

### The party leader

The most important elected member of a party's group of councillors is the party leader. The party group leader will generally also be leader of the council if his or her party enjoys a majority of seats on the council and, if the authority has an elected mayor, will normally be the party's nominee for this position. The leader will expect to initiate the major policies of the council group, set the tone and style of its strategy, co-ordinate its activities, mediate between its members and determine which colleagues will serve in the cabinet for the authority or, if the party does not enjoy a majority, be its chief spokesperson on important policy areas.

The power and authority of a party leader will, however, vary depending on personality and political circumstances. The position is achieved through election by the party group in what may be a strenuous and sometimes bitter contest between rival political leaders. The outcome of the vote may dramatically change party policy. For example, the election of Ken Livingstone in 1982 as leader of the Greater London Council was a triumph for more radical forces within the Labour group of councillors and signalled the beginning of confrontation with the Thatcher Government.

Although party leaders, like many prime ministers, are not necessarily all powerful, some can, over time, reach a position of dominance over the local authority to the extent that no policies are enacted without her or his acquiescence. Dominant party leaders achieve their status partly by careful and judicious appointment of friends or potential, but subournable, rivals to senior positions in their entourage. The executive of the party group will often be composed of individuals who are indebted to the leader for their political status and fully in accord with his or her policies. Some local politicians such as Sir Jack Smart, leader of Wakefield District Council throughout much of the 1980s and for a time Chairman of the Association of Metropolitan Authorities, occupy not only the position of leader but several other strategically important party posts such as chair of the district party or of a locally dominant trade union branch. It is possible in such a position for leaders to influence the attitudes of party members and, without recourse to overt discrimination, ensure that dangerous opponents to their policies are not often nominated as council candidates.

The image of a city 'boss' – a dominant politician who controls the governance of a community – is most firmly identified with the United States, where some mayors have been in a position through dominance in the local Democrat or Republican Party machine to dictate not only who holds office in local government but also who represents the area in State and federal elections. Generally, it is thought that city bosses are more a pre-1945 phenomenon. Mayor Richard Daley of Chicago was in the 1960s viewed as such a leader although he had limited powers in the State of Illinois. Powerful political leaders, the *local notables*, are perhaps more strongly entrenched in France, which has a more disciplined party system. For example, Gaston Defferre, who in the 1980s reformed French local government structures as Minister of the Interior, was simultaneously mayor of Marseilles, where he dominated both local and departmental government and represented the City in the National Assembly.

### Local party structures and the selection of candidates

Political parties do not regard their groups of councillors as isolated organisations that are unaccountable to the party at large. There are important connections between local political parties and their councillors, especially in relation to the procedures for electoral campaigns and the selection of candidates. In theory, the Labour Party is a democracy in which policy is determined by its rank and file membership, unlike the Conservative Party, which has never pretended to organise itself internally under democratic principles. It was argued by Robert McKenzie (1963) that both organisations are, nevertheless, at least as regards national policy making, oligarchies.

*The Labour Party*

When the Labour Party was formed in 1900 it was composed of trade unions and socialist societies which affiliated to the organisation. A new constitution, written in 1918, in a flush of post-war radicalism, grafted individual membership to the structure so that the Party established members' branches at local government ward level as the basis of an organisational hierarchy. Ward parties nominate delegates to the constituency party which covers the area returning an MP to Parliament. This body also includes delegates representing affiliated Labour members by virtue of trade union or socialist society membership.

Each local authority is shadowed by a committee which is called, as appropriate, the county or district Labour Party. These organisations are relatively large and may have a membership of up to 300 members. Most of the active delegates to these bodies are chosen from constituency parties, although, in practice, it is common for many constituency parties to select at least one delegate from each ward in their area. Affiliated party members are also represented on the county and district parties but, normally, few trade union branches bother to send a delegate, either through indifference or because the nominee must also be an individual party member. Each year the district or county party will choose a small executive which may have considerable authority in steering debate within the party and undertaking its day to day functions. In wealthy or electorally marginal areas the secretary of the district party may be a professional party agent. The function of the district or county party is to consider issues pertinent to the local authority area, and to organise and fight the local elections. This role includes powers to approve members who are willing to stand as candidates for local elections and to supervise their selection for local authority elections. Through its executive the local party has joint responsibility with the councillors' group for drawing up the manifesto for local elections. The party is also entitled to send a few delegates who are not councillors to the Labour group.

Most local parties take their powers seriously. In a large city with strong Labour Party representation, the district party will generally meet once a month and debate resolutions concerning the policies of their councillors and may expect reports from the leader of the council and his or her senior committee chairpersons. Some district Labour parties establish standing working parties composed of district party delegates and councillors to monitor the decisions of council committees and devise policy to be presented to the joint executives of the Labour group and district party who draw up the election manifesto.

Potentially the most effective power held by a district or county party is its control over the selection of electoral candidates. The executive of the district party must draw up a panel of party members who are fit and proper persons to be chosen as party candidates for future elections. Ward parties can only select as their candidate a member who has been placed on the panel. Members are included on the panel if they are nominated by a ward party or affiliated trade union branch, approved by their constituency party and then by the district or county party. In the past in some areas inclusion on the panel was almost automatic following nomination by a ward and constituency party. However, since 2001 the national Party has made selection a far more rigorous process, with potential candidates being obliged to demonstrate some political understanding before they can become a candidate.

Once established on the panel of candidates, the prospective councillors may be shortlisted by a ward party and invited to attend a selection meeting. Even the sitting councillors must be placed on the panel and stand for re-selection along with other hopeful candidates. Shortlisted candidates will be asked to address the branch delegates and then be asked questions. The final selection is undertaken by an exhaustive ballot, so that if no candidate gets a majority of votes on the first round of voting a new ballot is held in which the candidate with the lowest vote drops out of the contest. This process is continued until a candidate emerges with the majority of votes. The selection is supervised by a representative from the executive of the district or county party who will ensure that the selection process was conducted according to the rules. The candidate is not officially adopted until the county or district party approves the selection.

If all is well for a local party, the selection of a new candidate will be made from a number of very capable shortlisted Party members. In reality, in areas of the country less favourable to the Party, there will be serious difficulty in finding anyone willing to stand, and hence circumstances will effectively make much of the selection procedure only a formality. It is not unusual even in city parties for the shortlist to contain fewer potential candidates than there are vacancies, so that once the safe seats have been allocated the unattractive no-hope candidatures are foisted on any Party member who can be cajoled to put his or her name forward to fill an otherwise embarrassing vacancy (Chandler and Morris 1984).

### The Conservative Party

Locally, the Conservative Party does not have the structural uniformity that exists in the Labour Party. At the lowest level the Party is organised into branch associations which are formed in accord with the number of members attracted to the Party within a particular area. Thus, the branch structure does not necessarily coincide with the pattern of local government electoral wards. On occasion, there may be more than one branch per ward or, in areas of little faith in Conservative values, a branch may cover several wards. At the next level is a constituency association, composed of delegates representing local branches. This body, as in the Labour Party, is primarily responsible for selecting and monitoring the activities of an MP or a prospective parliamentary candidate.

Most local authority areas will be shadowed by a Conservative Party organisation specifically created to consider the Party's policies and oversee selection of candidates and the conduct of local election campaigns for that area. The composition and procedures of the district or county Conservative associations are not, however, established to a standard formula. The county and district associations of the Conservative Party are, in formal terms, much less influential concerning the policies of their councillors than is the case within the Labour Party. Tradition in the Conservative Party ascribes the policy making role to the Party leader at both national and local levels although the practice of politics obliges most leaders to consult with potential rivals and lieutenants. The Conservative Party is more ruthless in ridding itself of its failed or pensionable leaders than its supposedly more divisive rivals. The Party is not given to public displays of dissent and division but relies on the influence of its respected leaders to call failed leaders to account. Although, in constitutional terms, the chairman of a district or county Conservative association may have less power than his Labour Party equivalent, in practice many incumbents of such a post are respected elder statesmen of the Party with the authority to suggest and secure the resignation of an insecure politician.

The method of selecting Conservative candidates for local government is determined by model rules published by the national Party; there is no requirement to follow these but most parties do so. It is generally considered within the Party that candidates should apply for vacant posts of parliamentary or local government candidates and, at least in respect to local government, candidates may be put forward who were not previously Party members (Copus 2004: 75–6). Many established district Conservative associations will provide a panel of members who have expressed an interest in being considered as a candidate for election to the local council but, normally, no effort is made to prune the list and it is simply a guide to hopeful aspirants. There is rarely any obligation on branches to select candidates from the list and in some areas where there are either sufficient candidates in a branch, or none at all, no effort is made to construct a panel of candidates. Selection of candidates is made by the branches covering a particular ward through a joint meeting if this is necessary. The executive of the branches concerned may draw up a shortlist of party members who have applied for the vacant post and then a full meeting of members of the branch will be held at which the shortlisted candidates are interviewed and then selected following a vote from those present at the meeting. There can, however, be startling variations in this pattern.

### The Liberal Democrats

In the mid-twentieth century the Liberals were regarded as on the fringe of British politics. The Party had usually little need for strongly developed organisations to deal with local policy making and candidate selection procedures, and in keeping with a traditional support for local autonomy established a federal structure in regard to local politics. This framework persists despite the growth in importance of the Liberal Democrats in local politics. Even though the Party has won control of several local authorities, including the cities of Liverpool and Newcastle, it still maintains a federal structure allowing considerable autonomy to local branches. Like the Conservatives, the Liberal Democrats establish local party groups in relation to the strength of the party in a particular area. If there are relatively few members, the grassroots meeting will be based on a parliamentary constituency but in areas where Party membership is more robust the constituency level may encompass a number of branch parties covering a single or two or three local electoral wards. The Party does not necessarily form a formal party machine to cover a local authority area as a whole that would be similar to the district or county Labour parties.

Candidate selection is generally a process determined by the local constituency or ward grassroots meetings although they are obliged to submit their rules for selection for approval by the regional tier of the national Party organisation. The usual format allows the local party to request applications from Liberal Democrats who wish to be considered for selection as a candidate. In some areas where there is competition to become a candidate for safe seats, the local party may draw up a panel from which potential electoral candidates are selected. Selection procedures where there is competition for nomination usually require the candidate to address a selection meeting and the final choice is made by a single transferable voting system, either by members at the meeting or, if the local party prefers, through a postal ballot.

### Other parties

It is difficult to make generalisations concerning the structures and selection procedures for local government within the minor parties apart from the nationalist parties of Wales and Scotland. Unless a minor party has a very strong local presence, branches may well cover the whole of a constituency or even a local government area and there will be little need for any formal district or county party structures. Selection, in these circumstances, is almost certainly the result of an informal process in which an enthusiastic stalwart is wholeheartedly approved as candidate in the absence of any opposition or through a process in which somewhat unwilling members are cajoled by their party colleagues to put their names forward in order to help their cause.

### The influence of the local party

Potentially, a district or county party or association will have considerable powers to influence the activities of its local councillors, especially in respect to its capacity to approve candidates for selection as councillors. In reality, however, local parties rarely realise this potential. In many cities the executive of the district organisation is dominated by councillors who are able to control its proceedings as a consequence of their cohesion in the face of external criticism and their authority as prominent local politicians (Hall and Leach 2000: 162). In areas of the country where a party elected few, if any, councillors, the district or county party may meet infrequently and its debates have but an academic quality.

Complete domination is not always the case however, and there can be bitter conflict between the district party and councillors. During the Banham Commission's restructuring of local government, the District Labour Party of Chesterfield supported by the County Labour Party successfully undermined Chesterfield District Council Labour Group's policy on advocating a unitary authority status for the area by threatening to deselect councillors favouring such a policy (Hall and Leach 2000). In some areas councillors may also share some influence with a few powerful and respected party members who, whilst not elected to any authority, command leading positions in the local party organisation. In rural areas within the Conservative Party, these worthies once and, occasionally still, exert very great power. A landed gentleman, perhaps with a hereditary title, may retain some of the glories of the eighteenth century Whig aristocracy. In the Labour Party and, to a lesser extent, the Conservative Party, considerable influence may accrue to able individuals who are disbarred from being councillors by virtue of employment. A school teacher or social worker can, for example, become the chair of a district party as an outlet for frustrated ambitions in order to use this position to steer policy. Some active trade unionists may also choose not to serve as councillors and yet exert local influence. Richard Caborn, a Sheffield MP and former Minister of State, when a local trade union official, was, as Chair of the District Labour Party, highly influential in Sheffield local politics even though he was never himself a local councillor.

> In the United States, which has compared with Britain, generally weak and less disciplined party systems, it is far easier for directly elected mayors to appeal to the electorate on the basis of their personality rather than party loyalty and, thus, be more able to circumvent whatever controls the local party may impose on them. Similarly in Italy elected mayors are popular, in part, because of the widespread dissatisfaction over the corruption within the major parties and the delays and in-fighting caused by coalition government.

### The national machine

Routinely there are channels for central–local consultation within the major parties. The Labour Party holds an annual conference lasting two days for local government representatives, who are usually delegates from council groups and district parties. The conference is dominated by speeches from Party leaders and debates issues of mutual interest, although the resolutions are not binding on the leadership and are simply a guide to local feeling. The principal purpose of the conference is to generate publicity and allow councillors and district party politicians opportunities to meet colleagues from other parts of the country. The Conservative Party holds a similar conference where councillors fortunate enough to be selected as delegates may mingle with the great and the good and listen to speeches that will occupy some fragment of the headlines in the national press or television news.

More serious deliberation takes place in the Labour Party within a standing committee on local government composed of Party members from the National Executive of the Party, Parliament and government and from local government councillors. The committee serves as a forum in which local party leaders may exchange ideas with the senior Party policy makers on local government issues. Its function is, however, wholly in the area of policy making at a national level towards local government and it is not a forum for closely monitoring the policies of individual Labour groups or district parties. The strength of these committees to influence policy is also much greater when the Party is in opposition rather than in government, when national Party leaders as secretaries of state receive advice primarily from civil servants and powerful interest groups rather than the Party machine.

In the Conservative Party, following a restructuring of the Party machinery after the defeat of 1997, advice from local authority members was channelled through a Conservative Councillors' Association. All elected Conservative councillors are expected to be members of the Association, which, although officially independent, is organised by a Board consisting largely of councillors who can feed in ideas to the policy forum of the Party, which provides a channel for debate between national Conservative leaders and the rank and file. The chair of the Councillors' Association is a member of the national Board that runs the organisation of the national Party. It is questionable how far a Conservative minister or shadow minister will accept advice that he or she does not find to their taste. In the important debates on the Redcliffe-Maud Report that led to the overhaul of local government structure by the Conservatives in 1972, the then Secretary of State for the Environment Peter Walker roundly criticised consultative meetings of Conservative councillors for their objections to his ideas for fewer and larger district councils (Chandler 2007: 217). The Councillors' Association does however involve itself in many useful functions on behalf of the Party by providing advice on how to become a councillor and giving training to candidates. Advice on local government policy is also available to Conservative councillors through the research department of the central office of the Party and from the several right wing research bodies such as the Adam Smith and the Policy Studies Institutes. It is difficult to discern how much influence radiates to localities from this source.

Both the Conservative and Labour Party central machines can provide advice and guidance to local councillors but they have no mechanism for regular control of local government by the central Party. Intervention by the national Party offices may occasionally take place in the affairs of district and county parties or associations when local politicians are causing severe embarrassment to the national leadership. The Labour Party acted firmly in the 1980s to disband local parties in Merseyside which were seen to be infiltrated by Militant members and in 1995 suspended the local party machine in Walsall as left wing councillors embarked on a radical decentralisation policy opposed by the local MP and some members of the Labour group (Hall and Leach 2000). The action of suspending local party organisations and controlling local Labour politics from the central and regional offices of the Party is to use a sledgehammer to crack a nut but the occasional necessity for such action indicates the difficulty that the Labour Party has in controlling disaffected local party organisations. Given the even more federal structure of the Conservative and Liberal Democrat Parties, there is similarly in these organisations no effective machinery to steer local party policy in the direction that is favoured by their national Party leaders.

Overt attempts to manipulate local government through the national Party machine may end in disaster and embarrassment for the Party. Many rank and file members of the London Labour Party resented interference in selection procedures by the Party headquarters that were clearly aimed at undermining the chances of Ken Livingstone becoming the official mayoral candidate for London and, in the wake of much bad publicity, Frank Dobson, the choice of Blair, was heavily defeated. A similar strategy to manipulate the choice of leader of the Welsh Assembly was successful only in so far as the chosen candidate, Alun Michael, was selected by the Party with a narrow majority sustained by trade union and MPs votes. The chosen leader was obliged to resign as leader after less than a year in office as he failed to gain any enthusiasm from his backbench members of the Welsh Assembly. These misadventures may well have taught national politicians to be cautious in seeking to control local politics through selection by the Party hierarchy of candidates to stand as elected mayors.

### The ideological influence of the national Parties

Whilst there is no evidence of direct control over local party groups by the offices of the national Party, the values of local councillors may be set by their deference to the ideas of their national Party leaders. Dunleavy (1980: 135) has argued that

> local policy making is in large part constituted by stereotyped ideological responses to issues and problems with relatively little distinctively local reference.

Dunleavy's argument is difficult to substantiate since there is always likely to be considerable coincidence of views between members of the same party who come together on account of shared values. There is, however, sufficient evidence of widespread divergence of opinion within both the Labour and Conservative Parties on local authority policy to suggest that some councillors, and local authorities, despite their party affiliations, are sufficiently free thinking to disagree with the views of their leaders. The local socialist defiance of rate capping in 1985 demonstrated different attitudes within some city Labour groups from those of the national Party leadership.

Within the Conservative Party there is also widespread evidence of local challenges to the new-right policies of the Thatcher Government. At its most extreme the councillors of West Oxfordshire resigned *en masse* from the Party in protest at continued financial cuts to local authorities. Few Conservative councils followed the pure Thatcherist policies of Wandsworth or Westminster and preferred to act as parsimonious paternalists who valued the need for some local public services in housing and social services. It must, therefore, be concluded that whilst the views of the majority of local councillors coincide with nationally held orthodoxy, not all local politicians are unthinkingly uncritical of their leaders and some are capable of generating their own local ideologies.

## The many roles of councillors

There have been several attempts to classify councillors in terms of their motives and attitudes. Newton (1976), for example, developed a six fold typology relating to their orientation towards policy making. The problem with such schemes is that they tend to consider but one aspect of a highly complex pattern. Councillors' attitudes will be determined, in part, by their own character, by the type of authority in which they operate, their community, and the issues with which they are faced.

### *The parochial member*

Most typologies identify members who may be termed the 'parochial councillor'. They are predominantly motivated by a concern to represent their particular ward and to solve local problems on behalf of their constituents. The parochial councillor will see his or her task as listening to complaints and worries from local citizens about the state of council services and then seeking redress, either by action within council committees or by galvanising local government officers into resolving the issue. The parochial councillor is, therefore, the member who hears about a hole in the road and then looks into it. He or she leaves major policy initiatives to others. The 2000 Local Government Act attempted to enhance this vocation among backbench councillors by ensuring that they are free of many policy making tasks and have time to listen and represent the local parochial concerns of the citizens of their local ward but, as yet, there is no evidence that this has happened.

### *The policy orientated member*

Policy orientated councillors will try to steer the direction of the local authority as a whole or of some important element of its work. Although they will not, necessarily, ignore complaints from their constituents, such work will be seen as secondary to influencing the policy of the authority. New members when first elected will seek to gain positions on the executive of the local authority rather than remain tied to parochial tasks. The precise interests of such councillors will, of course, vary depending on political persuasion, interest and ambition. Some councillors acquire an overwhelming interest in some specific aspect of the work of a local authority. Before the advent of cabinet government, a councillor with modest, even parochial ambitions, could be put in charge of a minor committee and suddenly gain such an enthusiasm for its work that she or he became an advocate within the authority for the expansion of that particular function.

Councillors may be motivated by predominantly political rather than administrative ambitions in that they see their role on the council as a stepping stone to a major career in politics. They will be eager to develop policies and show managerial skills that gain them promotion within their authority and the applause of party colleagues at large. Other members may be motivated less by personal ambition but, more altruistically, by the desire to forward political aims and strategies. In Liverpool many Militant councillors were concerned to use membership of the local authority as a means of establishing a particular political viewpoint (Taaffe and Mulhearn 1988) and it is probable that some new-right activists are attracted into Conservative councils for similar, but ideologically wholly opposed, reasons.

Many councillors are, however, naturally conservative, regardless of political persuasion, and yet ambitious enough to want a major role within their local authority. They may be motivated by personal pride, the desire to become at least a big fish in a little pool, or a feeling that they should make their mark on their community. For some local politicians the responsibility of running a local authority presents an opportunity for job satisfaction that they could not dream of achieving in their ordinary working life. These members will be uninterested in radically new policies but wish to ensure the retention of conventional techniques of local government management to ensure effective and efficient provision of local services and a growth in the local economy. It can be suggested that the greatest number of local authorities are controlled by councillors of this persuasion. Among the local authorities in Britain only a very few adopt radical policies of either socialist or new-right persuasion. The majority pursue conventional aims and methods which, for the most part, accept the prevailing ethos of stewardship in relation to their dealings with central government.

## The background of councillors

The most comprehensive survey of councillors in Britain shows that, as a group, they are drawn from what are normally regarded as the more privileged

Table 8.1 *Characteristics of councillors*

|  | % |
|---|---|
| *Gender* | |
| Male | 70 |
| Female | 30 |
| *Age* | |
| Under 30 | 2 |
| 30–39 | 6 |
| 40–49 | 13 |
| 50–59 | 27 |
| 60–69 | 37 |
| Over 70 | 15 |
| *Ethnicity* | |
| White | 96 |
| Non-white | 4 |
| *Employment* | |
| In full time employment | 24 |
| In part time employment | 10 |
| Self-employed | 16 |
| Unemployed | 2 |
| Retired | 41 |
| Disabled, not in work | 1 |
| Looking after home/family | 3 |
| Others | 3 |
| *Education* | |
| Educated to degree level | 50 |

*Source:* IDeA, LGA, 2006, National cenusus of local authority councillors in England.

sectors of the population. They are predominantly male, middle class and middle aged and are better educated than the average population. This tendency confirms the findings of most surveys of political participation in liberal democracies, as shown in Table 8.1.

To some extent the apparent discrepancies between the population and the background of councillors are not as great as they may seem. Many Labour and some Conservative councillors who have middle class jobs will have been brought up in working class backgrounds and cannot be presumed to have lost touch with their origins. Despite this caveat, there are nevertheless still serious areas of under-representation in town halls. The numbers of women councillors are slowly increasing. Only 20 per cent of councillors were women in 1985 (Widdicombe 1986: 20, vol. II) but the day when there is approximately equal male and female representation seems still to be distant and it is clear that the proportion of councillors from a non-white background is considerably lower than their numbers in the population.

## The working environment of councillors

An important factor that may deter many would be councillors is the rigour of the job. Once elected, councillors spend a considerable proportion of their time on local authority work. In 2006 councillors were occupied with the work of their local authority on average for nearly 22 hours per week although councillors in non-metropolitan districts were less active, 18 hours per week, than those of metropolitan districts, who were engaged for 29 hours per week (IDeA 2006: 13). Cabinet members are also likely to work on local authority business much more intensively than their backbenchers and for many leaders and most directly elected mayors the task is in effect a full time paid occupation. This amount of time is clearly possible for retired or unemployed persons but becomes extremely arduous for anyone who has a full time job or is caring for children or the elderly.

### *Amateurs or professionals?*

Council work was until recently unpaid although councillors received an attendance allowance and compensation for lost earnings. There were many complaints about the allowances system on the grounds that it deterred people in full time work from becoming councillors and did not reward sufficiently leaders and chairs who spent most of their time working for their authority. In order to resolve some of these problems a system of payment for councillors was devised based on an annual allowance with further sums payable for committee responsibilities. Initially the maximum allowance was set by the government but since 1995 local authorities themselves have determined how much should be received by their members. The 2000 Local Government Act allows payments to some leading councillors to be pensionable. Most authorities have consequently substantially increased the payment to councillors. Sheffield City Council, for example, in 2007 provided each councillor £10,500 as an allowance with further payments being made to members with responsibilities of up to £17,000 for the leader. It became in the 1990s possible for a leading councillor to secure a living wage although the resultant standard of life was still not what would normally be expected from someone with responsibility for an organisation employing several thousand workers. Following the adoption of cabinet government the members of the executive will be mainly professional councillors and it is even more probable that all directly elected mayors will be full time salaried politicians. The restructuring of the policy process has, in part, been motivated by the argument that, if substantial power were given to a small group of local authority policy makers, they could be paid substantially for their work and involve themselves full time on local authority work. It is also hoped that higher salaries and greater responsibility will attract better qualified candidates to these positions. However, it remains to be seen how far these hopes can be realised, particularly when the lot of most councillors will be to remain poorly paid part time politicians serving as rather weak petition-ers to the small coterie of powerful professional local politicians on behalf of their constituents. Given that the financial rewards will be small and the time required substantial, it is not surprising that the position is extensively popu-lated by the retired over 60s.

### Training

There is no system of formal, nationally established training for councillors and it could be argued that such a scheme might be undesirable since it could be feared that any compulsory training scheme might deter would be candidates and more seriously be a means whereby the government's ideological values and assumptions about the role of local authorities are inculcated into minds harbouring different values. Only 42 per cent of councillors in the 2006 survey thought they would like a formal NVQ style qualification as result of being a councillor (IDeA 2006: 15). However, most councillors had attended some form of training and development during the preceding year. In some large authorities the political parties attempt to ensure that potential councillors understand their role and obligations through careful sifting of candidates and by organising training courses for candidates to ensure they are aware of the basic structure and organisation of their local authority.

Apart from this rather sporadic element of basic training, councillors receive few opportunities to gain more specialised understanding of the operation of the services which they are required to govern. On occasion, a councillor may secure funds to attend conferences or short courses organised by a professional body or college into some new technical innovation or change in legislation. In general, however, local councillors are expected to find out how their authority operates and the requirements and potential of their technical services through their own and unaided initiative. Many will, therefore, be educated as a result of personal, and on occasion, painful experience, through talking to fellow councillors, and probably, most extensively as regards technical issues, from officers of the council.

### Political ambition or civic duty?

The reason for becoming a councillor will rarely be for immediate financial gain and less than 2 per cent admit to such a motive. Most councillors (87 per cent) agree that their main reason is to 'serve the community' (IDeA 2000: 16) but the question is not asked as to whether for many it is also for the pursuit of polit-ical power. It is not infrequently alleged that any prominent councillor is moti-vated by the thought of becoming an MP rather than serving his or her locality, perhaps eventually emulating the Prime Minister, John Major, who was once a London borough councillor. J.S. Mill (1975: 379–80) argued that this was a highly creditable motive and that service in local government was a valuable training ground for national politicians. It is, of course, difficult to ascertain how many councillors harbour thoughts of political progress but it is undoubtedly the case that many of the most active and prominent council leaders have an eye on a national political career.

> The nature of the British political system, contrary to France, makes local government service a stepping stone, rather than an addition, to a role in national politics. A political structure that more closely integrated local and national politics might not create tensions between service to the locality and to the nation.

Whilst the desire for a political career may motivate some ambitious councillors, their aspirations are usually framed in local terms. The parochial politician is often concerned to aid their community and provide themselves with a worthy purpose of helping others. Many local politicians still believe in ideals of service to the community. For some councillors labouring in menial jobs the responsibilities provided by council work stretch their abilities and interests way beyond what they could have received from a less political life. These motives may be self-interested, but are rightly self-interested, since they are motivated not only towards self-fulfilment but the achievement of a better life for others.

### The competence of councillors

It is argued that many of the ills of local government stem from the quality of councillors, 'people of such modest abilities . . . controlling such large organisations' (Henney 1984: 326). This view has a long pedigree. J.S. Mill wrote in 1861 of the 'low calibre of men in local government' (1975: 369–70). Dame Evelyn Sharpe, as Permanent Secretary to the Ministry of Housing and Local Government, mourned the absence of councillors 'from business, from industry, from agriculture, from the professions' (Clements 1969: 14). This long established view was one of the factors behind the pressures to reform local government structures that culminated in the Redcliffe-Maud Commission and the 1972 Local Government Act. It was hoped that by decreasing the number of councils and, therefore, the number of councillors, local government would be served by more competent members. Such hopes do not appear to have been realised for official circles. Later, the Audit Commission concluded that

> a reduction in the number of elected members would be desirable, combined with an enhancement of their terms of service. Without such a change the worrying reluctance of well-qualified citizens to serve as elected members will grow and councils will increasingly face rapid turnover of young and inexperienced members. (1988: 9)

This attitude was a significant factor motivating the Blair Government's restructuring of local decision making.

The source of the established complaint concerning the quality of councillors has its roots in Utilitarian theory and, in particular, the writings of J.S. Mill. Liberals turned to democracy with some reluctance since they feared what Mill described as the tyranny of the majority. There was, they felt, a serious danger that the uneducated masses would overrule wiser counsels of the more educated and perceptive few. In countries in a state of barbarism where they could discern none of the cultured values of Western civilisation, some form of benevolent despotism was the only answer. Mill, and many of his fellow liberals, were sufficiently confident in levels of education in Britain to believe that in a democracy the masses would select the better educated and intelligent to positions of power. He would not be disappointed as far as central government is concerned.

The reasons for the disappearance of the notable from local politics has been analysed in Chapter 6. The nineteenth century roots of the critique of councillors lie in distaste for parish government, but more recently it has been an expression of concern over the departure of capitalist elites from local government and their replacement by labouring stock. The complaints concerning the unsatisfactory quality of councillors must be viewed in the light of the consequent development of central government's ethos of stewardship towards local authorities. Absent from these criticisms of the quality of councillors is any thought for the role of a councillor as a community representative. The humble parochial councillor who is concerned to articulate the worries and complaints of her or his constituents is not to be despised. Many grievances concerning local people can be forestalled through their timely intervention. Indeed, it may even be tentatively suggested that some of the violent tensions that disfigure present day society, from race riots to child abuse by parents housed in appalling conditions, could be assuaged if there were more, rather than fewer, councillors who could be closer to their electorate and more capable of dealing with their needs and complaints.

The criticism of the quality of local councillors is also dangerous since it implies a serious critique of democracy. If councillors are of poor quality then this must be a reflection of the choice of local people who must, therefore, appear to be unfit to make informed political decisions. In essence, it is a class based critique which Stanyer rightly berates as

> Impertinent, because it tells people what they ought to value, and undemocratic, because it denies that local elections should fulfil the role ascribed by the system of government to them. (Stanyer 1976: 278)

### Further reading

The role of local parties is considered most fully by Colin Copus (2004) but Gyford and James (1983) and Bulpitt (1967) still have relevance. Hall and

Leach (2000) produce useful case studies of conflict within local Labour parties and conclusions on the relationship between district Labour parties and the Labour groups.

Data on the background of councillors are now regularly surveyed by IDeA. A useful article on the role of non-executive councillors is provided by Snape (2004). Earlier but still relevant studies of the working conditions of councillors are provided in Barron, Crawley and Wood (1991) and the research conducted for the Widdicombe Report (1986).

The study of councillors, officers and interest groups was particularly enhanced by community studies of local government that cut across many themes and issues. These studies are often easily read and enjoyable but such research is now rather unfashionable. Among studies of Britain an early but excellent study is Birch (1959), which looks at the rather non-political small town of Glossop. Another influential early study is Bealey, Blondel and McCann (1965), which studies Newcastle under Lyme. Perhaps the most important British studies are Dearlove (1973) on Kensington and Chelsea, and Newton's (1976) study of Birmingham, which has a clear theoretical interest in democratic theory. Lee (1963) is a valuable study of the decline of notables in county government and more recently Goss (1988) considers the rise of the Labour Party in Southwark. Other interesting studies include Hampton (1970) on Sheffield and, from a disgruntled right wing perspective, Green (1981) on single party politics in Newcastle on Tyne.

# 9

# Bureaucracy and employees

The size of local authorities and the diversity of their tasks ensure that, in comparison with most private sector organisations in Britain, local government is big business. Birmingham City Council spent in the 2005/06 financial year nearly £2.9 billion (Birmingham City Council Summary Accounts). Its Chief Executive has an exacting and powerful position with a capacity to influence greatly the social and economic development of an area of over one million inhabitants.

Since local authorities in Britain are very large relative to those of other liberal democracies, they are much more complex bureaucracies and employ far more staff than local authorities in most other countries. The small communes of France may have very few if any workers as many of their services will be contracted out to private companies. Similarly a small United States city with a population of a thousand or less may employ a police chief and a deputy and a few clerks and workmen but rely mainly on contractors to undertake their tasks although, in some large cities or the State governments, the number of employees and complexity of the bureaucracy may be as labyrinthine as in Britain.

## The structure of the local government service

As Table 9.1 shows a large number of citizens are directly dependent on local government for their wages. This extensive workforce encompasses numerous skills and professions and includes several occupations such as teachers and traffic wardens who are not always thought of as local government employees. In recent years it has become even less clear who might be a local authority employee as opposed to someone working for an arm's length agency or a contractor for the local authority. Housing officers may be employees of a local authority sponsored housing association and many a refuse collector is an employee of a private contractor rather than the local authority.

Table 9.1 *Full time equivalent employees in local government in England, 2005/06*

| | |
|---|---|
| Teachers | 450,000 |
| Police and support staff | 202,000 |
| Fire service | 45,000 |
| Other local government services | 998,000 |
| Total | 1,695,000 |

*Source:* DCLG (2007), *Financial Statistics*, London, HMSO, Table 6.3a.

Despite its diversity, the local government service has been based on several traditional understandings and these tend to flow over into arm's length organisations and the corps of private contractors working with the public sector. There remains a tendency to divide the workforce, like the British army, into officers and the other ranks. The officers have white collar jobs and are considered to be middle class. The manual grades are considered to be blue collar working class involved in one of the many skilled or unskilled labours of local government. The officers start work at 9.00 a.m. in the morning and go home around 5.00 p.m. in the afternoon, if not employed on flexi-time, where, within proscribed limits, they can set their hours of work. Manual workers, unless on a round the clock shift rotor, will tend to begin work at 8.00 a.m. and end at 4.00 p.m., enjoying fewer holidays, generally lower pay and poorer working conditions than officers. Between the officers and the manual workers is a considerable coterie of clerks and typists who enjoy officers' conditions of work but not their salaries.

There are also sharp horizontal divisions among local authority employees, who are usually not transferable to other departments. Officers tend to be specialists, qualified and trained specifically to undertake the work of their department. Chief education officers began their careers as teachers, directors of social services must be qualified social workers and chief constables began their working lives as police cadets. This feature of the local government service contrasts with the generalist ethos within the higher levels of the civil service, which is based on the belief that administrative competence is more crucial than specialist knowledge. The specialist structure of the local government service emerged in the nineteenth century and is, in part, a reflection of the technical tasks performed within the local government system. This was to a considerable extent manufactured by central government. In as much as the value of local government to the centre was to ensure that detailed managerial and technical tasks were implemented to suit central needs, the proper functionaries to carry out these tasks were technicians rather than general administrators with a policy advisory role. This ethos was conveyed through the then existing central–local links in the late nineteenth century and later imposed by statutory demands which require certain functions to be filled by professional qualified personnel.

A distinction was also traditionally made between local authority staff who work in the field, providing services directly to the public, and those who work largely in the town hall or its satellite offices. The outworking professionals,

Table 9.2 *Local authority general administrative grades*

---

Chief executive – chief officer to the authority
Chief officer – head of a department
Deputy chief officer
Assistant chief officer
Principal officer
Senior officer
Administrative officers
Clerical officers

---

who include school teachers and social workers, may often pay little attention to their status as an employee of local government. Teachers may feel that their allegiance is to a school rather than the town hall and its councillors. Although these field workers are part of the local government system, their working conditions often have little or nothing to do with what goes on in the town hall. These issues are determined at a national level through bargaining between local authority associations, trade unions and the government.

## Management and leadership

Within each sector of local government there are numerous stratifications that determine the status of personnel and their attendant pay and conditions. The typical ranking for non-technical and professional staff working in general administrative or managerial roles is illustrated in Table 9.2.

### *The chief executive and senior officers*

The most senior position in the local government bureaucracy, following the recommendations of the Bains Report in 1972, is the chief executive. The post strengthened the powers held formerly by the town clerk or county clerk, who was, as the most senior legal officer, usually, but not always, regarded as the senior officer for the authority. The town clerk did not, however, normally have direct line management control over other chief officers. The post of chief executive, at least in theory, established an undisputed head of the local government service in each local authority to whom all officers, outside the police and fire services, would be responsible.

The chief executive is appointed by the leader or a directly elected mayor of a council with the support of cabinet members and often with the advice and help of an executive headhunting agency. As the senior officer of the authority the chief executive will usually be instrumental in determining the management structure of the authority although his or her ideas will require the approval of the senior councillors. It is expected that he or she will preside over a management team of senior officers who would include the treasurer, who is the head of the local authority's financial services, and usually the head of human resources and the heads of major services such as housing and education. In recent years many local authorities have restructured their management arrangements to create smaller senior management teams in which a few very senior officers co-ordinate policy over a range of services. The City of York, a unitary authority, is for example led by a chief executive and five directors, each of whom is responsible for a substantive number of services. The Learning, Culture and Childrens' Services Directorate, for example, deals not only with the LEA role but also libraries, sports, arts and parks.

In most European countries there is a post equivalent to the chief executive heading the administrative system. In the United States the city manager usually takes this role. However, in France, Italy and Spain the second tier of government is run by the centrally appointed civil servant, the prefect. In Ireland the central government rather than local councillors appoints the chief executives of its local authorities.

Chief executives are generally seen as managers whose major task is to create a uniform strategy that brings together the disparate elements of the local authority and forge partnership links with other agencies involved in local governance. The chief executive may, therefore, be the key leader in ensuring the enabling strategy for the local authority (Norton 1991). The position was once regarded as predominantly the preserve of lawyers, following the older tradition of the town clerk being the leading official in most local authorities. Since the post of town clerk was transformed into the more managerial role of chief executive the post has, over the decades, become more open to senior officers from all areas of local government activity.

### *Rank and file*

Although the local government service is not a national service, in that, unlike the civil service, there is no one employer for local government workers, there is considerable standardisation in the pay and conditions of service in local authorities. Below the level of senior officers the administrative staff of most local government departments are graded as indicated in Table 9.2 according to a structure devised, initially in the 1930s, in what were known as the Whitely Councils, through negotiations between the trade unions and representatives of the local authorities. Within each grade are numerous scales of remuneration and status that form endless sources of argument, grievance, elation and gossip in the daily soap operas of local government service. At exactly what point on a senior officer scale should a particular post be established can be a matter for local custom and practice. Manual staff negotiate their career structures through joint trade union, local authority committees, although the differing circumstances and requirements of individual local authorities lead to much bargaining on re-grading and local working practices.

Most field workers such as teachers, the police and fire officers are governed by separate scales of remuneration developed by negotiating committees for each service composed of the appropriate trade unions or professional bodies and representatives of the local authorities. Teachers, for example, are paid standard rates agreed by an *ad-hoc* national negotiating committee made up of teachers' unions and local authority representatives. The negotiating committee can, however, only recommend increases in teachers' salaries, which is the largest single item of any county council budget, if the government agrees to provide the extra grant income to pay for the rise. In effect, therefore, teachers' salaries, or similarly the salaries of lower grade staff or manual employees, are determined as much by a government confronting trade unions as by the local authorities themselves, which may become impotent by-standers in trials of strength between national trade unions and central government.

## Professionalism

The world of many local authority officers is circumscribed not only by their position within the hierarchy of the authority but also by their professional association. These are organisations composed of members who consider that they have common skills and interests. They behave in some senses like trade unions in that they safeguard the quality standards of their members' work although they may not necessarily be concerned with negotiating wage levels or conditions of service. The more powerful professional groups such as the British Medical Association, however, effectively take on this role. In other respects their influence may exceed some of the wildest ambitions of trade unions in determining work practices. A professional association that achieves widespread recognition can determine who can join the profession and discipline members if they stray from their approved codes of conduct.

The role of professionals is less prominent in many European states where smaller authorities, such as the French commune, leave many basic tasks to the mayor. More specialist legal or technical help within a commune may be provided by the bureaucracy headed by the departmental prefect, who is a civil servant controlling a considerable bureaucracy of more specialist civil servants. In Italy until recently many local officials owed their position as much to political contacts as to professional training. In the United States professionalism established outside a civil service framework resembles more the British pattern and city managers themselves form an established professional group.

Many senior positions within local authorities are only open to members of specified professional associations. The most influential professions ensure that anyone practising in their areas of competence has been trained to standards that they consider acceptable. The influence of an association may then continue throughout an officer's career. The profession will hold regular conferences and produce newsletters to keep its members up to date with the latest developments relevant to their work. The strongest professional associations establish detailed codes of practice for the benefit of their members and any officer who strays from the security of these commandments may be liable to serious criticism, if not disciplinary procedures.

The Chartered Institute of Public Finance and Accountancy is an example of a powerful profession within local government which can be assured of a near monopoly on all senior financial posts in local government. Long standing practice, reinforced since 1989 by legislation, requires that the chief financial officer of a local authority must be a professionally qualified accountant. CIPFA is the accountancy association most favoured by local government as it is concerned primarily with the public sector. To become an officer of any importance in a county or district treasurer's department it is necessary to have taken a series of professional examinations set and marked by representatives of this association. For local government finance officers the several volumes of CIPFA work practice, a document continually updated by the professional body, is their constant companion, at least in the workplace. Since senior members of a professional body are likely to be influential members of promotion panels, career advance will also be influenced by the concerns of the professionals. With its headquarters in London senior officers of CIPFA will be asked to advise not only local authorities but also central government on issues of public accountancy. A more recent but potentially powerful professional body is SOLACE, which was formed in 1974 to bring together chief executives of local authorities and now represents the views of all senior local authority managers. The organisation can be highly influential in moulding the prevailing management practices of local authorities and is listened to seriously by civil servants. Indeed, as observed in Chapter 5, as the numbers of former local government officers increase within Whitehall some civil servants will be former members of the organisation. The professional body is also promoting a further characteristic of a professional body by organising training courses for graduates who aspire to senior positions in local government management.

Given the importance of professional bodies, control over these organisations can assume important consequences for local government. In theory, professional associations are democratic societies whose members vote for a council or delegate conference to serve as its governing body. As the delegate meeting is usually too unwieldy to meet frequently, an executive will be elected to deal with policy issues in between the meetings of the sovereign body. Crucial to the operation of a large professional association will, however, be its elected officers and senior professional staff. The senior officers of an association will be elected by the membership and be recognised as being among the pre-eminent professionals in their field. In associations with a specifically local government remit senior members will usually be chief officers of major local authorities.

In addition to the elected officers, an association will appoint a secretary or an equivalent officer who will be the head of a small team of professional servants to the association. Although subject to the policy of the association, the professional staff may be able to exert a powerful presence within the organisation and their general secretaries can sometimes be seen by the public as their principal spokesperson. Noel Hepworth, a former Director of CIPFA was, for example, the author of one of the most authoritative textbooks on local government finance (Hepworth 1984). Recruitment to full time posts in professional associations can be through a slow process of rising through the ranks but often the highest posts are awarded to individuals who hold senior professional appointments in, for example, a local authority.

Although some professional bodies may appear to be present at the birth and death of a local government officer's career, the extent to which they exert an influence over their members varies widely. Whilst some professional associations, such as CIPFA or the Law Society which regulates solicitors, have an effective monopoly over entry into their area of expertise, in other sectors membership of a profession can be an advantage but is not essential. Officers in housing departments may join the Institute of Housing but membership of the organisation is not vital for promotion since members of other professional groups such as the Royal Institution of Chartered Surveyors can be employed as housing managers. Laffin (1986) charts the slow and painful moves towards recognition of the Institute of Housing which, although established in the 1930s to co-ordinate the work of senior officers in local authority housing departments, has never become the most powerful of professions.

Some local government posts are scarcely touched by organised professionalism. The relatively new, but expanding, sector of economic development has recruited personnel from a wide variety of backgrounds, including experienced industrialists, social economists and town planners. There is no set qualification or examinations necessary for obtaining posts in this field and there are only the glimmerings of co-ordinated organisation among economic development staff. Another more established area, municipal catering, has developed its own association to represent members' interests but the organisation does not include the majority of officers working in this field and cannot impose its rules and standards on local councils.

## Trade unions

Local government is a heavily unionised organisation and almost all levels of the service are represented by at least one and, in several areas, a veritable bouquet of trade unions. Manual workers in local government who have no professional bodies to serve their interest are particularly reliant on their trade unions to safeguard their working conditions. There are three principal unions representing these workers: UNISON, the GMB, which would like to be known as Britain's General Union, formed from the amalgamation of several smaller unions, and UNITE, the largest British union following the merger of the Transport and General Workers' Union and AMICUS in 2007. Most manual grades such as refuse collectors, parks attendants or caretakers will be members of the GMB or UNITE, depending on individual preference or the number of fellow members in a particular department. Some more specialised manual workers will, however, join the appropriate union dealing with their trade. Builders will be members of the Union of Construction and Allied Trades and Technicians (UCATT).

The clerical and officer grades were, until the 1970s, almost exclusively represented by the National Union of Local Government Officers (NALGO), which was formed in 1906 as a very respectable association for officers. It was not until 1964 that it recognised that its work lay in the same realm as manual workers and joined the Trade Union Congress. In conformity with a trend towards fewer, but larger, unions, NALGO merged in 1993 with the National Union for Public Employees and the health service union COSHE to form UNISON, which represents white collar workers in not only local government but also the privatised utilities and the health service.

Local government manual trade unions have, historically, never been the most militant, reflecting a view that whilst work for the local council was relatively low paid it represented a secure and socially respected job. The ethos of service before self and the honour of serving the community has, however, ceased to be widely cherished and also the security of employment is far more akin to that of the private sector than it was 50 years ago. Appeals to local government workers not to strike because of their service to the community could not easily be sustained when the gap between private and public sector became ever greater and the prestige of the service ever smaller. Local government workers during the 1970s and 1980s spearheaded major strikes that had serious political implications. These included the industrial unrest of 1978/79, christened by the press 'the winter of discontent', that did much to undermine the Callaghan Government and brought to power Mrs Thatcher.

The subsequent confrontation with trade unions by the Thatcher Government greatly reduced the influence of trade unions in general and those representing local authorities in particular. New legislation making it more difficult to call strikes, along with far higher levels of unemployment, ensured that many trade unions found little support among their workers for militant action. Within local government the development of CCT ensured that blue collar unions had a further reason to avoid militant action since they would run the risk that their local authority would lose the contract to supply a service and their members may not be re-employed by the new private sector contractor or, as is frequently the case, re-employed on even worse conditions of service. The process of contracting out has also tended to weaken union strength as some private employers may be less inclined to recognise the trade unions accepted by the public sector although such a trend is by no means universal (Doogan 1999).

Paradoxically, during the 1980s the white collar unions became more militant as conditions of pay and government support for public sector work seriously declined through the competitive individualist policies of the new-right Government. Values also changed as local government began to attract radical and militant minded graduates who saw public service as a career untainted with capitalist values and, hence, worthy of an uncompromising socialist. Some left wing local authorities attracted as officers militant political activists who were not loath to turn against their political masters when they were forced to retrench their activities by the Government. However, in the 1990s with the introduction of CCT for many professional and clerical services, and the decline of left wing militancy, much of the white collar radicalism in some UNISON branches melted away.

### Training and socialisation

The professional associations have had major importance in many of the long established spheres of management and service provision through their monopoly over recruitment and training in these fields. By the 1920s, almost all senior local government functionaries had joined the local government services from school at either 14 or 16 years of age and reached positions of influence through part time study towards professional qualifications and practical experience of their work acquired in the workplace by 'sitting next to Nellie'. In comparison with the senior levels of the civil service the formal educational achievements of local government officers were until recently generally modest. Up to the 1950s, apart from the education service and medical officers, few local government officers were graduates. Most were recruited into a local government department after leaving school with acceptable GCSE ordinary or advanced level grades and set to work in junior capacities (Poole 1978: 150). If they showed any promise and ambition their senior officers would enter them for appropriate professional qualifications and they would be expected to grind through several painstaking levels of vocationally orientated courses leading to a professional qualification through either attendance at a further education college or late night sittings over a correspondence course. The curricula for most professional exams emphasised a need to acquire a meticulous grasp of facts and legal procedures rather than any ability to think innovatively. The emphasis on competence rather than understanding and innovative capacity within the new NVQ qualification thus exerts a considerable attraction for more pedestrian local authorities.

The recruitment and training pattern reproduced the tradition that local government officers were specialists rather than generalists. Senior officers were, usually, well versed in the technicalities of their functions but had no training in how to manage their department or appreciation of the political and social consequences of their work. In certain areas of activity, lack of social awareness has, arguably, had disastrous consequences. Had borough surveyors, planners and architects greater understanding of social attitudes and values they may not have so enthusiastically turned to high rise housing developments. The emphasis on specialism has further serious implications in the wider context of the role of local government in the British polity since, as was argued earlier, it fits the system into the framework of stewardship, the implementation of centrally determined policy, rather than a culture that perceives local government as the legitimate representative of local interests.

In the 1960s concern over the in house professionalised structure of local authority senior management prompted a Government Enquiry published as the Mallaby Report (1967) into local authority recruitment and training. The Report, written as steps were being made to increase the numbers of University graduates, argued that local authorities should, like the civil service, recruit to its most senior ranks university trained administrators and that specialist courses in public administration should be established to meet this need. Since the 1960s the massive increase in student numbers has ensured that most local government officers are now graduates. Despite this change, professional training remains, however, a crucial step for progression to senior posts in many public sector specialisms and, for the most part, these courses still emphasise a factual and legalistic rather than imaginative approach. The rethinking of local government training of the 1960s led also to the creation, through the joint efforts of the local authority associations, of a training board to monitor and encourage vocational programmes by local authorities. Among its varied functions this organisation, currently named the Improvement and Development Agency for Local Government (IDeA), tries to ensure that local authorities seriously promote the educational and training needs of their staff.

Although the Mallaby Report argued that generalist administrators should study courses, such as public administration, based on a range of social science subjects, the impact of the Thatcher Governments' emphasis on business efficiency and profitability has moved local government personnel departments to favour management training developed largely for private sector enterprise. Courses leading to a Masters in Business Administration have been particularly popular with aspiring senior managers in local government. The development of management training in local government is, at one level, to be welcomed as helping to secure more economic, efficient and effective service delivery. The innovation does, however, have serious limitations when it solely imitates training to sharpen the '3Es' of efficiency, economy and effectiveness cherished by private profit making organisations. Such an approach recognises the 'price of everything and the value of nothing' by giving a limited appreciation of what generalism or efficient management entails without regard for the ethical, democratic and representational role of public service. Given the narrow curricula of most management education in Britain, the value of a generalist outlook is, once again, lost to the public service.

### The power of officers

The extent to which senior local government officers rather than the councillors determine the policy of their local authorities is a much debated subject. It has been argued by Dunleavy (1980) that some professional bodies representing local government officers are highly influential in determining local policy outcomes but Laffin (1986) argues that, although some officers are certainly important, many professionals have little impact on the policy process. It is a question with no set answer since different local authorities will foster very different administrative cultures. Potentially, local government officers have a number of powers they can use to gain their own way, many of which are not unique to local government but are available to any professional bureaucrat who is theoretically subservient to elected lay politicians.

Local government officers are full time employees and, therefore, have more time than most councillors to devise policy and influence its implementation. A senior officer can spend many hours aided by subordinate staff drawing up a watertight report supporting his or her views, whereas a cabinet member who might have a full time job in an unrelated field will scarcely have the time even to read the final document. Officers are also specialists, more so than their civil service equivalents, and can argue strongly that a particular course of action is either imperative or unthinkable for technical reasons. Few councillors will, for example, be able to challenge an architect's report alleging that a building is unsafe due to the failure of concrete beams. Since local government officers are permanent employees protected from arbitrary dismissal by trade unions they can, on occasion, act with a measure of insubordination without much fear of adverse consequences. A decision of Sheffield City Council to ban corporal punishment in schools was undermined when, either deliberately or in error, officers informed schools that this was a policy for consideration by school governors and not a firm commitment of the local authority.

The traditional structure of the local government system provided bureaucrats with further means of controlling their councillors. In contrast to civil servants, who serve only the government, the local authority officer was a servant of the full council and not just its majority party. Thus, they advised not only committee chairs but any councillor, including the opposition spokesperson, and could insist that information embarrassing to the party in power was made known to the opposition. The new executive arrangements for local government policy making tend to draw officers closer to the cabinet of the authority and, if opposition parties are excluded from this circle, they are likely to be less able to gain information from officers in their position as backbenchers. In the more adversary climate of scrutiny committees, officers may be less inclined to reveal issues that the executive policy makers would prefer to remain hidden. Studies of scrutiny committees suggest that they have in many authorities been allocated few senior officers to guide and resource their research and deliberations (Hopkins 2007).

In some circumstances officers have a statutory duty to act contrary to the demands of their councillors. A chief executive and city or county treasurer must warn the full council if they are spending or raising funds illegally. Should they fail to provide such a warning and publicly repudiate the council's policy these officers will be regarded as as legally culpable for the decision as the councillors. The 1989 Local Government and Housing Act further entrenched these powers by requiring local authorities to designate some senior employees as monitoring officers with a duty to inform all councillors and, in the case of financial issues, the district auditor, if they believe a decision of the council will be unlawful or a case of serious maladministration.

The influence of councillors over their officers is further diminished by the networks of linking professional interests within local government. Many local councillors will receive their understanding of the role of a department from professional officers and hence, like the officers themselves, be highly susceptible to receiving as gospel the values according to a well organised professional body. A professional body may be so influential that it can persuade not only its members but the government to accept its values. Patrick Dunleavy (1981) demonstrated that a passion for high rise tower blocks that began within the Royal Institute of British Architects infected not only local authority architects but also the senior civil servants in the Ministry of Housing and Local Government. Government ministers consequently provided such generous offers of grants to build tall that councillors could not refuse even though many may in their bones have had no wish to create such impractical and untraditional housing.

### Limits to bureaucratic power

Although it is possible to pile argument onto argument in support of the power of chief officers, it is essential to keep many of these points in perspective. Councillors are not necessarily naive, uncouth amateur politicians. Even in the 1930s, no one considered that Herbert Morrison, the Leader of the Greater London Council who later became one of the most senior members of Attlee's Government, could be easily fooled by his senior officers. Local politicians tend to be better educated and informed than the general public and some will be able to devote many hours to local authority work. Although it is difficult to measure factors such as ruthlessness or cynicism, many councillors who reach the position of a committee chairman are not likely to be made of the stuff that accepts every advice tendered or is unwilling to enter a political fight if their personal views are opposed.

Simplistic assumptions about the power of professionals are now being undermined with the development of cabinet government and professional elected mayors. The leaders of many of the larger city authorities and many cabinet members are effectively full time councillors and spend probably more time on local authority work than their chief officers. Many councillors enter the local authority with some measure of professional expertise given that a greater number of graduates and professionals are occupying council positions. Once on the council, members specialise and can within a few years achieve a considerable expertise on, for example, housing matters or social services. Indeed, they may assume a role which, in central government, is argued to be an ideal administrative attribute for a permanent secretary, the capacity to grasp intelligently the implications of technical knowledge and relate this to the wider needs of community and the prevailing political climate.

The entrenchment of senior professional local politicians ensures that larger local authorities operate rather like central government in Whitehall, where a full time secretary of state or the prime minister receives advice from an established permanent secretary. In local government the relationship that develops between the leader or elected mayor and the chief executive is in most cases supportive. However, the two individuals can be in conflict and the officer will be prepared to use his or her resources of biasing information, hiding awkward facts from the politician and acting without his or her consent. The greatest policy tensions have emerged when a local authority changes its political control, leaving a cautious chief executive in charge of a radical policy or a radical officer stifled by conservative politicians. The new-right London Borough of Westminster obliged its Chief Executive to resign largely on account of his reluctance to endorse policies that are now subject to criticism from the press and the local authority auditors. Derbyshire County Council in its local socialist phase during the 1980s similarly forced the departure of senior officers who had policy differences with the council leaders. Currently, a far less tense ideological division between parties ensures such action on political grounds is far less likely.

In the United States city managers are very vulnerable to sacking by the mayor and senior councillors and have a tenure in office not unlike that of a football coach. If this pattern were replicated in Britain, elected mayors and leaders would normally have the final word on policy decisions. Frequently an American city manager who loses a job in one city gains re-employment in another and hence loss of a post is not necessarily the end of a career; thus confident city managers may not always worry too much about losing the mayor's confidence.

The relationship between a councillor and chief officer is, in practice, rarely an adversarial contest with each side seeking to gain the advantage over the other. Committee chairs and their senior officers will usually be aware that they need to work in a close harmonious relationship using each others' abilities if they are to extract the best possible results for their departments. If a chief officer and his or her cabinet members cannot agree on policy then it is probable that their department will fail to develop convincing policies or be in a strong position to gain and defend its resource base. Because of the need for such a relationship, councillors usually try to ensure when appointing a chief officer that the incumbent will be politically attuned to the values of the local authority. The relationship between the councillor and chief officer can at times be so close that it is not only impossible but rather meaningless to discern who actually devises policy initiatives. Laffin and Young (1990: 110–12) identify four roles that emerge from the accommodation of professional values to the differences in policy and management style in local authorities. These are controllers, who are powerful figures determining a parsimonious and orderly operation of a department; enablers, who, in contrast, use their expertise to facilitate the policy objectives of the politicians; professional advocates, who seek to pursue the objectives associated with their profession; and finally policy activists, who are appointed to senior posts and are professionals with a strong view of how they wish to shape the development of their local authority or department.

Since councillors have the ability, save, perhaps in case of the chief constable, to appoint chief officers, they will often secure the degree of co-operation and ideological viewpoint from their leading professionals that they deserve. Local authorities can and often do select chief officers who are sympathetic to their political views. Conversely a cabinet member with no wish to radically overturn established policies will choose a chief officer who will take complete control of his or her department and maintain the generally conservative mainstream tenure of their profession. In many of the predominantly Conservative rural counties and districts, where councillors do not become involved in the day to day running of the authority, chief officers tend to be cautious managers of the authority's affairs. Apparent domination of a local authority by its officers may be fully acceptable to the councillors and is not necessarily a product of some victory for bureaucracy in an internecine strife between officer and councillor.

## Further reading

There has been no very recent study solely devoted to changes within the local government service since the study by K.P. Poole (1978), which, whilst informative, is now a study of a system based on professionalism and departments rather than executive government, partnerships and contracting out. Dunleavy (1980) presents a theoretical challenging scenario on professionalism which he extends in his study of high rise housing which has relevance for the present (1981). More recently, but again not reflecting the Blair years,

Martin Laffin's books on professionalism (1986) and trade unions in local government (1989) are insightful and much of the argument still holds today. Laffin and Young (1990) analyses further the growth and development of professionalism and Doogan (1999) discusses the changes in local authority employment brought about by CCT.

# 10

# Management and accountability

It is sometimes argued that a private sector business differs from a local authority in that it must make a profit whereas a local authority can operate its services inefficiently and simply make up any shortfall through taxation (Henney 1984: 285). This is, however, an urban myth. Local authorities are required to make a profit on some of their services and must, for all their activities, ensure that they are making the most efficient use of public resources.

A more substantive difference between private sector business and local government is the overall aim and objectives of each enterprise. Most private sector firms have as their principal mission the aim of making money for their shareholders and have responsibility to society in general only in so far as the pursuit of profitability does not damage public welfare and ethical codes. A local authority, however, not only must demonstrate it uses resources efficiently but also it must have as its mission the preservation and enhancement of the economic, social and environmental well being of its community. As a democratically elected public organisation the local authority is also subject to realising these goals in accordance with the wishes of the populations it serves. This chapter will discuss both the demands on local authorities to ensure efficient, cost-effective management and the corresponding pressures this requirement places on what are essentially democratic organisations.

### New Public Management

By the 1950s a new discipline of management as an applied social science had taken root in the private sector. Its classic founding theories were developed early in the twentieth century by businessmen such as F.W. Taylor and Henri Fayol who believed that it was scientifically possible to produce greater efficiency and profitability in private businesses. These ideas led to the generation in the 1920s of time and motion efficiency studies and the acceptance of hierarchic line management in which each individual was given a specific range of duties to be undertaken under the supervision of a higher manager. These ideas were never wholly acceptable to the public service values of either the civil service or local government in Britain, which were much influenced by management theories that argued that efficiency was not the only measure of the worth of strategies for the delivery of public services and that regard had to be given to the quality of provision and concern for the well being of the citizen (Thomas 1978).

It was not until the 1970s that the growth of new-right values and the consequent criticism of public and nationalised services seriously eroded any belief that there was more to local government than just the efficient delivery of services. One of the most trenchant critiques of the efficiency of the public sector that swept into Conservative Party thought stems from the ideas of a group of United States economists who are seen as the founding members of rational choice theory. They argue that it must be assumed that individuals are rational and seek to maximise their own self-interests. Politicians and public officials, therefore, have a vested interest in building bureaucratic empires that are far larger and more costly than are needed to provide a necessary public service (Niskanen 1973a, 1973b; Tullock 1975). This is partly a consequence of the rational self-interest of individual bureaucrats who gain better pay, chances of promotion and personal aggrandisement through the growth of the public sector. Government bureaucracies also expand in size because politicians win votes by promising greater expenditure and thus build up increasingly large financial commitments which they find impossible to decrease. This, it is argued, will not happen in private sector businesses facing competition as the higher costs of an over-large bureaucracy lead to higher prices and the departure of customers. Local government, as a public monopoly, can, however, provide services with less efficiency in the absence of competition. The crude nature of democracy, requiring voters to support packages of policies rather than express opinion on individual programmes, prevents the ballot box from becoming a successful device for restraining mismanagement.

The new-right view has arguably not stood up well to empirical investigations. Whilst the majority of studies show that competition saves costs and improves technical efficiency of service delivery, this is far from certain when account is taken of the wider considerations of the cost of establishing a competitive framework or the extent to which any savings are actually retained by the local authority. Boyne (1998) argues that adoption of this strategy probably has more to do with ideological favouritism towards private sector provision and lessening government intervention in economic provision than the pursuit of better and more efficient public services. He concludes there is as yet no convincing evidence to support the public choice case.

Despite empirical evidence, the new-right of the Thatcher years argued that local government should allow its services to be provided by the private sector but where this was not possible they should be managed under the more efficient and ruthless methods operated by successful business corporations. Under the Thatcher Governments local authorities, along with other public bureaucracies, were either forced or strongly encouraged to follow this path, which began to be termed New Public Management (NPM). Rhodes (1991: 548) has refined a definition from Christopher Hood (1991: 4–5) of NPM as

1 A focus on management, not policy, and on performance appraisal and efficiency.
2 The disaggregation of public bureaucracies into agencies which deal with each other on a user pay basis.
3 The use of quasi markets and contracting out to foster competition.
4 Cost cutting.
5 A style of management which emphasises *inter alia* output targets, limited term contracts, monetary incentives and freedom to manage.

The extent to which these values have been adopted by local authorities is far from uniform and there are differing interpretations as to how change should be secured in management practices between the post-1979 Conservative Government and the Blair Government. As Vivien Lowndes (1999: 37) observes, in local government, 'management change is a non-linear process, involving continuities between old and new processes, movements forward and backwards and change at different levels'.

---

Considerable impetus behind the New Public Management approach in Britain stemmed from the influential study of public sector management in the United States, *Reinventing Government* (1992) by Osborne and Gaebler. They suggested that public sector bodies should be operated as a business and praised those that made money from entrepreneurial risk taking. Such action, whilst possible for many United States cities, is generally ruled out by existing legislation in Britain that restricts local authorities from profitable trading unconnected with the central duties of a local authority.

---

Enthusiasm for NPM began to be applied to local government during the later years of the Thatcher Governments by Nicholas Ridley, Secretary of State for the Environment from 1986 to 1989. Ridley's solution to enlarged self-interested local bureaucracy was the 'enabling authority'. As outlined in Chapter 3, local government should not build huge bureaucracies to deliver services but contract out its services to private companies. The enabling authority has a few councillors and senior officers responsible for determining public needs and drawing up, awarding and monitoring contracts with private sector bodies which will supply these services. The local authority should, therefore, purchase services from the private sector and, therefore, needs only a small number of largely white collar staff.

A central pillar of the enabling concept as established by the 1988 Local Government Act was the principle of compulsory competitive tendering. The

Act required local authorities to invite sealed bids from any organisation that wished to operate a number of local services specified by the government. The contractor who agreed to fulfil the local authorities' requirements at the lowest price had to be awarded the contract. Initially established to cover manual tasks such as refuse collection, the Major Government widened the framework to encompass professional roles such as legal and financial services, although before contracts in these sectors were fully developed the CCT regime was replaced by the Best Value strategy of New Labour.

A consequence of CCT was that many local authorities divided the departments which were required to contract out services into teams that drew up the contracts and teams that implemented the service if the contract was won in house. Where the contract went to an outside body many of the employees who carried out the function, such as collecting refuse, became employees of the private contractor rather than the local authority. Thus, under the Conservatives, partly due to CCT and also to cuts in funding to the public sector, employment in local government ceased to be a job for life and many authorities began shedding staff to become smaller bureaucracies composed of proportionately more professionals involved in policy advice and management rather than manual operatives.

In addition to the development of CCT, the Major Government came up with a 'big idea' to ensure public agencies that could not be subject to market forces were controlled by their 'customers' through Citizen's Charters. In the context of local government this idea had been anticipated by a number of authorities that had schemes to set targets for their service departments and invite members of the public to complain if standards were not fulfilled. York City Council and the Scottish Region of Lothian were notable pioneers of this approach. The Citizen's Charter initiative required local authorities and many other public agencies to set targets for efficient standards of service delivery that had to be approved by a section housed within the Cabinet Office. If the authority could not meet the required targets, members of the public could expect some form of compensation and improvements in the delivery of the service. The idea of the Major Government was not wholly out of step with long term thinking within some sectors of the Labour Party. As early as the 1920s Fabian thinkers such as Sidney and Beatrice Webb had suggested local authorities should attain minimum standards of service provision as a means of ensuring equality for all citizens, and this idea had been incorporated into Labour Party manifestos during its 1980s wilderness years.

## Targets and inspections

New Labour did not accept that private businesses operating under the discipline of a free market unrestricted by government intervention would necessarily provide a better service than the public sector and were concerned ideologically that such a system might create an unacceptable measure of inequality. Nevertheless many of Blair's modernisers considered that without externally imposed restraints in addition to the electoral system, public sector organisations, including local government, would become inefficient and complacent unless central government placed compulsory demands upon them as to their output and costs. For the Blair Government the driving force to secure better management in the public sector has involved setting targets for public bodies with the threat that failure to achieve a required level of output could lead to an organisation losing control of the service to a potentially more successful provider, be it in the public or private sector.

### Best Value

The revised strategy for ensuring efficient management for local services was outlined in the 1988 White Paper *Modern Local Government* and became, for service efficiency, legislative reality in the 1999 Local Government Act. The Act restructured CCT into a framework for managing service delivery called Best Value. The principle behind the idea of Best Value is that local authorities should set, or have set for them, performance targets for the efficient delivery of services and be required to maintain these standards or lose the capacity to run the service. The performance targets are many and varied depending upon the particular service concerned. In some sectors such as education these are set by the national government and comprise, for example, targets for the numbers of children at key stage two of the national curriculum achieving an acceptable grade in their standard attainment tests for literacy or numeracy. Whilst the government sets the standards for sectors such as education and social services, the standards for many less crucial services are established by the local authorities themselves and encompass factors such as the extent to which socially provided houses are fully occupied or the administration costs for dealing with each housing benefit claimant. It is expected that the local authority sets the level of service provision following consultation with its citizens using survey methods usually conducted on a regular basis by private polling agencies. The Blair Governments have constantly urged local authorities to use forms of regular opinion sampling such as citizens' juries and focus groups to ascertain public expectations.

Although set by the local authority, the targets have a generally common structure so that it is possible for local authority attainment on, for example, refuse collection to be compared with data available for a neighbouring authority of similar size. Thus, a competitive element is built into the strategy to ensure that authorities which deliver services at a lower level of efficiency or quality than other comparable authorities can be identified and pressured into improving performance. A branch of the Audit Commission has the task of monitoring whether local authorities set themselves appropriate targets and efficiently meet their goals unless there is another appropriate national inspection agency

Table 10.1 *Comprehensive Performance Assessment*

|  | **Criteria** |
| --- | --- |
| Direction of travel | Improving strongly |
|  | Improving well |
|  | Improving adequately |
|  | Not improving |
| Use of resources | Financial reporting |
| (largely financial measures) | Financial management |
|  | Financial standing |
|  | Internal control |
|  | Value for money |
| Service assessment | Various factors dependent on service |
| Performance assessment | Various factors dependent on service |

for a specific service. The Best Value strategy does not abandon the view that many local services can be supplied by the private sector. Local authorities are encouraged to develop partnerships with private sector bodies and other agencies in order to supply services as efficiently as possible. If a local authority chooses to operate a service in house it must demonstrate to the satisfaction of the Best Value inspectorate that there are sound reasons why it should be implemented by the local authority rather than a private business or a voluntary agency. A carrot and stick approach was used towards ensuring local authorities took note of the Best Value findings. The best performing authorities would be given the status of beacon authorities and be requested to guide other less able councils. Should a local authority fail to set or consistently attain acceptable standards in relation to a service, the Audit Commission or an agency such as OFSTED can, following a series of inspections, recommend to the government that the service to be taken over by another organisation. This entails contracting out the service a private sector business or not for profit agency chosen by the government.

The evaluation of efficient management by local government was further extended after the 2001 General Election in a White Paper, *Strong Local Leadership – Quality Public Service*. The subsequent legislation incorporated Best Value in a system termed Comprehensive Performance Assessment (CPA), which evaluated the overall corporate performance of the authority based on its plans and achievements and how much the authority was improving. These assessments culminated in the award of four stars to the best authorities and none at all to what the Audit Commission regarded as the worst authorities. The framework for the assessment is shown in Table 10.1. The 2007 Local Government Act replaces the CPA from April 2009 with a new system for Comprehensive Area Assessment that is intended to evaluate the provision of services more from the point of view of the local consumer within a specific area and will not so much emphasise solely the role of the local authority but the range of local partnerships and organisations delivering services to that community.

The Audit Commission and the Government claim that the introduction of these reviews has greatly improved the performance of local councils and currently no county council or unitary authority is assigned no stars whilst the majority bask in the satisfaction of three or four stars. Almost everyone it appears is a winner and the Government may claim on the basis of this evidence that its stewardship of local government is highly successful. The procedures to secure this impression are, however, expensive and often appear to concern more matters of detail inappropriate for comment by a central agency than matters of substance. For example, a service assessment of libraries in Cumbria comments that 'Internal signage could be improved . . . at the one in Carlisle it was difficult to identify where the lift was situated' (www.audit-commission.gov.uk/reports).

It must be questioned how far this form of assessment in reality has caught the imagination of the public, who do not appear to be particularly aware of the grade achieved by their local authority. Despite excellent reports from the Audit Commission, the ruling Labour Party in Sheffield lost ground to the opposition in the 2007 local elections. The assessment of the performance of local authorities by a crude, even childish system of awarding stars for pleasing teacher, undermines the whole concept of democracy that is based on the view that an elected authority is accountable to its electorate and may be an expression of the interests of its citizens. If local citizens are happy with a measure of inefficiency in the provision of local services that is their choice.

### Local Area Agreements

The Government of Gordon Brown in its first weeks in office stated it was interested in cutting the number of targets set for local authorities as a means of cutting the costs of inspection and facilitating greater local autonomy. The creation of Local Area Agreements is meant to help in simplifying the number of targets and ensuring they apply more closely to local needs. There are, nevertheless, in 2008, 198 indicators of local success in the armoury of the Government. The system for establishing target and assessment of local authority performance is being folded into a framework for Local Area Agreements which from 2008 are mandatory for all unitary and county councils. The idea for LAAs began in 2005 but on a voluntary basis, and schemes could attract extra funding but, following considerable changes in the system, a new framework was established in the Local Government Act of 2007. The Government claims the scheme will provide local authorities with far greater discretion as to how they develop their services. Following negotiations with the appropriate regional government office, single tier authorities can set targets for up to 35 outcomes but must additionally meet 16 performance targets for education set by the Department for Children, Schools and Families.

The targets must also be developed in consultation with other agencies in the area and for two tier authorities this will involve the district councils, which may be given different targets from each other. Specified public sector organisations such as police authorities, the Highways Agency or Sport England also have a duty to co-operate with the local authorities on the development of LAAs. It is expected that the cost of achieving the targets will be met through their normal funding arrangements but there will be some reward grants available to encourage councils to achieve their targets.

The consequence of this arrangement has been the production by single tier authorities and the county councils of statements of targets they wish to achieve over a three year period through joint working with a number of specified public agencies. Bedfordshire County Council, for example, has agreed as one of its targets to secure a reduction in the numbers in the county claiming unemployment benefit in the Mid-Bedford District to 5.0 per cent in 2008/09, 4.0 per cent in 2009/10 and 4.8 per cent in 2010/11 in partnership with, among others, the Learning and Skills Council, Job Centres and the Learning Partnership. There are similar targets negotiated with other agencies for services such as reduction of land fill sites for domestic waste, carbon dioxide emissions, smoking or the number of elderly people unable to live independently. The scheme clearly gives further emphasis to joined up working and continues the target driven approach to securing management efficiency. However, in an economy at near recession levels with little capacity to increase public spending, it remains to be seen how many of the wish lists of agreement will be attained.

## Beacon scheme

The Blair Government added a further carrot, as opposed to stick, for the most innovative and efficient authorities through a beacon authority scheme. Each year a number of authorities are awarded for that year beacon status if they show innovation and effective management ideas in one of a number of management or service delivery themes. An advisory committee to DCLG designates these services over a year in advance of the awards being made. In 2007 applications from authorities were invited for 10 themes that included tackling climate change, dignity in care and reducing re-offending. Successful councils can apply for a small measure of financial support for their work on a particular theme but are enticed to join the scheme more on the grounds that it will enhance the status of successful officers applying for these programmes. The work of successful officers involved in making a bid is likely to be publicised by organisations such as IDeA and they may be held nationally as upholders of good practice from which other authorities may learn something useful. The successful councils and their incumbent party or party coalition leaders will also be able to boast to their electorate of their success.

## Inspectorates

In addition to the Audit Commission are the several agencies that have been established to review the quality of specific public services. Some of these agencies can trace their origins to the nineteenth century. Perhaps the most well known is OFSTED, which was established in 2002 by the Major Government to be more independent of the government than the previous system that had begun in 1840 as the schools inspectorate. The system of inspection was partially privatised. Teams of approved private inspectors are contracted to undertake the inspections of particular schools. Much criticism was faced in the earlier years of OFSTED about the inequalities between assessments from different inspectorates. In 1997 the powers of OFSTED were further extended to include not only inspection of schools but the LEA itself. OFSTED assesses whether all parts of the LEA's activities are of a standard it considers appropriate and recommends to the government that, where an LEA is failing to meet appropriate standards, the service is removed from the local authority and transferred to another agency. The power has been used on several occasions with the greatest blow falling on the London Borough of Hackney, which in 2002 lost control of its education service for at least 12 years to an independent non-profit making education services trust whose Chair appointed by the Government is a former Chief Inspector for Schools.

Since the development of the reformed poor law in 1834 there has been some form of inspection of social service provision. In 2003 a range of inspectorates were brought together as the Commission for Social Care Inspection which regularly assesses the standards in care homes and also inspects the social services departments in local authorities and awards stars for good practice. The Commission can closely monitor and require improvements within local authorities that it considers to be poor performers. Fire services have an inspections service which falls within the remit of the Audit Commission. The Police Inspectorate rates standards of support for police services provided by local police authorities, as do inspectorates for the probation services and the administration of courts. The Government's strategy to merge inspectorates led to a proposal to amalgamate these groups with the Prisons Inspectorate to form a huge single inspectorate for all matters judicial and custodial but this was too much for Parliament and the idea was quietly withdrawn.

## The ethical dimension

A criticism of New Public Management is that concentration on the 3Es of efficiency, economy and effectiveness pays no regard to a further and more important 'E' word, ethics. Any business whether private or public, let alone a democratically elected organisation, must ensure that its policies and the conduct of its policy makers and employees can be justified in terms of the established moral standards of the society in which it operates. Unethical conduct encompasses a wide range of improper actions such as embezzlement of public funds, giving favours to friends and relatives at the taxpayers' expense, racial discrimination and sexual harassment.

Corruption has been endemic within local government although, given the numbers of councillors and local government personnel, it is not a particularly widespread problem and, debatably, has been less of an issue in recent decades than in the nineteenth century despite a much higher standard of expectation of what may be acceptable conduct. In the 1970s serious attention to issues of corruption concerning local government came to light with the unmasking of the most organised and pervasive case of bribery of the last 50 years. A firm of architects created by John Poulson was found to have secured a large number of contracts with local authorities through advancing bribes, such as expensive holidays, to councillors and senior officers. Leading national politicians and civil servants were also implicated in the scandal. The Poulson issue led to a Government Enquiry under Lord Salmon which, among its recommendations, suggested that councillors must declare any personal financial interest in matters being discussed by their authority and also enter their outside financial interests in a publicly available register. The Salmon Enquiry, however, observed that

> We have heard no evidence to give us concern about the integrity and sense of public duty of our bureaucracy, or to suggest that it is common for members of the public to offer bribes . . . in the day-to-day administration of central and local government. (1976: 11, para 35)

The Salmon Report did not mark the end of corrupt practices in local government. In the 1990s the most sensational case involved Lady Porter, who, as leader of Westminster City Council, was found by the District Auditor to be arranging the sale of council houses within the Borough so as to fortify the Conservative vote.

In order to ensure that there were further safeguards against corrupt practices than the system of audit, the Thatcher Government in 1989 required local authorities to designate a senior official as a monitoring officer, who is empowered to investigate charges of improper administration and take appropriate action by informing, if necessary, the auditors or police of serious misconduct. Tony Blair came to power partly on the wave of a number of widely publicised scandals concerning the misuse of power by MPs during the Major Government and set about consolidating his popularity by establishing far stronger codes of ethical behaviour in public life that were later to haunt his final years in office. In the context of local government, stronger ethical regulation was promised in *Modern Local Government: In Touch with the People* and was delivered as part of the 2000 Local Government Act. The Act establishes a

Standards Board for England with the task of recommending to Parliament a code of ethical conduct for local authorities and assigns this task to a commissioner. In Wales the role is effectively assigned to the Ombudsman. A parallel Scottish Act in 2000 set up a Standards Commission for Scotland.

---

Corruption is endemic in European and United States local governments; at least as much as in Britain. Problems have ranged from the serious accusation that the President of France, Jacques Chirac, used his position as mayor of Paris to squirrel away funds to support his political party, to the established tradition of political favouritism as the basis for selection of local government officers in Italy and in some cities of the United States.

---

Each major local authority is also required to establish a standards committee to monitor compliance of the ethical code. The committees are made up of backbench councillors and some appointees not connected with the authority. The monitoring officer effectively serves as the chief officer servicing the committee and in many cases sets its agenda. Each councillor must sign a declaration agreeing to abide by the code once it is adopted and if they refused to accept the document they would lose their position on the Authority. The code requires councillors to show respect to others and thus avoid racial or sexual discrimination and bullying and harassment, declare when they have a personal interest in a policy that advantages themselves, respect the need for confidentiality and generally ensure they do not act in a way that harms the moral standing of the authority.

The Standards Board, whose members are appointed by the government with the advice of the LGA, ensures that all principal local authorities have established acceptable monitoring committees and will also become involved in investigating difficult or disputed cases that are too problematic to be dealt with by the standards committee of a particular local authority. The Board also reviews complaints about unethical behaviour within parish and town councils, and almost half of the issues considered by the Board relate to rows within these institutions. However, on occasion such matters may afflict the higher reaches of local government, as in 2006 when Mayor of London, Ken Livingstone, was subject to investigation for accusing an over-intrusive journalist of behaving like a concentration camp guard. If the Standards Agencies in England or Ombudsman in Wales consider that there has been a breach of ethical codes they can refer the case to an Adjudication Panel whose members are appointed by the Department of Justice. These tribunals consider the case, allowing legal representation to the accused councillor, determine whether accusations of misconduct are valid and, if appropriate, order that the councillor is suspended from office or disqualified for a number of years from standing as a councillor. In Scotland the Standards Commission has the powers of a tribunal to suspend councillors from office.

## Redress

In the first half of the twentieth century it was assumed that the electoral system and the courts were sufficient means to ensure that citizens could ensure that they were not treated unfairly or fraudulently by their local authority. Whilst the courts still remain as an option for those with the wealth to pay for civil action against their local authority, the decreasing confidence in the capacity of local democracy to change the behaviour of individual councillors or local political parties has led to the accretion of a number of agencies to help secure the interests of the citizen against their local authority and also changes in democratic management to ensure more open government.

### *Open government*

Local government has in recent years become a much more open structure whose inner workings can be revealed and brought into the light of day. All meetings of a full council and its sub-committees are, by law, open to the public although the 2000 Local Government Act does allow local authority cabinets to meet in private if sensitive issues affecting individuals or companies are to be discussed. The 1985 Local Government Access to Information Act ensured that all documents relating to the meetings of a local authority should be made available to the public.

Institutionally, local authorities are fully open to influence by interest groups. There is no barrier to the freedom of association and communication at the local level, provided the groups involved are not indulging in slander or meeting for some criminal purpose. The rights of association at local level are not differentiated from nationally set restrictions on forming societies and groups or assembling for protest marches and rallies. The right to communicate dissent is, in practice, less restricted at the local level. Central government can more easily prevent publication of what it regards euphemistically as 'sensitive' material through the use of the Official Secrets Act. Local authorities do not enjoy these powers of protection and have no formal powers to restrict press comment on their actions.

Local authorities have also been made more accessible to public scrutiny with the advance of the internet and the development of systems of e-governance. Every major local authority has established a web site that can be accessed either directly or, through the index to local authorities, on the government's web portal, www.direct.gov.uk. Local authority web sites vary in their structure and quality but most sites are orientated towards ensuring the public can readily gain access to information needed on particularly well used services such as refuse collection and school standards. Most sites will also file details of the minutes of their council meetings and their executive cabinets and will provide a resumé of their accounts. All sites will inform the public how to contact directly their local councillors and the results of recent elections.

Some, however, may have richer material on the history of their area and will provide details on the functions of their committees and departments. Reference to these sites can be a useful additional supplement to this study.

### Ombudsman

If, following contact with councillors and officers, someone feels they have been harshly treated by their authority they can seek redress from the local authority ombudsman. The office was established for England and Wales in 1974 and two years later in Scotland. The institution followed in the wake of the establishment in 1969 of the Parliamentary Commissioner, popularly known as the ombudsman, to investigate complaints against the civil service. The office was designed to deal with cases where local authority officers or councillors may have acted within the moral code but have made serious errors of judgement or failed to act effectively. Such cases, referred to as maladministration, can be sent to the local ombudsman or, to give the position its official title, the Commissioners for Local Administration. There are three such Commissioners in England, who work on a regional basis, and one each for Scotland and Wales. Citizens may complain to the appropriate Commissioner, in the first place through their local councillor but if this individual will not take up the case, then directly to Commissioner. The office received over 19,000 complaints in 2005 and found that the local authorities should amend their action in 27 per cent of these (www.logo.org.uk/surveys.htm). The largest number of cases relate to planning decisions.

The system has a number of serious flaws which are also present in the national ombudsman system. Access is initially through an elected representative and so the office is not well known or very readily approachable. The Commissioners have no power to take the initiative themselves to investigate failings or to prosecute or compel authorities that have acted unreasonably to mend their ways. The Commissioner issues reports on its investigations which are communicated to the erring local authority and can be made public. Most local authorities take notice of the complaint and compensate the aggrieved citizen but they can, and on occasion do, sit out the criticism.

> In contrast to Britain, the Swedish ombudsman, the office which was the model for the idea, can prosecute authorities that have neglected their duties and investigate cases on its own initiative or as a result of a direct approach from an individual or interest group.

### The role of the tribunals and courts

Many services operated by local authorities that require the payment of benefits or raising money through property taxes are likely, from time to time, to embroil a local authority in disputes between itself and aggrieved citizens who believe they are being shortchanged or are paying too much. These matters, if unresolved to a complainant's satisfaction by the authority, can usually be presented to a tribunal, a quasi judicial body but without the formality of the courts. The exact form and procedures of tribunals vary but they can usually resolve problems more speedily and cheaply than the courts and have members with specialist knowledge of the subject matter. Established by legislation they can involve local government on matters such as housing benefit payments or council tax and business rate charges.

Should the many schemes for testing public opinion and evaluating efficiency still break down, especially in relation to the problems that may be faced by the individual, citizens still have the right, if not always the financial means, to take their local authority to court. A local authority may be, and many are, sued by citizens who have, for example, fallen on uneven paving and suffered injury as a result or believe that a school has wrongfully excluded their child. Such action can, however, be difficult for the ordinary citizen to finance unless their case is taken up by a well heeled interest group. Court cases for damages can, if contested, be very expensive and if they fail the court may expect the complainant to bear the costs of the case. As many solicitors now pursue cases on a 'no win no fee' basis the capacity to risk a court case against an authority has much increased but at the expense of the lawyers getting a higher proportion of the settlement than might otherwise have been the case. Most authorities will, however, at any particular time expect to be embroiled in a number of on-going court or tribunal cases.

### Further reading

Management practices in local government have a long established literature and major studies on corporate management are referred to in Chapter 7. New ideas of management developed in the 1980s can be approached through Walsh (1995) and Stoker (1999). Boyne (1998) is the most comprehensive study of empirical work on the results of new-right management theory. The application of these ideas more specifically to local government has an extensive literature. A useful guide is provided by Kerley (1994) and also of importance are Leach, Stewart and Walsh (1994) and Fenwick (1995). Clarke and Stewart (1990) and Stewart (1986) develop an influential framework for citizen focused management although their views are not in the new-right perspective of NPM. Stoker (1999) provides a number of valuable articles on recent changes in the management process. Fergusson (2005) outlines the use of e-governance by local authorities in Britain.

Prior (1995) and Chandler (1996) contain material on the citizen's charter and local government. Hunt (2006) discusses access to information and local government. Details of how Best Value and CPA operate can be found through reference to the Audit Commission's web site. Similarly the ethical code for local authorities can be found on the Standards Board's web site at www.opsi.gov.uk/si/si2007/20071159.htm. OFSTED and other inspectorates' Reports are available through the web.

# 11

# Interests, business and the media

Local government is not 'an island pure and entire unto itself' but operates as an actor amidst a maze of voluntary and business organisations that may be delivering services in partnership with the local authority. There are also numerous less well connected groups that seek to influence a council's policies. Traditionally, it has been routine to depict these organisations as pressure or interest groups. In the 1960s and 1970s academic studies of interest groups in local government were greatly stimulated by a theory of pluralist democracy maintaining that successful politicians achieve popularity by listening to the many voices of disparate groups and then steer a policy direction that successfully satisfies as many of these interests as is possible.

R.A. Dahl in his classic study of pluralism *Who Governs?* (1961) studied the power of the mayor in New Haven, the City in which the University of Yale is established, and argued that the position required the mayor to mediate between numerous interests within the town so as to secure the policies that best fulfilled the demands of numerous complementary and conflicting interests. Thus democracy was secured as decisions generally reflected the most strongly supported policy outcomes.

Studies of power in communities in Britain in the 1970s (Hampton 1970; Dearlove 1973; Newton 1976; Green 1981) argued that pluralist theory, especially where local government is concerned, was misleading and only a few well connected wealthy groups were ever successful in influencing local policy. Over the last 30 years this adversary view of interest groups has changed substantially. Whilst a great many interest groups seek to change local policy by putting pressure on their councillors, the most successful, with strong encouragement from national government, work in close partnership with local authorities.

149

## Policy networks, partnerships and communities

The most important interests affecting local government policy and service delivery have no need to stir up mass demonstrations or laboriously assemble petitions but work quietly behind the scenes. It is misleading to depict these efficacious interests primarily as organisations locked in internecine strife with the government or public sector agencies. Successful groups do not have to resort to expensive strategies of confrontation but achieve their aims through the development of close working relationships with officers or members of a local authority. The patterns of frequent interaction between interests and government and political parties can be complex since it is far from being a one way process of an isolated group putting pressure on government. In practice, influential groups may modify their actions as much as politicians so as to co-ordinate their interests for mutual benefit and groups may often interact with one another to achieve their goals. These intricate patterns have been described as policy networks to demonstrate the presence of many inter-linking relationships between organisations that devise and deliver policy (Rhodes and Marsh 1992). On many occasions these networks form well established stable relationships that are referred to as 'policy communities'. The rhetoric of the post-1997 Labour Governments has been to promote the close relationship between interests, including local government, as partnerships of planners and providers both seeking the common goal of producing better services for the citizen.

Some of the most important examples of policy networks within local government have already been analysed in discussing the professional interests of officers. A professional association such as CIPFA is at root an interest group acting on behalf of its members. Similarly, trade unions may enjoy an important status in policy communities and expect to be regularly consulted on matters concerning the working conditions of their members. They can also be influential in forming Labour Party policy through their affiliations to the Party. However, rarely is there a concerted effort by a trade union to control a local authority and in many cases where leading councillors are also prominent members of a trade union it is impossible to determine whether they act as union members, councillors or Labour Party members (Barker 1982). As will be discussed below the influence of major business interests can, given the Government's insistence on partnership, be such that they can insinuate themselves in many aspects of service delivery, economic redevelopment and planning.

However much governments use the language of partnership to describe the relationship between local authority and favoured interests, the concept of policy networks leads to the conclusion that there is a rather large elephant in the local room. Powerful interests in Britain do not operate solely on a local level but influence politics through close working relationships with government ministers and senior civil servants. Groups can secure such a favoured status because of their economic importance to the nation. These comprise the large multi-national firms and banks and insurance companies. They may also be groups with a monopoly of expertise and authority in a particular area, such as the British Medical Association or the Law Society, or organisations that share strong ideological links with a political party, such as the trade unions enjoy with Labour Governments or business interests with both the Conservatives and Labour. If a local authority chooses to thwart the interests of any of these powerful groups it may not only have to contend with direct local pressure from the offended interest but also with pressure from central government acting on behalf of that interest.

The effectiveness of interest groups in comparative terms is also dependent on deeply ingrained attitudes within the political culture of a nation. Whilst in Britain and the United States there is a widespread acceptance that interests negotiate with each other and central government to secure policy change, in France there is far greater suspicion of interests with the result that disaffected groups such as farmers are more likely to resort to direct confrontational action than negotiation to achieve their aims.

Critics of these arrangements argue that the development of corporate relations between local authorities and big business is an inevitable consequence of the capitalist system. Even in the most left wing council the interests of capital will oblige a local authority to follow its own interest and co-operate with business. Cynthia Cockburn's (1977) study of the rise and fall of local authority funded community associations in Lambeth suggests that the good intentions of local councillors to consult residents on their future could not be sustained against pressures by big business to redevelop large areas of the Borough. A combination of economic power and influence by business at local and national level defeated any attempt by community associations to assert their individuality. It may be suggested, therefore, that local authorities can play a partnership role with industry and commerce in local economic development provided they swim with the interests of the private sector partner and provided central government does not see fit to impose a national solution to local economic problems.

## Local authorities and the business community

Among the most influential groups are large businesses that command extensive financial resources and expertise and have a major influence on the local economy. As discussed in earlier chapters, since the development of the 'enabling authority' under the Thatcher and Major Governments and the emphasis on partnership and Best Value under Labour, the relationship between local government and business has become closely intertwined. Under Best Value local authorities must justify why they implement a service 'in house' rather than work in partnership with a private company. Thus, most authorities have contracted out services such as refuse collection and waste disposal, recreation facilities, housing and provision of social care. Many clerical services such as auditing, payment of wages and collection of taxes are also contracted out to the private sector. New buildings are often financed, constructed and leased back to local authorities through PFI and almost all local urban regeneration schemes are expected, if they are to attract government grants, to involve partnerships between the local authority and businesses or voluntary agencies. A consequence of these developments has been to bring businesses in far closer co-operation with local authorities. As a private company develops the resources to provide a local service at the expense of any capacity within the local authority in terms of detailed knowledge and machinery to run that service, it becomes difficult for the local authority to return to providing a service on its own and forces the organisation to be dependent on the private or voluntary sector to provide the services it needs.

> In the United States links between business interests and city governments are generally much closer and in some cities, such as San Antonio in Texas, the government of the city is predominantly controlled by business representatives. More often, as demonstrated by Clarence Stone (1989), in his study of government in Atlanta, Georgia, city politics revolves around the co-operation between business groups and community based interest groups.

### Voluntary or third sector organisations

Local authorities are dependent not only on the activities of business but the work of what are popularly seen as voluntary charitable groups. To some extent there is an image of voluntary groups as small well meaning organisations run on rather amateur lines by teams of enthusiastic volunteers. Whilst there are many local charities based on purely voluntary help that enhance the sense of local community throughout the country, the largest voluntary organisations, although often using un-paid help, are major public service organisations employing full time professional staff. Many of these groups have a crucial role in filling the 'gaps' within the welfare state by providing services that have not been fully met by the state at both local and national level. For example, an organisation such as the National Society for the Prevention of Cruelty to Children (NSPCC) investigates cases of child abuse that would otherwise be the province of local authority social services departments. The large scale not-for-profit organisations that fill important gaps in state provision are frequently referred to as 'third sector organisations' as opposed to 'voluntary agencies'.

The Conservative Government encouraged the growth of third sector organisations in many public service sectors in order gradually to supplant public sector and particularly local government activity in these areas. As shown in Chapter 3, this was a central aim of the Thatcher Governments in relation to housing where the Governments reinforced the previously rather small sector of rented housing provided by housing associations to the point where the majority of publicly owned housing is now constructed by housing associations (Malpass 2000). The role of the local authority housing department is to work with housing associations in identifying those in need of subsidised housing and there was discussion even within the Blair Government, let alone the Conservative Party, on the possibility of transferring complete responsibility for subsidised public housing to the third sector housing associations. Similarly many social services functions are delivered by voluntary agencies acting in partnership with local government.

## The occasional interest groups

Whilst the most influential non-governmental or party groups influencing local authorities may be those working in partnership with a local authority, there remain many organisations that have no close contractual ties with the authority but need on occasion to interact with their local council. Since interest groups comprise all organisations involved at some time in political action, apart from the institutions of central government and political parties, their numbers are scarcely calculable. Most groups are formed for purposes other than political representation and only become incidentally involved with governments. A football club may become an interest group if it discovers that the local authority is about to grant permission to a large multi-national firm to dig up its playing field. Similarly, the large chemical manufacturer will be an interest group if it attempts to persuade the local authority to allow it to build on the council owned playing fields beloved by the football club. In addition to sports clubs and large firms, local authorities will receive demands from groups as varied as chambers of commerce, neighbourhood watch schemes, rate payers' associations, anti-road lobbies, Green Peace, local radio stations and women's shelters.

Newton (1976: 38) attempted to assess the number of groups active in the City of Birmingham and reached the figure of 4,264 before he stopped counting. A more recent count of Birmingham interests reached 5,781 (Maloney, Smith and Stoker 2000). The majority of Newton's groups had not however been involved in political activity, at least in the two years preceding the survey, and hence only around one third could be classified as political interests. However, groups that are politically active frequently relate to the local authority, and Maloney, Smith and Stoker (2000: 807) found that 82 per cent of voluntary and community groups believed that Birmingham City Council was an important source of information.

The variety of groups requires some classification if sense is to be made of their political characteristics and influence. Most basic theories of interest groups make a distinction between those that are formed to fight against a particular cause or issue and those that represent an on-going interest. Single issue groups include committees formed by irate home owners threatened by a road development or a group seeking to prevent dumping of nuclear waste in its community. Once the group has succeeded or irrevocably failed it will disband or have to restructure itself around some new cause. Because of the usually limited nature of their concerns, single issue groups are not usually as important as promotional groups representing an on-going interest. These include organisations as varied as trade unions, trade associations of employers, religious bodies and community groups. They are formed to represent the concerns of groups that have an interest in promoting or pursuing an activity that will continue for the foreseeable future. Classification of such groups must be arbitrary since the complex diversity of human interest does not lead to neat logical packaging of interests.

Newton assigned groups into 13 functional categories (1976: 38); Stoker (1991: 115–17) has suggested a four fold classification into producer groups (which encompass businesses and trade unions), community groups, cause groups and voluntary groups. However, such one dimensional classifications do not do justice to the complexity of the relationship between government and interests. The subject area of a particular group needs to be considered alongside its attitude towards local policy makers. Frequently, established groups may behave differently towards the local authority on certain matters and take a different approach on other issues. Larger, more powerful groups often tend to be multi-purpose organisations conducting a range of activities which may lead them to oppose and criticise a local authority on one particular issue whilst in another area they may be actively working in amicable partnership with the local authority. A business may, for example, work in partnership with a local authority on the delivery of a service but also attack the authority over its policy on car parking or tourist promotion. It is therefore necessary to develop a classification based not only on the broad subject area of the interest group but also on its relationship of interest to local authorities. This has been portrayed in a simplified relationship matrix as depicted in Table 11.1.

## Single issue groups and campaigns

A glance at a local newspaper often suggests that the majority of interests are groups protesting about some aspect of local authority policy. This impression is, however, misleading as the most visible are often not the most successful. Examples are numerous and include groups opposing building developments, closures of local authority facilities such as a school or an elderly persons' home or protests from groups enraged that the local authority may not have clamped down on 'rat running' through a residential neighbourhood or kerb crawling

Table 11.1 *Interest group and local authority relationships*

| Attitude to local authority | Single issue group | Community Group | Business and economic interest | Voluntary welfare group |
|---|---|---|---|---|
| Hostile | Xville by-pass protestors | Xville residents group against the by-pass | Xville Chamber of Commerce opposing high council tax | NSPCC criticises Xville social services |
| Supportive | Xville by-pass supporters | Xville residents group for the by-pass | Xville Chamber of Commerce for the local authority trade fair | MIND praises social services for help to mentally ill |
| Partnership | The Xville by-pass supporters and local authority working group | The Xville residents and local authority area committee | Chamber of Commerce and local authority promoting a trade fair and SRB bid | Xville Housing Association builds sheltered housing for mentally ill on local authority register |

in a red light district. A not untypical issue is campaigns by local residents to oppose the construction of a large supermarket in their community that would cause even greater congestion on an already overcrowded road. A few campaigns gain national prominence as in the case of the objections by wealthy residents of Gerrards Cross in Buckinghamshire against the construction of a Tesco supermarket.

Often the more successful groups campaigning over a single issue are less visible than some less efficacious groups since they can ensure that the local authority is fully in agreement with their cause and deals with the problem. They therefore have no need to further publicise their concerns and work to support rather than oppose the authority. On occasion alliances on single issues between the local authority and campaign groups develop when both organisations are in agreement over their opposition to policies of the central government or a large business group. In the 1980s several left wing authorities with the co-operation of the Campaign for Nuclear Disarmament declared themselves nuclear free zones as a gesture that had little practical impact but gave publicity to the cause of CND. Local authorities in South Yorkshire have sided with local residents' campaign groups against open cast mining in their areas.

## Community groups

An important class of interest groups that affect local authorities more than central government are the numerous community groups that have been established to look after the mutual concerns of people living in a specific locality or to represent a particular group of city wide residents who have a common set of values. Often such groups are the source of single issue campaigns and their interest in a particular area or community of interests ensures they will constantly refer issues to the local authority. In Sheffield, for example, residents of the Nether Edge area may voluntarily join the Nether Edge Society, which issues a regular newsletter informing its members about the history and personalities of the area but, in political terms, has much to say on building development and road improvements in the area and may be important in forming local opinion on, for example, replacement of council owned trees on the local streets.

Community groups representing localities within a local authority are a necessary creation of the growth of local government units into what are effectively sub-regional rather than genuinely local organisations. Professionals living in prosperous suburban communities are governed by the same authority as the unemployed residents of a run down council estate. Both groups may have reason to support and defend their localities but will make very different demands on the local authority. Within rural districts encompassing an area of many square miles there will be many small towns and villages that have concerns that are wholly different from those of communities many miles distant. For example, the small industrial town of Workington is governed by the same District Authority as the Lake District tourist town of Keswick. The interests of villages and towns may be taken up and promoted by the parish or town council and many of these minor authorities can effectively act as local community interest groups by pressuring the local authority to respond to their needs. In cities these groups may be replaced by an informal network of community associations and, on occasion, area consultative committees created by the local authority itself.

The term 'community' may not only describe the links between people living in the same area but people of similar interests and background even though they may not live close to one another. Thus, many towns have city wide communities of people with common ethnic, religious or sexual backgrounds. Ken Livingstone when leader of the GLC gave particular prominence to such groups as he sought to provide support to many London wide minority interests. On occasion a local authority may even foster and fund groups in order to gain an insight into the needs of a particular community. Most local authorities support tenants' associations or advice centres as a valuable means of gaining feedback from citizens even if this may at times be highly critical of their actions.

### The success or failure of single issue and community groups

The probability of single cause groups achieving success depends on factors that affect the majority of interests although many single cause groups have far fewer resources to help them secure their goals. Newton's (1976) study of Birmingham was an attempt to evaluate in a British context the pluralist theories established in Dahl's earlier writings. He concluded that the most politically active and influential interest groups tended to be those which had a larger membership and substantial financial resources and staff and that these factors tended to cluster together. This finding confirms most national studies. A group with a large membership will be more likely to have an electoral impact. Many members provide a higher income and a greater ability to pay for professional workers and expert advice. Professionalism and an ability to recruit expert help allow interests to fully research their arguments and present their ideas in a clear well documented form. These factors will, in turn, ensure that leaders of the better resourced and supported interest groups are more likely to get the attention of policy makers.

Perhaps the most crucial factor is the nature of their cause and the values held by the policy makers within the local authority. A group that seeks support on an issue that is consistent with local authority policies and values is likely to find it far easier to succeed in its aims. It is also important for the group to show that it is representative of opinion and that its views are not likely to be opposed by a significant number of individuals or interests. The success of a group may also depend on its campaign strategies. Councillors will not enthuse about groups that seek to coerce and politically embarrass them. Dearlove (1973) showed that councillors in Kensington and Chelsea preferred to be approached through ward councillors or committee chairs, whilst actions such as demonstrations or complaints through the press were frowned upon.

If the two sectors promoting success are put together it is clear that groups led by well educated middle class activists campaigning on an issue likely to gain the sympathy of councillors and senior local government officers will be most likely to have their concerns considered sympathetically. Within such a framework lies a further crucial characteristic of a successful group: the ability to have close personal links with senior policy makers. As was demonstrated in relation to business, voluntary and professional groups, the most effective interests work within the local authority through close linkages with senior officers and councillors and have, usually, little need to campaign against the authority.

### Communication and the media

The press and local radio and television have an important role in the interaction of interests and local government. The media can itself be a very powerful interest in its own right as local newspapers or radio stations may have decided views as to the activities of the local authority and forward these ideas as part of their editorial policy. They also act as an important means of communication between councillors, local interests and the electorate.

## The national media

Local government is of interest to television, radio and the national press largely in so far as it has an impact on national government. Thus, local electoral contests are reported and monitored on national television, usually late at night, and normally as a form of opinion poll on the rating of the national parties. Similarly, major issues affecting local government, such as the poll tax, are reported not so much because of their local consequences, but in so far as they are issues that divide the parliamentary parties and affect national voting opinions. Even when the reported local issue appears to concern a single local authority, such as the tabloids' false accusations in the 1980s of 'looney left' antics of local socialist London boroughs, the subject is used to discredit national political tendencies. In this context, therefore, the national media is an important factor undermining any value for local government as the representative of specifically local opinion.

## The local media

Locally, the most potent communicators of local politics are the press and local radio. Since the range and scope of these media are varied, there is a considerable variation in the coverage of local politics. In the large cities there are local daily and evening newspapers that will have a significant coverage of local political issues. In recent years the established press has been rivalled by free news-sheets geared to maximising advertising revenue, but many of these include local political comment. Some local authorities are seeking to emulate this tendency by issuing their own periodic news-sheets to households in their areas. A city will also have at least one, and increasingly several, local radio stations. It is normal for most BBC local radio networks to devote some attention to local authority issues. They will interview leading councillors and their opponents concerning major issues before the authority and will also cover local election campaigns. The political coverage of many independent stations devoting their output to popular music may be minimal but a few may have coverage as extensive as the publicly owned stations.

> In the United States, where there is far more substantial development of local television largely through cable channels, it is possible to gain far more detailed coverage of local politics and in some towns the local cable television company will each week show live the proceedings of their local city councils for the benefit of the community.

Whilst there are many sources of local information in urban centres, the coverage of local issues in rural areas may be much less thorough. Before 1939 most small towns or groups of neighbouring villages had a local weekly newspaper which would have reported extensively the proceedings of local authorities in their areas. There has been a steady decrease in the number of local weekly papers as a consequence of amalgamation and closures. This trend has, however, paralleled an increase in the size of local authority areas so that it is not infrequent for a weekly newspaper to cover one county or district area. In as much as this takes place, it is more by coincidence than by design. For many parts of the country there is no particularly local press and hence district and county council issues are reported either in special editions covering a particular area or, more usually, as local items that are often given relatively little detailed coverage. J.M. Lee reflected on this fragmentation in Cheshire:

> There were no newspapers that thought in 'county terms' – no county society existed to buy them – and a considerable amount of anti-ministerial feeling directed against county officials sprang from ignorance occasioned by this lack of publicity. (1963: 205)

It is difficult to assess what impact reporting of local politics may have on the fortunes of a local authority. There appears to be a strong coincidence of local and national voting behaviour which has reinforced the argument that local policy making is not determined by local interests. This is, as is argued in Chapter 12, a doubtful assertion and there is plenty of evidence to suggest that able local politicians are usually concerned to cultivate the electorate by working through the local media. It is also argued that variations in the national and local vote can occur, but these are too little researched to evaluate the effect of the local media in this process.

Evidence on the attitude of councillors to the media is conflicting. Dearlove (1973: 182), comparing the attitudes of councillors in community surveys, showed that few councillors thought the press was a major source of influence as regards the needs of their electorate. In reality, councillors' opinions on the media will be determined by their political stance. Where, as in Kensington and Chelsea, the press is not regarded as politically supportive of the local authority, the councillors will be negatively influenced by the media and hostile to its reportage. In many local authorities where the press is at least tolerated, leading councillors will try to form good working relationships with favoured editors, journalists and broadcasters. Thus, a council leader will be prepared to provide news to a local editor provided he or she reports the issue in reasonably balanced and fair terms.

Mutually self-interested but cordial relations between local leaders and the press are, however, only sustained where the local media support, or at least tolerate, the policies of the council. In some cases the press may be seen by councillors as unhelpful and, therefore, can be ignored, presumably with the hope that no one would seriously read the offending rag. It is probable that such a breakdown of trust between the press and councillors is more likely within Labour rather than Conservative groups. Although some newspapers are favourable to the Labour Party, it takes money to run a newspaper or local radio station and those with money tend to support the Conservative cause.

### E-governance

An increasingly important strand of communication for local government and the public is through the internet. It is now possible for citizens to obtain through their personal computer volumes of information about local government services. All local authorities now have a web site and can provide basic information about their services to the public. It is possible through the web to pay bills to some councils or to apply for grants or request a specific service. Most local government web sites also provide news about recent developments and initiatives of the local authority. A temptation for some authorities is to use this medium to praise the ruling council although the convention remains that the local government officers who provide and download the information should not show preference to a particular party or politician.

However, this means of communication can be used to facilitate a flow of information from the citizen to the local authority as well as in the other direction. Members of the public can through the internet pass comments on to their local councillors or request answers to questions. In the future it is probable that councillors may be less likely to have constituents turning up at their regular surgeries or phoning them up at some unlikely hour about a problem. Councillors will need instead to be ready to scrutinise their e-mails and provide prompt answers to constituents in reply to their messages or be prepared to receive and reply to text messages through mobile phones. The use of e-governance may also enable computer literate citizens to express in their 'blogs' their views on the performance of their authority or councillor and attempt to reach a wide public with their comments. It remains to be seen how far the use of instant and widespread communication will undermine the traditional role of the local press or even local radio in shaping public opinion on the local authority as the formation of opinion shifts to other more instantly accessible electronic media.

### Further reading

Whilst many community studies and textbooks refer to interest group activity in local government there is no substantive work solely dedicated to reviewing this field. However, Newton (1976) is of crucial importance and contains important research on the role of local groups, and Saunders (1979) is also invaluable in the case of powerful economic interests, as is Cockburn (1977). Studies relating to professional groups and trade unions were considered in the previous chapter. Hain (1976) provides some useful case studies. There are few studies of the relationship between racially united groups and local government with the valuable exception of Ben-Tovim et al. (1986).

There is now a considerable literature on local authorities and business partnerships which touches on the role of interest groups. This includes Campbell (1990), Harloe, Pickvance and Urry (1990), a number of contributions to Stoker (1999, 2000) and Sullivan and Skeltcher (2002). Of earlier interest is Moore and Richardson (1989). Chandler and Lawless (1985) is beginning to date in a rapidly changing era but should still have useful material.

There are few studies of the impact of local government on the media although Fergusson (2005) outlines the use made of electronic media by local authorities.

# 12

# Patterns of government

One of the more intriguing aspects of the study of local government was that it dealt with a diversity of elected organisations that demonstrated differing tendencies and behaviour. During the 1980s the politics of a radical left wing authority such as Lambeth differed sharply from the neighbouring new-right London Borough of Wandsworth. In the early years of the twenty-first century differences between the policies of local authorities are not as sharp as they were in the 1980s. This is, in part, a reflection of increasing central government control over local authorities driving them to adopt similar policies. In addition, the third way agenda of New Labour has established a compromise between Old Labour and Thatcherism that has been adapted by most local authorities. Local government leadership is also not as sharply defined by a single ruling party dominating every local authority given that the rise of third parties ensures that many local authorities have no party in overall control and are steered by the compromises reached through party coalitions.

### Does party politics matter?

As Table 12.1 demonstrates, most local authorities of Britain have experienced changes in political control during the last 20 years. From a low base the Liberal Democrats have become a significant force within local government and their re-emergence has ensured that many local authorities are hung councils with no single dominant party in control.

Although many local authorities appear to be firmly partisan, there has been considerable debate about whether, at the local level, party politics has any bearing on the policies adopted by local governments. The concept of the 'end of ideology' developed by Daniel Bell (1960) promoted the idea that the stability of mature capitalist systems meant an end to class polarisation between left and right and that the ideological differences between parties were increasingly of little relevance. Political rivalry in these circumstances becomes a contest

Table 12.1 *Party control of local authorities, 1979–2007*

|  | 1979 | 1989 | 1995 | 1998 | 2006 |
|---|---|---|---|---|---|
| Conservative | 262 | 169 | 13 | 28 | 169 |
| Labour | 79 | 163 | 206 | 210 | 75 |
| Liberal or Liberal Democrat | 1 | 12 | 51 | 44 | 33 |
| Other parties | 39 | 12 | 4 | 19 | 2 |
| Independent majority | 57 | 32 | 23 | 19 | 14 |
| No overall control | 77 | 127 | 157 | 148 | 147 |

*Source:* Municipal Yearbook 1979 and 1989; *Local Government Chronicle*, 13 May 1995; Llewellyn 1999; Local Government Chronicle Election Centre, 2006.

between parties claiming to be better managers of a nation's economy and social well being rather than a conflict over ideology. Considerable evidence was marshalled in the 1960s to back up this view. In Britain, electoral studies of the major political parties argued that they were less and less divided in terms of ideology (McKenzie 1963). Surveys of local government policy output at this time did not, however, support this thesis. A study by Noel Boaden of spending by county boroughs in England and Wales showed that 'as predicted, Labour councils were more active in services with a significant impact on the overall role of government. They were bigger spenders on the bigger services' (1971: 112). These findings were supported by Sharpe and Newton, who concluded that 'parties are a much more potent factor in influencing governmental outputs than much of the previous output research has recognized' (1984: 215).

Studies of individual local authorities led by the 1970s to a received wisdom on the characteristics of Conservative and Labour controlled authorities that still has some resonance today. These will be described in the following sections, but the arrival of Thatcherism in the 1980s and her onslaught on many of the traditionally accepted roles, values and freedoms of local government led to serious schisms within local parties of both the left and the right, and established for a decade a radicalism in local government that had not been visible since the 1920s to be followed, especially during the Blair years, by a new consensus on party policy within local government and the eclipse of radical and polarised positions. The following discussion of the characteristics of differing values within local government explains the rise and fall of these movements but it is also essential to emphasise how far the once established assumptions on where political power lay within local government have changed since the 1970s.

## Labour local authorities

The Labour Party gained control of seats in local authorities almost as soon as it was formed in 1900 and by the 1920s Party members controlled a number of city councils. Many of the early Labour Party activists, especially Fabian intellectuals such as Sidney and Beatrice Webb and George Bernard Shaw, encouraged local councillors to secure socialist objectives through the municipalisation of productive and welfare services. Socialist authorities tried to buy out gas, electricity and transport undertakings as well as enthusiastically implement new powers to build houses. Attempts to become involved in the productive and commercial economy were, however, blocked by a Conservative Parliament which refused to sanction the private bills that would enable the development of municipal socialism. Expansion was, however, possible in the provision of welfare and many Labour authorities led the way in the development of council housing.

Following the reconstruction of local government functions by the 1945 Labour Government, much of the innovatory enthusiasm of Labour controlled authorities appears to have run into the sand of the professionalised routines of their Tory rivals. The moderacy of many Labour authorities stemmed in part from a desire to demonstrate to the electorate that the Party was not, as claimed by many Conservatives, a hot headed revolutionary body, but instead a respectable, efficient and prudent Party that was fit to govern. These old-Labour stalwarts tended to support the existing range of services held by local government with its emphasis on education, housing, social services and recreation, and sought the development of these activities as public welfare services which should be exclusively designed and controlled by the local authority. Many were suspicious of alternative methods of delivering these traditional local services as undermining the centrality of their local municipal empires and throwing open public welfare to what they saw as the vested interest of the private sector. Like their traditional Tory counterparts they tended to be deferent to professional advice. Both old-Labour councillors and professional officers had a stake in the *status quo* of incremental expansion of municipal welfare.

The conservatism of many Labour authorities before the arrival of local socialism was also a consequence of their domination by long established leadership cliques of, by the 1970s, ageing councillors. There are a number of studies that attest to a decline in Labour Party membership and activity since the 1940s. Hindess (1971) argued that in Liverpool, under the leadership of the Braddocks, most working class wards dwindled to a tiny membership of stalwarts who had little impact on their community. David Green observed that

> The Labour party in Newcastle . . . was large neither in terms of total membership nor in terms of active membership. The party was kept going only by the energy of a few individuals. The selection of electoral candidates, the most important function of the party, was carried out in such a way that the vast majority of Labour councillors were assured of continued reselection more or less regardless of how well they performed their duties. (1981: 34)

In such circumstances, the mainstream Labour authority was not greatly given to innovation and many leaders of Labour authorities at the time of the rate capping conflict in 1985 refused to support the radical socialist leaders.

In the late 1970s there was, however, growing dissent among younger councillors in some cities against the established Labour oligarchies that controlled city politics. The generation of radical younger councillor coincided with Thatcher's attacks on local autonomy at a time when the national leadership of the Party was so riven with conflict it provided little leadership for Party supporters. The energy with which the radical socialist local authorities attempted to challenge Thatcher, therefore, earned their leaders great respect and support among rank and file Party members. The older oligarchies of Labour politicians were in a number of cities swept aside by younger radical councillors. David Blunkett became leader of Sheffield City Council in 1980 and Ken Livingstone was elected leader of the GLC in 1981. Radical socialism was, however, only partially successful and many cities continued to be dominated by more moderate politicians whilst some Labour groups, as in the City of Manchester, were torn apart by a bitter struggle between new and old styles of leadership.

Local socialism was not a consistent phenomenon and there are marked differences in policy. Radical Labour authorities followed or paralleled each others' example, not so much by always imitating the actions of fellow travelling authorities, but by a preparedness to rethink traditional policies and innovate into new areas. Sheffield City Council and the GLC put much effort into developing their local economies through establishing funding agencies for new co-operative business. Islington, in contrast, concentrated more on the innovation of decentralisation and popular participation in local policy making. South Yorkshire County Council emphasised its strategy for subsidised public transport. A differing concept of socialism took root in Liverpool, whose moribund party machine had been captured by the Militant Tendency which aimed to overthrow the capitalist state through populist revolution to form a classless society (Crick 1986). Militant strategy in Liverpool sought to revive the local economy by large scale public spending on housing regardless of budget restraints. In 1984 they appeared to have gained a considerable victory when, following a threat to set a deficit budget, they gained more funds from the Government. The following year the Government was determined not to give way and, after surcharging errant councillors, the movement went into eclipse. After the rate capping crisis of 1985 radical local authorities of the left were

Many of the strategies adopted by the local socialist councils, although vilified in the tabloid British press as products of a 'loony left', were policies that had long been established in many European countries. For example, many German and Italian cities substantially subsidise public transport to develop highly efficient integrated bus and tram services and many European, let alone United States, cities were active in promoting local economic regeneration before this became a major issue pioneered by local socialist authorities in Britain.

forced to retrench many of their more expensive policies and thus rethink their programmes. Nevertheless, there remains in place an important legacy from this period such as the strategy that local government should be a focus for local economic development and social equality for alienated minority groups.

*New Labour*

Local government was never central to Tony Blair's experience or concerns although the institution could be valuable in implementing policies or even in policy innovation, provided it followed the Government's overall strategy. The first years of the New Labour Governments, nevertheless, led to a dramatic change towards a closer partnership between local and central government than had existed under Thatcher and Major. However, within this idea of partnership, local government was never to be the equal of central government or even the exclusive voice of local interests. As New Labour had accepted much of the new-right concern that governments unreasonably restricted individual initiative, delivery of new services should be shared even at local level with private sector and voluntary agencies or in co-operative organisations with representation from a number of interests. Behind the New Labour Governments' relationship with local government was an overwhelming concern to retain power through a policy based on the Administrations' capacity to deliver on their manifesto promises for improved services, especially in education and health. Blair could not, therefore, afford to allow local agencies to stray too far from the Party's manifesto promises and self-imposed targets. Local government needed, thought Blairites, to be modernised in order to more effectively fulfil his ambitions for improved services.

Policies such as executive cabinet government and elected mayors were, therefore, attractive to New Labour as they seemed to promise more streamlined policy implementation and a more visible charismatic style of leadership. Best Value and later CPA along with the Standards Board were essential to motivate local authorities to improve on the delivery of the Government's promises and show that targets had been reached. Partnerships ensured local government was not the only instrument for delivering local services and that the local authority could be by-passed if it failed to deliver. It was hoped that new executive structures and new systems for voting would re-engage public opinion with local government and enhance citizens' participation. The strategy is all very well as far as it goes, but it submerged any idea of local authorities having substantive discretion to follow policies preferred by their local electors as opposed to those established at the centre.

New Labour rejected both the independent innovatory values of local socialism and the conservative oligarchs who characterised the old pre-war Labour Party. An attempt by a group of left wing Labour councillors in Walsall to create a highly decentralised structure for local government in the District resulted in its leader, David Church, following a visit by Party deputy leader John Prescott, being thrown out of the Labour Party (Parker 2003). The consequence has been over the decade of Blair's Governments the development of generally colourless and rather subservient local governments and, with the exception of Ken Livingstone, who was never Blair's choice as mayor of London, the disappearance of local government leaders as nationally known individuals. The typical New Labour councillor is, as suggested in earlier chapters, a rather ineffective toiler in scrutiny committees and, if a cabinet member, a full time head of a service closely working with his or her senior service directors on means to secure the targets required by the Audit Commission. It is perhaps only the Labour leadership that might be surprised that electoral turnout has continued to decline and that few citizens have an ambition to become local councillors.

## Conservative local authorities

The Conservative Party began life as the Tory Party, which emerged in the seventeenth century in support of the Monarchy and the Anglican Church. It was a Party that predominantly represented the interests of the smaller landowners, the village squires, who, although relatively well heeled, did not have the resources to modernise their farms as did the wealthier, generally Whig, aristocratic landowners. Many feared the Whigs' potential to buy up the smaller estates. The Tory, therefore, opposed rapid social and technological change and believed that society should evolve, if at all, through slow incremental steps. The squire should remain, with the parson, the focus of village life and receive respect and deference from the lower status tenant farmers and labourers. However, the squire also had duties towards his inferiors and, at least in theory, protected the lower classes in his domain from the disasters of infirmity and economic misfortune.

The Tory tradition of the nineteenth century valued community government. The parish represented an organic unit of order in which the squire and parson were dominant and the lower orders provided the minor offices according to their station in life. The more dominant landowners were JPs who met to co-ordinate their work and supervise parishes in the quarter sessions of the county court. These local worthies frequently socialised together in house parties and the hunting field and formed the elite county set. This Tory tradition still falteringly survives in mainstream Conservative local government, especially in the rural counties and districts. Local leaders who accept this strand of thought govern their communities with a light, paternalistic hand. The Tory councillor does not seek to develop radically new policies within his or her authority and is usually willing to defer to accepted professional practice provided this does not lead to policies that are particularly radical or expensive. Many shire counties which are usually Conservative controlled consequently have a three month cycle of meetings which leaves much detail in the hands of officers and is not geared to promoting radical restructuring of policies. The Tory council does not choose to spend large sums of money or substantially raise taxes since it is opposed to policies that would redistribute resources to the extent that the privileges of the affluent are levelled down to the benefit of the poor. It is not, however, opposed to the principle of paternalistic welfare and accepts that it is important to provide educational opportunities and social services to all deserving families. The local authority also has an important duty to maintain law and order and funding of this sector is seen as an important function.

### *The new right*

During the nineteenth century the progress of industrialisation might have assigned the Tory Party to obscurity and then oblivion if its leaders, such as Peel and Disraeli, had not realised that to survive the Party needed to accommodate leaders of industry and commerce. By the early twentieth century the Party had gained the adherence of industrialists who had earlier supported the Liberal values of *laissez faire*, arguing that government should interfere as little as possible with commerce. This strand of thought made little progress until the 1970s, when the Party had run out of ideas that caught the electorate's imagination. The term 'new-right' has been used to describe the followers of this classical Liberal thought. In reality it would be better to describe the theory as neo-liberal since this approach revives ideas, developed in the eighteenth century, favouring individual competition as a means of progress. These beliefs were reasserted in the context of twentieth century capitalism by Nobel prize winning economists F.A. Hayek and Milton Friedman, who argued that the state had grown out of control and interfered with so much of the lives of its citizens that there was little individual freedom and scope for personal initiative and progress. The welfare services produced by the state diminished the potential for innovation through high taxation and enslaved the poor in an inescapable cycle of servitude as they were given no incentive to develop their lives through productive work. The state had become parasitic on individual entrepreneurship and thus a barrier to progress.

In Chapters 5 and 6 it was shown how these values helped prompt the Thatcher Governments to reduce the powers and spending of local government as part of the over-extensive apparatus of the state. These attacks led to protests not only from Labour authorities but, in more veiled form, from the many Tory led shire counties and districts that found these ideas inimical to their own ideology. Whilst interested in thrift, the Tory councillor also values, as a duty, the welfare role of his or her local authority. Mrs Thatcher found that her radical new-right values had far less appeal to the older Conservative of the shire counties who entered local politics partly as a duty required for membership of the 'county set' and a charitable desire to support good work in the community. There were, therefore, only a handful of major Conservative authorities that wholeheartedly accepted a new-right direction. The flagships for new-right values were the London Boroughs of Westminster and Wandsworth, which began pursuing elements of the theory when Conservatives won control from the Labour Party in 1978. Against the tide of national electoral opinion, they have held on to the Boroughs in successive elections. A scattering of smaller district councils, such as Southend, also adopted new-right values for a brief period in the late 1980s and, among county councils, Kent has flirted with this ideology.

The strategy adopted by these local authorities has been to reduce their expenditure through ensuring that all their services are either abandoned in favour of private sector provision or, if they must be provided by the public sector, opened to competition with the private sector. Thus, in Wandsworth, its former leader, Paul Beresford (1987: 6) described his strategy as

1) The efficient management of services: to cut waste; to ensure high quality and to test all Council services, where possible, against the private sector and to contract out, where appropriate.

2) A vigorous sales policy involving: a) the sale of land and buildings where such action proves economically efficient; and b) the sale of houses to families on low incomes, thus breaking up enormous housing estates and providing a stimulus to the maintenance of such housing.

3) Major capital investment, using capital receipts from sales and capital allocations to rebuild the local commercial and industrial infra-structure.

This policy led to a major reduction in expenditure by the authority and, with the help of favourable government manipulation of grant, for a time the lowest local taxes in London. It also resulted in a major reduction in the number of employees and a substantive decrease in the number of council houses and land held by the Borough.

It can be questioned whether these policies are pursued in line with new-right theory or whether, as Beresford argues, they are the product of 'ordinary common sense' (1987: 5). There is, in at least some supposed new-right authorities, a strong business ethos that does not so much denigrate welfare provision but the manner in which it has been provided by traditional local authorities. Eric Pickles, who led the radical new-right of Bradford City Council in the late 1980s, maintained that he has little interest in new Conservative philosophy and received little help from the Conservative central office as to how to manage his authority. His principal attack was against an overlarge inefficient bureaucracy and he saw his role as that of a management expert seeking to oust waste and inefficiency from a stagnant private business in order to improve the welfare of the city (Smitham 1991).

There is insufficient research on the ideas of the new-right authorities to make any definitive statement on their values and, indeed, it may be shown that, as in the case of local socialist authorities, there are many different variants within this category. The evidence that does exist suggests that whilst these authorities are not particularly ideological in outlook, they are led by ambitious and enthusiastic political activists who do not accept the traditional Tory values of gradual change and deference to authority and expertise. It may be suggested that the proponents of new-right values at the local level, as in central government, represent a relatively new type of Conservative attracted to the Party not as the upholder of tradition and privilege but as the best means of forwarding individual progress through ruthless business efficiency rather than collective welfare. These values were not lost on the young Tony Blair, who continued many of the values of the 'new-right' within the post-1997 Labour Governments.

The success of the Blair Government and failure of the Conservatives in opposition to revive public enthusiasm for new-right policies unalloyed with an element of social concern has led the Party under Cameron to seek to out-Blair Blair's success rather than soldier along a far right path. Cameron informed the LAG's annual conference in July 2007 that 'This is a ridiculously over-centralised country and I stand before you a convinced localist.' Whether policies seriously reflect this view is debatable. They currently comprise abolishing elected regional assemblies, which are QUANGOs carrying relatively little policy weight, removing the Standards Boards and allowing local authorities more choice over spending by removing ring fenced grants. The Party has also nailed its colours to a New Labour modernist agenda by persuading Michael Heseltine out of political retirement in order to press for an idea he unsuccessfully proposed when Secretary of State for the Environment in the Major Governments of extending the strategy of directly elected mayors. As it currently stands the Cameron leadership appears to have rejected the new-right policy of undermining local government in favour of minimal government but does little to suggest a deep interest in the institution *per se* or a strategy that is radically different from the Blair and Brown Administrations.

### The Liberal Democrats

By the 1950s the Liberal Party had almost disappeared from local politics as they had from the national Parliament. They were once a dominant force in local politics, particularly in the cities, but were upstaged by the Labour Party, and clung to enclaves of support in the West of England, Wales and some areas of Scotland. The revival of Liberal electoral fortunes, whilst a reflection of dissatisfaction with both of the major parties, was also promoted by local Liberal parties developing community based campaigning to improve local services rather than emphasise their national policies. Liberal leaders began to emphasise the value of gaining support at the local level through attention to community politics. Party leader Joe Grimond urged his rank and file in 1960 that

> The Liberal Party should be the party to which the people look to reforms which affect their daily lives . . . let us get things done and let us start in local government. (Bulpitt 1967: 106)

This prescription was enthusiastically endorsed in Birmingham by local activists. Wallace Lawler became a Birmingham councillor and then the Liberal MP for Ladywood in a surprise by-election victory in 1969, as a consequence of cultivating widespread cross party support for his efforts in helping local residents with their individual local problems (Cyr 1977: 260). Lawler's example was followed by a generation of later Liberals and culminated in the Party gaining control of a number of local authorities. The most dramatic success for Liberal community politics has been in Liverpool, where it became the largest single Party in 1973 after holding just one seat five years earlier in a city which, even in the nineteenth century, did not have a strong Liberal tradition. The Liverpool success was engineered by a local businessman, Trevor Jones, who perfected the techniques of local campaigning. Stress is placed on ensuring that local residents are in frequent contact with Liberal activists who are prepared to act as a channel for their complaints. Liberal Democrat community politics is concerned with getting done many simple things that are important in people's lives, such as securing a new dustbin, ensuring council house repairs are properly carried out and leading local campaigns for safer roads. These strategies were publicised by house to house canvassing backed up by frequent community newsletters.

Nationally the Liberal Democrats have well entrenched constitutional demands particularly concerning electoral change to facilitate proportional representation at local level. They are also, traditionally, more inclined to support devolution of power to the regions. The success of community politics has also ensured the Party encourages policies that devolve decision making from the remote town hall to local communities. Liberal Democrat authorities such as Tower Hamlets, South Somerset District Council and Rochdale Metropolitan District Council pioneered structures for decentralised services.

Whilst it is clearly evident that Liberal Democrat politicians have developed new campaigning styles in local politics, it is much less easy to discern the extent to which they run their local authorities differently from the other parties. There is little evidence to suggest that they spend more or less than their rivals. Where the Liberal Democrats have taken over from Labour councils as in Liverpool or Sheffield, it appears that the Party is much more inclined to prune budgets, but they are, in general, more adventurous on spending than Conservatives. In general, the Party pursues different policies in different areas and is just as prepared to collaborate with Labour as Conservative authorities in hung councils (Leach and Stewart 1992). As a Party often supported by disaffected Labour voters in poorer areas and disenchanted Conservatives in wealthier areas, its supporters do not give the Party the basis for any homogeneity in its policies from one area to another.

**Independents and others**

At the beginning of the twentieth century the majority of local authorities, especially those covering rural areas, were non-partisan in the sense that councillors did not stand under party labels but as unaffiliated individuals. The fully independent councillor thus voted on issues without reference to any political leader. In practice, however, independent councillors are often supporters of a political party, particularly the Conservatives (Grant 1977: 3), but they do not believe that, at a local level, their views should be marshalled into a particular direction by a party machine. There has been since 1945 an insidious erosion of the capacity of councillors to stand as independents. This is due to many factors, such as the growth of the more organised Labour Party at the beginning of the century which required non-socialists to organise in opposition to its success; the disappearance of smaller local authorities, where individuals could be known by many in the community; and the growth of national media focus on party politics. Only a few independent authorities therefore remain and, as Table 12.1 indicates, their number is declining.

Whilst there are but a few obviously independent local authorities, there probably remain others that tend in practice to be non-partisan. Bulpitt (1967) found that in Lancashire and Cheshire local elections were often fought on party lines in smaller authorities but once councillors were elected the party groups did not co-ordinate the policies of their members or expect them to vote at all times with their party colleagues. Birch (1959) relates how a debate on finance in Glossop, a largely non-partisan council, produced divisions based as much on length of residence in the area as party stereotypes on spending preferences. The restructuring of local government in 1974 to create much larger local authorities brought to an end much of this local non-partisanship except within parish and town councils.

In addition to the big three parties of Labour, Conservative and Liberal Democrats, there has also been an ebb and flow of smaller party groups active within the local political arena. Among these the regionalist parties, the Scottish National Party (SNP) and Plaid Cymru have significant following in their Provinces. After the Scottish elections of 2007 the SNP was, with other parties, in control of 12 authorities as well as the Scottish Assembly. Like the Liberal Democrats the exact policies of SNP councillors can vary considerably from one authority to another or even within authorities. In Wales Plaid Cymru has also had local successes and in 2008 had 205 council seats. In contrast to the SNP, the party more uniformly tends to position itself to the left of New Labour.

In England minor parties have historically at times made a substantial impact in local politics. In the 1930s a rate payers' movement seeking lower local taxes gained substantive support but eventually became largely absorbed by Conservative interests. However, remnants of this movement remain in

Table 12.2 *Types of hung council*

|  | Number |
| --- | --- |
| Formal coalition | 7 |
| Power sharing | 8 |
| Minority administration | 53 |
| No administration | 8 |
| Unidentifiable | 4 |
| Total | 80 |

*Source:* Leach and Stewart (1992: 13).

some authorities such as in Barnsley, where they have been the strongest opposition to the dominant Labour Party. Gaining more publicity than council seats, the British National Party has found some favour in largely poorer white working class areas where there are fears of rivalry for jobs with non-white communities. The most promising new Party on the block is perhaps the Green Party, which is beginning to secure sufficient support to gain executive cabinet posts and influence in some hung councils.

## Hung councils

Analysis of party values in local politics has been muddied by the increase in local authorities where no one party has had overall control. In such circumstances there have been a number of strategies for dividing power. Leach and Stewart (1992) classified these councils in terms of working relationships between parties. In the majority of hung councils one party, usually the largest in terms of seats, is permitted to take the lead role and select the committee chairs. The party will, however, only secure enactment of its policies if it makes concessions to the opposing parties. Less frequently in some authorities two or more parties form an effective working coalition in which they agree to divide the committee chairmanships between them and form agreements on policy. A third category involves parties agreeing to distribute executive posts between themselves but making no further permanent agreements on policy. In only a few hung councils were parties unable to reach an agreement. In such a situation committee chairs may be elected for each meeting and policy emerges, if at all, by a long and painful process of inter-party wrangling. There are also a few authorities where party discipline is low and hence the fact that no party predominated made little difference to the cross party bargaining that had always characterised these councils, (Leach and Stewart 1985). Leach and Stewart classified hung councils in 1992 as shown in Table 12.2. After nearly two decades of frequently hung councils, as can be seen from Table 12.3 the pattern of coalitions under the cabinet system appears to be more orientated towards coalition rather than minority control.

Table 12.3 *Party rule in English hung councils with cabinet government, 2006*

| | |
|---|---:|
| One party taking all cabinet seats | 34 |
| Two parties sharing cabinet seats | 40 |
| Three or more parties sharing cabinet seats | 26 |
| Total | 100 |

*Source:* Municipal Year Book, 2006.

It is difficult to generalise about the party composition of the alliances that underlie hung councils in which a minority administration is able to govern as there are frequent changes in relationships given the volatility of party fortunes on local authorities. As might be expected, however, the most infrequent alliance is between Conservative and Labour Parties, with only four instances in 2006 of such a combination sharing power in a two party coalition and 14 in three or more party coalitions. However, in a few cabinets Conservatives in particular have brought in the leaders of the minority parties in posts usually without a portfolio so that they may co-operate with the opposition on certain issues but can be over-ruled if they have strong differences with the majority.

> Managing local authorities in which no party has an overall majority is the expected rather than the exceptional pattern in many European cities. In Italy the stagnation created by the competition between many opposing parties led to the creation of a system for directly elected mayors which has gained considerable popularity. The mayor of Rome, despite having no strong party identification, has been suggested as a future prime minister of Italy.

Regardless of the combination of alliances it is generally the case that hung councils develop policy through behind the scenes bargaining between parties that have developed some form of informal understanding between them. The result is the politics of compromise and accommodation. It is also a situation in which the ideas of senior officers may often be regarded as an important means of resolving differences. However, many chief executives prefer not to work with the uncertainty of a coalition arrangement which will also place difficulties in the way of any major proposals put forward by chief officers as much as for a councillor.

### An end of ideology?

A review of policy styles and orientation that stems from differing party ideologies must be treated with some caution. The idealised models of behaviour suggested under each category are not meant to precisely fit all local authorities. There are numerous variations on the basic themes. It can, however, be concluded that there are probably far more substantive areas of agreement between political parties in local government than substantive differences. Even in the 1980s the majority of local authorities were neither enthusiasts of the new-right or the radical left but had similar 'end of ideology' values concerning the role of local government as an element of a mixed economy welfare state.

At the beginning of the twenty-first century there appears to be far less that differentiates local authorities than 20 years earlier. There are no authorities that appear now to be radically socialist pursuing policies centrally geared to achieving greater social equality. There similarly remain few authorities wedded to a new-right philosophy although both Westminster and Wandsworth have continued under right wing Conservative domination despite the demise in the national fortunes of their Party. Effectively, with the Blair and Brown Governments pressing local authorities to adopt private sector contractors where this is found to be more efficient and with no effective relaxation on tight spending curbs on local government, it has been far more difficult for any local authority to follow the local socialist path of high local taxation to fund extensive subsidies to housing and transport budgets so as to benefit the poorer groups in the community. Thatcher ensured that socialist values could not be pursued by local government and the Blair Government has done nothing that effectively removes this constraint. The policies of the new-right are still more open for local authorities although Best Value may constrain some of the wildest shores of outsourcing key services should any local authority wish to pursue the path to the fully enabling but not implementing authority. However, sufficient remains of new-right values to ensure that all local authorities have been pushed to the right under Thatcher and Major and have been kept in such a position by Blair and Brown.

### Further reading

Community studies will clearly provide a profile of individual local authorities and, therefore, are a valuable background to this section. These studies have been summarised in Chapter 8. The importance of party politics in local government is broached by Bulpitt (1967) and considered empirically by Boaden (1971) and Sharpe and Newton (1984). Hung councils are analysed by Leach and Stewart (1992).

There are few general studies of the Conservative Party in local government although recent work by Holliday (2000) provides a useful summary of the present situation, but there are valuable insights into the Disraelian tradition in community studies such as Lee (1963) and Dearlove (1973). Further reading on the new-right was outlined in Chapter 3.

Local socialism received considerable attention when the movement was at its height, with Boddy and Fudge (1984), Gyford (1985) and Lansley, Goss and Wolmar (1989) being particularly valuable and, although not always as incisive as it could be, Blunkett and Jackson (1987) is also important. There is considerable writing focused on the attitudes of New Labour and Hall and Leach (2000) provides a valuable introduction to the values of the Party at the grassroots. Brooks (2000), Stoker and Wilson (2004) and Stoker (2004) are examples of studies considering the evolution of thinking on local government in the New Labour years.

The older traditions of the Labour Party are well illustrated by Donoghue and Jones (1973) in their biography of Herbert Morrison. However, some idea of the indifference of other Labour leaders to local government can be gleaned from works such as Williams on Gaitskell (1979), Pimlott on Dalton (1985) and Crosland on Crosland (1982), although I would not advise reading the whole of these biographies solely to discover the paucity of enthusiasm they demonstrate towards the subject of this book.

Details on local election results for Britain are summarised by the Local Government Chronicle Elections Centre at the University of Plymouth that can be accessed through the research centres listed on the web site of Plymouth University (www.plymouth.ac.uk). The founders of the Centre, Colin Rallings and Michael Thrasher, also edit a series of handbooks on local election results which are regularly updated. Davies and Morley are editing a series of studies on electoral results in county boroughs in England and Wales between 1919 and 1938, publishing so far three volumes.

# 13

# The future in a comparative context

Reforms to the structure of local government put forward by the Blair Government were aimed at reviving interest in local authorities. As illustrated in Table 13.1 there seems relatively little enthusiasm for local politics in terms of voting turnout and, as discussed in earlier chapters, the numbers of potential candidates seeking to become councillors. It is argued in this chapter that the Government and its advisors have failed to identify the reason for such an apparent lack of interest in local politics and have incorrectly seen the solution in terms of strong leadership, greater efficiency and partnership with other agencies rather than the issue of centralisation and lack of power at community level. Throughout this study a running commentary comparing features of the British system of local government with those of other major liberal democracies should have demonstrated that the system in Britain is in many ways an unusual local government structure. Many of the differences between British practice and that of continental Europe and the USA may explain an issue that appears to be baffling to the Blair and Brown Governments.

## How the British system differs from other systems

Local government most obviously and clearly differs from the systems in the larger countries of the European Union and the United States in respect to the size and number of tiers of units of governance. As illustrated in Chapter 2, Britain has far fewer local authorities than other liberal democracies and hence units represent far larger numbers of citizens. The implications of the 2007 Local Government Act are to move to a single tier structure of elected executive local government without much encouragement to revive local powers within the parish. In addition, unlike the situation in Britain, other systems have a generally well developed and often significantly powerful regional tier of government. The consequence of this structure is that British local authorities are, in comparison with other systems, large structures representing not so much localities but sub-regional

Table 13.1 *Voting turnout in local elections in England (%)*

|  | 2002 | 2003 | 2004 | 2005 | 2006 | 2007 |
|---|---|---|---|---|---|---|
| London | 32 | – | – | – | 38 | – |
| Metropolitan districts | 32 | 33 | 41 | – | 35 | 35 |
| Counties | – | – | – | 64 | – | – |
| English districts | 35 | 34 | 41 | – | – | 39(37) |
| English unitaries | 30 | 35 | 37 | 61 | 34 | 33(38) |
| All authorities | 33 | 35 | 41 | 63 | 37 | 37 |

*Note:* Figures in brackets are for local authorities with are third of seats elected in 2007. The 2005 results are higher than for most years as the local elections were held at the same time as the General Election.
*Source:* Local Government Chronicle Elections Centre, University of Plymouth. (www.plymouth.ac.uk/pages/view.asp?page=16191)

areas. There is little connection for most residents of rural areas between the local authority and the community in which they live. An inhabitant of a town that before 1974 may have been governed by an urban district or borough council for some purposes is now administered by larger district or unitary units that cover several similar but relatively distant communities. Engineers of the British system of local government have sought to ensure each unit is of roughly similar population size whereas in most other countries the arrangement takes on board the obvious fact that communities do not come in uniformly sized packages.

> Most Western European local governments and city government in the United States emerged through an organic growth of settlement patterns and the sense of community that grew around these areas has always been respected by the state. As a consequence there is little uniformity as to the size of communes in France or cities in the United States. Some may be tiny villages whilst others may encompass populations of many thousands.

## Centralisation

The second striking difference between British and United States or European local government systems is the extent of centralisation. It is, of course, much more problematic to measure levels of centralisation across countries than to observe the size in terms of population of each tier of local government. Nevertheless, there is substantial evidence to suggest that in Britain, local government is far more subject to central control than in the United States. Unlike most cities in the United States, British unitary authorities cannot determine how much they can spend or raise in property tax, they have less capacity to operate entrepreneurial businesses, they have little control over the operational activities of police or education, and have no safeguards to ensure that their boundaries cannot be subject to change if required by central government.

It has long been argued that in comparison with France, British local authorities exerted considerable independence as they were not subject to control by a centrally appointed official, the prefect, who had powers to disallow the local budget proposals and suspend a local authority if it was thought to be acting illegally. However, even before reforms to the prefectoral system in the early 1980s, the structure of French local government was much less centralised than outwardly it appeared. Local politics in many cities is governed by powerful politicians who may not only be the local mayor but also represent their community in the National Assembly. They can then use their leverage at the centre to control the local prefect and bargain with fellow local notables for their share of goods and services (Ashford 1982). Local government in Britain, as shown in Chapter 5, has in contrast few MPs who also serve as active local councillors.

In Britain there is little sense of territorial patron–clientelism within the Nation. Individuals do not look towards either local politicians or their national representatives to act on behalf of their community and secure gains for their locality through being able to pressurise central government. This is not to argue that some MPs do not work successfully on occasion to secure gains for their constituency but rarely if at all do electors choose between candidates let alone which party they support in a general election with reference to their local roots and capacity to influence central government on behalf of the locality. Party affiliation and national politics are all consuming in the media's interpretation of politics and by extension this is also applied to the prevailing political culture. Britain, unlike many other liberal democracies, lacks a sense of subsidiarity. This idea is enshrined in the values of the European Union and, using rather a different source in the United States in the writings of De Tocqueville, maintains that personal freedom is maximised if power is devolved to the smallest units that are capable of effectively dealing with an issue.

### The frequency of structural change

Public indifference to local government as suggested by electoral turnout has ensured that central government can change the constitution of the system with considerable regularity. Major structural reforms to the tiers and boundaries of local government have taken place since 1974 once every ten years and are currently again on the table following the 2007 Local Government Act. The restructuring of several counties to unitary authorities in 2007 created, moreover, almost no comment in the national media. In addition, there has been major restructuring of the decision making systems of local authorities, their powers in relation to many services and their funding regime. The only occasion where popular feeling has reversed a policy relating to local government that was deeply embedded in a Government's strategy was the poll tax but here the issue was not so much defence of local financial autonomy but concern over an unprogressive system of taxation.

In contrast to other European countries the status and prestige of local government have in recent decades been seriously questioned. Local government in Britain has always had its critics but from the 1980s was subjected to a vociferous largely new-right inspired onslaught on its democratic integrity. These views gained considerable currency in the Governments of Thatcher and Major. It was argued that lack of exposure to competition and the electoral system that created many one party dominated councils established a closed club of councillors and senior officers who could isolate themselves from public opinion. The system was, they argued, consequently overstaffed and inefficient and harboured widespread corruption (Henney 1984; Walker 1983). However, surveys of popular attitudes to local government even in the 1980s (Widdicombe 1986: 40) did not display general popular disaffection with the service citizens received from their local authority and the Best Value surveys conducted by the Audit Commission affirm that currently there is still widespread satisfaction with local services. There is, nevertheless, little enthusiasm for the system itself and the ideals of local democracy as a whole but more an indifference to what Harold Laski (1934: 412), quoting Virgil, termed 'the genius of place'.

---

A feature of the British system of local government that is not replicated in Europe is the frequency of change and reform. France established regions in the 1960s and significantly changed the roles of prefect and mayor in the early 1980s and on an incremental basis merged some communes. In the United States it is the States that change the structures and powers of local government but in most cases, and especially boundary change, major restructuring would only be approved by a referendum and rarely are these successful. Thus a 20 year old textbook on France or the United States local government largely describes the system as it is today whereas any British textbook on local government requires a substantively new edition at least every 10 years.

---

## New Labour's reforms: can they work?

The 1998 White Paper *Local Government: In Touch with the People* indicates through its title that a major element of its proposals concerns greater citizen identification and participation in local governance. The White Paper (para. 2.12) sets out a strategy to give

- A bigger say to local people by
  - creating new political structures for councils;
  - improving local democracy;
  - strengthening local financial accountability;
  - establishing a new ethical framework.

- A better deal for local people by
  - improving local services through Best Value;
  - councils promoting the well being of communities;
  - simplifying capital finance;
  - introducing some local discretion in business rates.

As described in the preceding chapters, these aims have been promoted through the 1999 and 2000 Local Government Acts but in practice, as with most legislation, the outcome did not fully mirror the intentions. The 2006 White Paper *Strong and Prosperous Communities* and the resultant 2007 Local Government Act attempt to restructure policy towards local governance in Britain in the light of experience. The policy now places less emphasis on voting turnout but retains an enthusiasm for strong leadership, greater efficiency in service delivery and partnership with other public, voluntary and private agencies. In addition the reforms aim to again restructure the system to gradually bring in even larger unitary authorities throughout England. Whether the revised direction will bring about a resurgence of public enthusiasm for local government is questionable.

Many ministers and probably most civil servants supported by some academics appear to believe that concentrating decision making in the hands of a visible mayor or leader, rather than a wider group of councillors who make decisions in the closed room of party caucuses, may provide local citizens with a figure who is visible and accountable to them. However, the impact of a move towards a smaller executive, in itself, does not suggest a move towards spreading power more widely within the community but rather concentrating power in the hands of a few individuals. Political visibility does not on its own necessarily equate with greater democracy. A single individual governing a large community is likely to be far less accessible than members of a larger collective group of decision makers. Elected mayors will have time to relate personally to only the most influential and powerful members of the public and are unlikely to deal with most ordinary citizens on a day to day basis. Unlike the mayor of a small French commune, who is likely to know and meet frequently the citizens of his or her community, the mayor of a big city, whether in France, the USA or Britain, will be, like British national government leaders, a remote figure seen by the population through the lens of media reporting rather than personal contact and experience. A consequence of such a system might initially be to create greater interest in local politics, especially in cities where the media find much in the personality or earlier career of the mayor to interest readers. Interest will not however be translatable into power and influence for the individual any more than readers of *Hello* magazine can influence the mind of the fashionably glamorous.

Whilst the elected mayor may be high profile but remote from the individual, the ordinary backbench councillor who is supposed under the new system to be able to devote more time to his or her constituents is likely to be an increasingly marginalised and insignificant figure. The cabinet system translated to local level has produced even more marginalised councillors. Under the old system a backbench councillor could busy themselves on what may appear to be an unglamorous sub-committee such as markets or allotments and through such work provide a fulfilling role that generated real improvements for their community. Instead all councillors are expected to bring general issues from their constituents to the attention of the great and the good in the form of the cabinet or the mayor who may wholly ignore their complaints and concerns. It seems unlikely that the strategies open to the new style backbench councillors will be adequate to redress the indifference of council executives to their work on behalf of their constituents.

Whilst the Blair Government has focused power and management of local government in cabinet governments or mayors and appointed managers, it has done little to encourage local initiatives to secure closer contact with the electorate through devolving power to area committees or to parish councils. Citizens may be more likely to be politically involved if they are given the resources to make observable changes, albeit small, to the communities in which they live and work. The Government has not prevented schemes for decentralisation but has also not seen such a move as central to its aim of reinforcing local democracy. This seems particularly strange given the preceding argument that Britain, with such large units of local governance, is more in need of decentralised government than almost any other European state or the United States.

### Controlling the local authority

The level of democracy within a local democracy is not solely dependent on the democratic framework of the structures and internal decision making machinery but also on the extent that those who control the local authority have freedom to govern through being given a high level of resources and political discretion by central government. The 2000 Local Government Act has granted local authority leaders at least some measure of discretion through clauses that define the broad purpose of a local authority to be to develop the economic, social and environmental well being of its community. Such a step moves local government in Britain more towards a framework that is less restrained by the principle of *ultra vires*. However, only a few of the barriers to develop potential new powers have been set aside. The Government, as indicated in Chapter 4, has not substantially changed many of the crucial limitations on local spending imposed by the Conservative Party in the 1984 Local Government Finance Act. Rate capping, although less visible, still remains a weapon in the Government's armoury. Determination of the extent of capital spending, although simplified, stays in the hands of central government. The Blair Government also increased its capacity to intervene in service delivery by local governments through the Best Value framework. Whilst local authorities do not now have to submit to the crude demand in CCT that they accept the lowest bid for the provision of particular services, they are bound by central inspection to provide services of a standard that is laid down not by local views and values but by the centre. There has also been no move to relocate the substantive powers to build and manage public housing away from the housing associations back to democratically elected local authorities nor to restore some of the controls local authorities held over education prior to the 1988 Education Reform Act. The increase in regulation of local government activities by the centre and the continued central imposition of financial restraints do nothing to suggest that the New Labour Governments trust local democracy and local government to be able to govern without central surveillance.

### The growing corporatism

One of the most significant and yet largely unnoticed changes to the system of local governance in Britain, which is perhaps the most radical transformation initiated by the New Labour Governments, is in the insidious incorporation of local authorities into the decision making machinery of central government. During the Thatcher and Major Governments the relationship between central and local government was one of deep hostility and suspicion. Over the 10 years of New Labour Governments, without any major fanfare of policy announcements, there has been a revolution in the relationship between central and local government. As discussed in Chapter 5 the door to senior positions in the civil service has been opened to senior local government officers. Chief executives from a local government background are increasingly chairing or represented in government enquiries or appointed to executive positions in major regulatory agencies.

Following the creation in 1997 of a single Local Government Association for England and Wales, local authorities themselves relate to central government with a more coherent voice and with the development following the 2007 Local Government Act there will be fewer major authorities with chief officers and leaders who can have individually and collectively a far stronger voice within Whitehall. The consequences of these changes may be that policy makers in Whitehall and the local authorities have far more of a common culture and outlook and will be prepared to work together to involve local authorities within the framework of partnership with other major agencies and private sector companies to steer local policy.

This may at first sight appear to be a much needed development that is to be welcomed as signalling an end to the conflicts that almost destroyed the autonomy of local government during the Thatcher years. However, such close co-operation through central government may have a rather different corrosive effect on local government by undermining the capacity for citizens in different communities or regions of Britain to have an individual and distinctive voice and the capacity to be different from one another. The move towards a local government structure composed of unitary authorities is likely to promote a system not dissimilar to the operation of police forces in Britain. The relatively small number of local authority chief executives will be positioned ever closer to the views and values of central government and present an amorphous outlook which will be developed predominantly by collaboration between a central and unitary authority professional network. Such uniformity could be partly countered by the creation of a lower stratum of community governments based on parish and town councils but community, as has been discussed earlier, has not been seriously encouraged by central government. Parish and town councils under the 2007 Act will be able to undertake more initiatives but only with, in many instances, the support and funding of the unitary or county authorities in which they rest.

This growing ethos of corporatism is also likely to flourish in a framework in which the political parties are closely aligned in policies and seek to gain power by appealing to the middle of the road majority within the electorate. During the 1970s and 1980s polarisation of politicians and a significant section of the electorate between right and left ensured that Labour controlled authorities were likely to be unwilling to co-operate with government politicians or compliant civil servants. The move towards acceptance of many aspects of Thatcher's policies concerning marketisation and competition and a reciprocal move towards concern for social exclusion on the part of Cameron's Conservatives have produced substantial consensus between the two largest parties on the role of local government in the first decades of the twenty-first century. In conformity with New Labour's view of partnership between public and private sectors this tendency may be leading to a relatively small number of unitary local governments operating under much the same framework as the many *ad-hoc* regulatory agencies that at arm's length seek to steer the economy and welfare provision within a predominantly market economy to have some regard for fairness and exclusion of the poor.

### What is needed to secure local democracy?

After seven years of the 2000 Local Government Act there is no electoral evidence that suggests it has succeeded in increasing the profile of local government. If local government were to be brought closer to the people in Britain, it might seem more appropriate than creating elected mayors to encourage far greater decentralisation of decision making to bring the opportunity of making decisions at the community level of village, town or district of a large city. This could be secured by legislation that requires each local authority to develop a strategy for decentralisation of policy making to neighbourhood committees or to parish councils and to establish a system of direct participation of citizens in such local decisions as opposed to discerning public opinion through questionnaires and focus groups.

At the opposite end of the spectrum of sub-national government, democracy would also be enhanced if a system of elected regional governments were created in England which would have powers to develop strategies concerning regional economic growth and also to provide a focus that secures public accountability for a wide range of regional services, such as the NHS, which are currently governed at the regional level by *ad-hoc* unelected agencies.

Serious democratisation, whether to the smallest communities or at a regional level, must also take subsidiarity seriously by ensuring that effective powers and resources to implement policy are passed to the appropriate level of government. A system in which financial resources given to localities are controlled effectively by the centre, and in which most authorities provide services to a standard approved by the government or subject to appeal to the centre from dissenting interests, is scarcely a structure facilitating genuine local democracy but rather a system of local management of centrally determined strategies.

Effective local democracy must also entail that accountability of the local politicians elected to make decisions for a community, county or region should be, not to the national government, but to the local electorate. The procedures that have been particularly developed by the Blair Government that demand, through Best Value, minimum standards of service provision or the adherence of councillors and local government officers to appropriate ethical codes demonstrate a distrust by the centre of a basic premise of democracy, that the voters are the most appropriate determinants of what an area should require by way of services and the standards to be expected from its representatives. If local government, as opposed to local management, means anything it is that communities differ in their needs and demands and will, therefore, choose to have different types and levels of service delivery, different styles of government and different codes of conduct.

It would, of course, be wrong to move too far in arguing for local autonomy and no one should expect local governments to be independent of state controls. Whilst differences in service standards or even ethical conduct may be acceptable and even expected at local level, there are clearly standards of morality that must be expected to be applied universally throughout a nation and certain services that must be made available to everyone in society regardless of class, race, sexuality or able-ness. Nevertheless, within such a framework most European states and the States of North America generally appear to strike a far better balance between local and central power than has developed over the centuries in Britain.

## Further reading

Reflections on the future of local government in Britain can be found from a number of perspectives. A robust defence of the system has been made by John

Stewart over a number of decades in, for example, *The Nature of British Local Government* (2000) and *Modernising British Local Government* (2003). George Jones and John Stewart write a frequent column in the *Local Government Chronicle* with trenchant comments on details of reform proposals. Studies of the development of local government up to the present day, such as Atkinson and Wilks-Heeg (2000), Stoker (2004), Leach (2006) and Chandler (2007), consider how the future may evolve.

# Appendix: major events concerning the development of local government in Britain

1832    Electoral Reform Act
        and the emergence of liberal values as a governing ideology in Britain.

1834    Poor Law Amendment Act
        Establishes poor law boards, removing powers from individual parishes, setting up *ad-hoc* amalgamations of parishes and also creating a central supervisory Poor Law Board.

1835    Municipal Corporations Act
        Gives larger towns and cities powers to create elected borough councils and thus lays the foundation for the modern system of local government.

1848    Public Health Act
        Creates *ad-hoc* health boards to provide clean water and sewage systems from amalgamations of parish councils.

1870    Education Act
        Establishes requirement for compulsory education for children up to 13 years of age and that school boards are created where no arrangement for administering public education exists.

1871    Creation of the Local Government Board
        The first government department specifically dealing with local government.

1888    Local Government Act
        Creates elected county councils and removes the powers of JPs over county administration.

1894    Local Government Act
        Creates elected urban and rural district councils based on health board areas and effectively transfers most parish duties to larger local government units.

1899    London Boroughs Act
        Restructures boroughs in London, thus completing the modernisation of the local government system in England and Wales initiated in 1834.

1919    Housing Act
        Establishes financial powers to enable local authorities to build large housing estates.

1919    Creation of the Ministry of Health, which takes over the Local Government Board functions.

1929    Abolition of poor law boards of guardians and transfer of their responsibilities to local government.

1935    Creation of centrally controlled National Assistance Board, ending local authority responsibility for alleviation of poverty.

1946    National Health Services Act
        Creates a national health service outside the local government system.

1947    Electricity Act
        Nationalises electricity production and supply and removes this power from local government.

1947    Town and Country Planning Act
        Greatly extends local government role in town and country planning.

1948    Gas Act
        Nationalises and de-municipalises gas production and distribution.

1952    Creation of Ministry of Housing and Local Government.

1960    Herbert Commission Report on local government in London published.

1963    London Government Act
        Creates the Greater London Council, 32 London boroughs, and the Inner London Education Authority to come into force in April 1965.

1996    Redcliffe-Maud and Wheatley Royal Commissions established.

1969    Redcliffe-Maud and Wheatley Royal Commission Reports published and broadly accepted by Wilson Government.

1970    Conservatives win General Election in June and Heath as Prime Minister announces major modifications in plans to restructure local government.

1971    Creation in October of the Department of the Environment, which takes over the powers of the Ministry of Housing and Local Government.

1972    Local Government Act
        Creates new structures for local government in England and Wales which come into force in April 1974 following deliberations of a Boundary Commission to determine the exact arrangements for the new authorities.

1973    Local Government (Scotland) Act
        Restructures local government system for Scotland, to come into force in 1974.

1973    Water Act
        Transfers municipal water and sewage disposal powers to unelected regional water authorities.

1974    Labour wins the General Elections of February and October.

1975    Consultative Council for Local Government Finance created.

1976    Layfield Report on local government finance published.

1978–79    'Winter of discontent', major strikes by municipal workers.

1979    Conservatives win the General Election in May, Mrs Thatcher becomes Prime Minister.

1980    Local Government Planning and Land Act
Establishes new system for local government grants, creates enterprise zones and UDCs, requires direct works departments to compete with private sector for building contracts.

1980    Housing Act
Requires local authorities to sell council houses to tenants.

1982    Local Government Finance Act
Further restuctures grants system, removes local powers to set more than one rate demand in a year and creates the Audit Commission.

1984    Rates Act
Provides the government with powers to cap the rates set by local authorities and thus effectively allows central government to determine local authority expenditure.

1984    Bill published to pave the way for abolition of the metropolitan counties and GLC.

1985    From March until July some local authorities attempt to defy the provisions of the Rates Act but all are unsuccessful.

1985    Local Government Act
Abolishes from April 1986 the metropolitan district councils and GLC, transferring powers respectively to MDCs and London boroughs or unelected agencies.

1985    Local Government Access to Information Act

1986    Transport Act
Deregulates public transport, removing local government powers to subsidise bus services and also allowing competition between bus companies on the same routes.

1986    Local Government Act
Prevents local authorities from publishing material critical of the government.

1987    Widdicombe Report published.

1987    Rates Act (Scotland)
Creates poll tax system to replace the rates for Scotland.

1988    Local Government Act
        Requires local authorities to put many services out to CCT and includes section
        28 banning local government support to homosexual groups.

1988    Housing Act
        Facilitates the sale of council estates to the private sector or their transfer to
        Housing Action Trusts.

1988    Rates Act
        Establishes the poll tax for England and Wales, abolishing the domestic rate,
        and removes local control over rates to businesses with the unified business
        rate.

1988    Education Reform Act
        Allows schools to opt out of local government control, sets up the national cur-
        riculum and creates local self-management for schools.

1989    Local Government and Housing Act
        Further measures to increase council house sales, gives local authorities
        powers to develop their local economies but curtails their capacity to own and
        control businesses.

1990    National Health Service and Community Care Act
        Places responsibility for care in the community to local government.

1990    Mrs Thatcher loses leadership of the Conservative Party in November and is
        succeeded as leader and Prime Minister by John Major.

1991    Further and Higher Education Act
        Removes further education from local authority control.

1991    Consultative documents announced by Michael Heseltine propose a restruc-
        turing of local government to favour a single tier system and directly elected
        mayors.

1992    Local Government Act
        Establishes a Local Government Commission under the chairmanship of Sir
        John Banham to restructure the local government systems of England. The
        Scottish and Welsh Offices conduct parallel studies.

1992    Local Government Finance Act
        Repeals the poll tax and replaces it with the council tax.

1993    Local Education Act
        Establishes a Funding Agency for Schools.

1995    Elections for some of the new unitary authorities created by the Banham
        Commission but also concerns over some proposals and replacement of
        Banham as Chair of Commission.

1996    New unitary and restructured counties following the Banham Commission
        fully established.

1997    Labour Party takes power with Tony Blair as Prime Minister.

1998    White Paper *Modern Local Government: In Touch with the People* published.

1999    Local Government Act
        Creates the Best Value framework for establishing standards for local government service provision and systems to replace CCT in ensuring competition and partnerships between local government and private sector service provision.

2000    Elections and opening of the Greater London Authority.

2000    Local Government Act
        Gives new general powers and duties to local authorities, creates cabinet government and elected mayors or mayor/manager structures, establishes new role for backbench councillors, scrutinising committees and new ethics and standards committees.

2001    Restructuring of Best Value to incorporate Comprehensive Performance Assessment.

2004    Defeat of North East Region referendum.

2006    White Paper, *Strong and Prosperous Communities*.

2007    Local Government and Public Involvement in Health Act
        Proposals to create further unitary authorities.

# References

Ashford, D.E. (1982) *British Dogmatism and French Pragmatism*, London, George Allen and Unwin.

Atkinson, H. and Wilks-Heeg, S. (2000) *Local Government from Thatcher to Blair*, Cambridge, Polity.

Audit Commission (1988) *The Competitive Council*, London, Audit Commission.

Bailey, S.J. (1999) *Local Government Economics: Principles and Practice*, Basingstoke, Macmillan.

Bailey, S. and Paddison, R. (eds) (1988) *The Reform of Local Government Finance in Britain*, London, Routledge.

Bains, M.A. (1972) *The New Local Authorities: Management and Structure*, London, HMSO.

Barker, M. (1982) 'The Relation between Trade Unions and the Labour Party in Sheffield', Department of Political Studies, Sheffield Polytechnic, Sheffield.

Barron, J., Crawley, G. and Wood, T. (1991) *Councillors in Crisis*, Basingstoke, Macmillan.

Batley, R. and Stoker, G. (eds) (1991) *Local Government in Europe: Trends and Developments*, Basingstoke, Macmillan.

Bealey, F., Blondel, J. and McCann, W.P. (1965) *Constituency Politics*, London, Faber and Faber.

Bell, C. and Newby, H. (1971) *Community Studies*, London, George Allen and Unwin.

Bell, D. (1960) *The End of Ideology*, Glencoe, The Free Press.

Ben-Tovim, G., Gabriel, J., Law, I. and Streddet, K. (1986) *The Local Politics of Race*, London, Macmillan.

Beresford, P. (1987) *Good Council Guide: Wandsworth 1978–1987*, London, Centre for Policy Studies.

Birch, A.H. (1959) *Small Town Politics: A Study of Political Life in Glossop*, Oxford, Oxford University Press.

Blunkett, D. and Jackson, K. (1987) *Democracy in Crisis*, London, Hogarth Press.

Boaden, N. (1971) *Urban Policy-Making*, Cambridge, Cambridge University Press.

Boddy, M. and Fudge, C. (eds) (1984) *Local Socialism?*, Basingstoke, Macmillan.

Bogdanor, V. (1999) *Devolution in the United Kingdom*, Oxford, Oxford University Press.

Bowman, M. and Hampton, W.A. (1983) *Local Democracies*, Melbourne, Longman.

Boyne, G.A. (1998) *Public Choice Theory and Local Government: A Comparative Analysis of the UK and the USA*, Basingstoke, Macmillan.

Bradford, M. (1988) *The Fight for Yorkshire*, Beverley, Hutton Press.

Branson, N. (1979) *Poplarism 1919–1925*, London, Lawrence and Wishart.

Brooks, J. (2000) 'Labour's Modernisation of Local Government', *Public Administration*, 78, 3.

Bulpitt, J.G. (1967) *Party Politics in English Local Government*, London, Longman.

Bulpitt, J.G. (1983) *Territory and Power in the United Kingdom*, Manchester, Manchester University Press.

Burns, D., Hambleton, R. and Hoggett, P. (1994) *The Politics of Decentralisation*, Basingstoke, Macmillan.

Butler, D., Adonis, A. and Travers, T. (1995) *Failure in British Government: The Politics of the Poll Tax*, Oxford, Oxford University Press.

Byrne, T. (1992) *Local Government in Britain*, 5th edn, Harmondsworth, Penguin.

Campbell, M. (ed.) (1990) *Local Economic Policy*, London, Cassell.

Castells, M. (1977) *The Urban Question*, London, Edward Arnold.

Chandler, J.A. (1988) *Public Policy Making for Local Government*, London, Croom Helm.

Chandler, J.A. (1992) 'Three Faces of Intergovernmental Relations', *Public Policy and Administration*, 7, 47–57.

Chandler, J.A. (ed.) (1993) *Local Government in Liberal Democracies*, London, Routledge.

Chandler, J.A. (ed.) (1996) *The Citizen's Charter*, Aldershot, Dartmouth.

Chandler, J.A. (1998) 'Regenerating South Yorkshire: How the Public Sector Dominates Business Partnerships in Britain', in Walzer, N. and Jacobs, B.D. (eds) *Public Private Partnerships for Local Economic Development*, Westport, Conn, Praeger.

Chandler, J.A. (2005) 'Comparative Inter-governmental Relations: Models that Need to Travel', *Local Government Studies*, 31, 3, 269–84.

Chandler, J.A. (2007) *Explaining Local Government, Local Government in Britain since 1800*, Manchester, Manchester University Press.

Chandler, J.A. (2008) 'Liberal Justifications for Local Government in Britain: The Triumph of Expediency over Ethics' *Political Studies*, 56, 2, June.

Chandler, J.A. and Kingdom, J.E. (1999) 'MPs and Local Government: The Case of Sheffield', presented to the Political Studies Association Annual Conference, University of Nottingham.

Chandler, J.A. and Lawless, P. (1985) *Local Authorities and the Creation of Employment*, Aldershot, Gower.

Chandler, J.A. and Turner, R. (1997), 'Pricing and Local Authorities', *Public Money and Management*, 17 (2), April–June, 37–43.

Chandler, J.A. and Morris, D. (1984) 'The Selection of Local Candidates', in Bristow, S., Kermode, D. and Manmin, M. (eds) *Redundant Counties*, Ormskisk, Hesketh Press.

Chandler, J.A., Gregory, M., Hunt, M. and Turner, R. (1995) *Decentralisation and Devolution in England and Wales*, Luton, Local Government Management Board.

Churchill, H. (2007) 'Children's Services in 2006', in Clarke, K., Maltby, T. and Kennett, P. (eds) *Social Policy Review 19, Analysis and Debate in Social Policy, 2007*, Bristol, Policy Press.

Clarke, M. and Stewart, J. (1990) *General Management in Local Government: Getting the Balance Right*, Harlow, Longman.

Clements, R.V. (1969) *Local Noteables and the City Councils*, London, Macmillan.

Cockburn, C. (1977) *The Local State*, London, Pluto Press.

Cole, A. (2006) *Beyond Devolution and Decentralisation: Building Regional Capacity in Wales and Brittany*, Manchester, Manchester University Press.

Cole, G.D.H. (1947) *Local and Regional Government*, London, Cassell.

Copus, C. (2004) *Leading the Localities*, Manchester, Manchester University Press.

Copus, C. (2006) *Party Politics and Local Government*, Manchester, Manchester University Press.

Crick, M. (1986) *The March of Militant*, London, Faber and Faber.

Crosland, S. (1982) *Tony Crosland*, London, Jonathan Cape.

Crossman, R.H.S. (1975) *The Diaries of a Cabinet Minister*, Vol. I, London, Hamish Hamilton and Jonathan Cape.

Cyr, A. (1977) *Liberal Party Politics in Britain*, London, John Calder.

Dahl, R.A. (1961) *Who Governs?*, New Haven, Yale University Press.

Dahl, R.A. (1971) *Polyarchy*, New Haven, Yale University Press.

Davies, S. and Morley, B. (2006) *County Borough Elections in England and Wales, 1919–1938*, Vol. 3: *Chester–East Ham*, Aldershot, Ashgate.

Dearlove, J. (1973) *The Politics and Policy of Local Government*, Cambridge, Cambridge University Press.

DETR (2000a) *The Single Regeneration Budget*, London, HMSO, www.regeneration. detr.gov.uk.

DETR (2000b) *Modernising Local Government Finance: A Green Paper*, London, HMSO, www.local.detr.gov.uk/greenpap.

Dod's (yearly serial) *Dod's Parliamentary Companion*, London, Dod's Parliamentary Companion Ltd.

Donoghue, B. and Jones, G.W. (1973) *Herbert Morrison*, London, Weidenfeld and Nicolson.

Doogan, K. (1999) 'The Contracting Out of Local Government Services: Its Impact on Jobs, Conditions of Service and Labour', in Stoker, G. (ed.) *The New Management of British Local Governance*, Basingstoke, Macmillan.

Duncan, S. and Goodwin, M. (1988) *The State and Uneven Development*, Oxford, Polity Press.

Dunleavy, P. (1980) *Urban Political Analysis*, London, Macmillan.

Dunleavy, P. (1981) *The Politics of Mass Housing in Britain 1945–1975*, Oxford, Clarendon Press.

Dunleavy, P. (1984) 'The Limits to Local Government', in Boddy, M. and Fudge, C. (eds), *Local Socialism?*, Basingstoke, Macmillan.

Dunleavy, P. (1991) *Democracy, Bureaucracy and Public Choice*, Hemel Hempstead, Harvester Wheatsheaf.

Dye, T. (2000) *Politics in States and Communities*, 10th edn, New York, Prentice Hall.

Elcock, H. (1991) *Local Government*, 2nd edn, London, Methuen.

Elcock, H. and Jordan, G. (1987) *Learning from Local Authority Budgeting*, Aldershot, Avebury.

Elcock, H., Jordan, G. and Midwinter, A. (1989) *Budgeting in Local Government*, London, Longman.

Fenwick, J. (1995) *Managing Local Government*, London, Chapman and Hall.

Fergusson, M. (2005) 'Local E Government in the UK', in Drüke, H. (ed.) *Local Electronic Government: A Comparative Study*, London, Routledge.

Fraser, D. (1979) *Power and Authority in the Victorian City*, Oxford, Basil Blackwell.

Goss, S. (1988) *Local Labour and Local Government*, Edinburgh, Edinburgh University Press.

Goss, S. (2001) *Making Local Governance Work: Networks, Relationships and the Management of Change*, Basingstoke, Palgrave.

Grant, W. (1977) *Independent Local Politics in England and Wales*, Farnborough, Saxon House.

Green, D.G. (1981) *Power and Party in an English City*, London, George Allen and Unwin.

Greenwood, J., Pyper, R. and Wilson, D. (2002) *New Public Administration in Britain*, 3rd edn, London, Routledge.

Greenwood, R. and Stewart, J.D. (1974) *Corporate Planning in Local Government*, London, Charles Knight.

Greenwood, R., Walsh, K., Hinings, C.R. and Ransom, C. (1980) *Patterns of Management in Local Government*, Oxford, Martin Robertson.

Griffith, J.A.G. (1966) *Central Departments and Local Authorities*, London, George Allen and Unwin.

Gustafsson, A. (1988) *Local Government in Sweden*, 2nd edn, Stockholm, The Swedish Institute.

Gyford, J. (1985) *The Politics of Local Socialism*, London, Allen and Unwin.

Gyford, J. and James, M. (1983) *National Parties and Local Politics*, London, George Allen and Unwin.

Hain, P. (ed.) (1976) *Communities in Conflict*, London, John Calder.

Hall, D. and Leach, S. (2000) 'The Changing Nature of Local Labour Parties', in Stoker, G. (ed.) *The New Politics of English Local Governance*, Basingstoke, Macmillan.

Hambleton, R., Savitch, H. and Stewart, M. (eds) (2003) *Globalism and Local Democracy: Challenge and Change in Europe and North America*, Basingstoke, Palgrave.

Hampton, W.A. (1970) *Democracy and Community*, Oxford, Oxford University Press.

Hampton, W.A. (1987) *Local Government and Urban Politics*, 2nd edn, Harlow, Longman.

Hardill, I. (ed.) (2006) *The Rise of the English Regions?*, London, Routledge.

Harloe, M., Pickvance, C. and Urry, J. (eds) (1990) *Place, Policy and Politics*, London, Unwin, Hyman.

Hennessy, P. (1989) *Whitehall*, London, Secker and Warburg.

Henney, A. (1984) *Inside Local Government*, London, Sinclair Browne.

Hepworth, N. (1984) *The Finance of Local Government*, 7th edn, London, George Allen and Unwin.

Herbert, E. (1960) *Royal Commission on Local Government in Greater London*, London, HMSO.

Hill, D. (1974) *Democratic Theory and Local Government*, London, George Allen and Unwin.

Hindess, B. (1971) *The Decline of Working Class Politics*, London, McGibbon Kee.

Hoggett, P. and Hambleton, R. (eds) (1988) *Decentralisation and Democracy*, Bristol, School for Advanced Urban Studies, Bristol University.

Hogwood, B. and Lindley, P.D. (1982) 'Variations in Regional Boundaries', in Hogwood, B. and Keating, M. (eds) *Regional Government in England*, Oxford, Clarendon Press.

Holliday, I. (2000) 'The Conservative Party in Local Government 1979–1997', in Stoker, G.(ed.) *The New Politics of English Local Governance*, Basingstoke, Macmillan.

Hollis, G., et al. (1990) *Alternatives to the Community Charge*, York, Joseph Rowntree Trust and Coopers Lybrand.

Hood, C. (1991) 'A Public Management for All Seasons?', *Public Administration*, 69, 3–19.

Hopkins, P.M. (2007) 'An Assessment of the Impact of Majority Political Groups on Overview and Scrutiny in Local Government', PhD thesis, University of Northumbria.

Hunt, M. (2006) 'Local Government and Access to Information', in Chapman, R. and Hunt, M. (eds) *Open Government in a Theoretical and Practical Context*, Aldershot, Ashgate.

IDeA (2006) *National Census of Local Authority Councillors 2006*, London, IDeA.

John, P. (1989) *Introduction to the Community Charge in Scotland*, London, Policy Studies Institute.

Jones, B. (1995) *Local Government Financial Management*, Hemel Hempstead, ICSA Publishing.

Jones, G. and Stewart, J. (1983) *The Case for Local Government*, London, George Allen and Unwin.

Jones, K. (2003) *Education in Britain: 1944 to Present*, Cambridge, Polity.

Keith-Lucas, B. and Richards, P.G. (1978) *A History of Local Government in the Twentieth Century*, London, George Allen and Unwin.

Kellas, J.G. (1968) *Modern Scotland*, London, Pall Mall.

Kerley, R. (1994) *Managing in Local Government*, Basingstoke, Macmillan.

King, D. (1987) *The New Right*, Basingstoke, Macmillan.

King, D. and Stoker, G. (eds) (1996) *Rethinking Local Democracy*, Basingstoke, Macmillan.

Kingdom, J.E. (1991) *Local Government and Politics in Britain*, Hemel Hempstead, Philip Allen.

Kingdom, J.E. (2003) *Government and Politics in Britain*, 3rd edn, Cambridge, Polity Press.

Labour Party (1997) *Manifesto; Because Britain Deserves Better*, London, The Labour Party.

Laffin, M. (1986) *Professionalism and Policy: The Role of the Professionals in the Central–Local Relationship*, Aldershot, Gower.

Laffin, M. (1989) *Managing under Pressure: Industrial Relations in Local Government*, London, Macmillan.

Laffin, M. and Young, K. (1990) *Professionalism in Local Government*, Harlow, Longman.

Lagroye, J. and Wright, V. (eds) (1979) *Local Government in Britain and France*, London, George Allen and Unwin.

Lansley, S., Goss, S. and Wolmar, C. (1989) *Councils in Conflict: The Rise and Fall of the Municipal Left*, Basingstoke, Macmillan.

Laski, H.J. (1934) *A Grammar of Politics*, 3rd edn, London, Allen and Unwin.

Layfield, F. (1976) *Report of the Committee of Enquiry into Local Government Finance*, Cmnd. 6453, London, HMSO.

Leach, R. and Percy-Smith, P. (2001) *Local Governance in Britain*, Basingstoke, Macmillan, Palgrave.

Leach, S. (1998) *Local Government Reorganisation: The Review and its Aftermath*, London, Frank Cass.

Leach, S. (2006) *The Changing Role of Local Politics in Britain*, Bristol, Policy Press.

Leach, S. and Copus, C. (2004) 'Scrutiny and the Political Party Group in UK Local Government' *Public Administration*, 82, 2, 331–54.

Leach, S. and Stewart, J. (1985) 'The Politics and Management of Hung Authorities', *Public Administration*, 66, 1, 35–56.

Leach, S. and Stewart, J. (1992) *The Politics of Hung Authorities*, London, Macmillan.

Leach, S., Stewart, J. and Walsh, K. (1994) *The Changing Organisation and Management of Local Government*, London, Macmillan.

Lee, J.M. (1963) *Social Leaders and Public Persons*, Oxford, Oxford University Press.

Llewellyn, A. (ed.) (1999) *The Guardian Local Authority Directory*, London, Alcourt Publishing.

Local Government Chronicle Election Centre (Various years) University of Plymouth, www.plymouth.ac.uk/elections.

Loughlin, J. (ed.) (1999) *Regional and Local Democracy in the European Union*, Luxembourg, Office for Official Publications of the European Union.

Lowndes, V. (1999) 'Management Change In Local Governance', in Stoker, G. (ed.) *The New Management of British Local Governance*, Basingstoke, Macmillan.

Lynch, P. (2001) *Scottish Government and Politics*, Edinburgh, Edinburgh University Press.

Lyons, M. (2007) *Lyons Inquiry into Local Government*, London, HMSO.

Machin, H. (1977) *The Prefect in French Public Administration*, London, Croom Helm.

Mallaby, G. (1967) *Report of the Committee on the Staffing of Local Government*, London, HMSO.

Maloney, W., Smith, G. and Stoker, G. (2000) 'Social Capital and Urban Governance: Adding a More Constitutional Top Down Perspective', *Political Studies*, 48, 4, 802–20.

Malpass, P. (2000), *Housing Associations and Housing Policy: A Historical Perspective*, Basingstoke, Macmillan.

McConnell, A. (2004) *Scottish Local Government*, Edinburgh, Edinburgh University Press.

McKenzie, R.T. (1963) *British Political Parties*, 2nd edn, London, Mercury Books.

Midwinter, A. (1984) *The Politics of Local Spending*, Edinburgh, Mainstream.

Mill, J.S. (1975) 'Considerations on Representative Government', in *Three Essays* ed. R. Wollheim, Oxford, Oxford University Press.

Miller, W.L., Dickson, M. and Stoker, G. (2000) *Models of Local Governance: Political Opinion and Theory in Britain*, Basingstoke, Palgrave.

Moore, C. and Richardson, J.J. (1989) *Local Partnership and the Unemployment Crisis in Britain*, London, Unwin Hyman.

Municipal Year Book (Annual Serial 1994–2007) *The Municipal Year Book*, London, The Municipal Journal Ltd.

Newton, K. (1976) *Second City Politics*, Oxford, Oxford University Press.

Newton, K. and Karran, T.J. (1985) *The Politics of Local Expenditure*, London, Macmillan.

Niskanen, W.A. (1973a) *Bureaucracy and Representative Government*, New York, Aldine-Atherton.

Niskanen, W.A. (1973b) *Bureaucracy: Servant or Master?*, London, Institute for Economic Affairs.

Norton, A. (1991) *The Role of the Chief Executive in British Local Government*, Birmingham, Institute of Local Government Studies.

Osborne, D. and Gaebler, T. (1992) *Reinventing Government*, Reading, Mass, Addison-Wesley.

Page, E.C. and Goldsmith, M.J. (eds) (1987) *Central and Local Government Relations: A Comparative Analysis of West European States*, London, Sage.

Parker, S. (2003) 'A Step in the Right Direction', *The Guardian: Society Guardian*, 12 March.

Parrott, L. (1999) *Social Work and Social Care*, Eastbourne, Gildredge Press.

Perri 6, Leat, D., Seltzer, K. and Stoker, G. (2002) *Towards Holistic Governance*, Basingstoke, Palgrave.

Phillips, A. (1994) *Local Democracy: The Terms of the Debate*, London, Commission for Local Democracy.

Pilkington, C. (2002) *Devolution in Britain Today*, Manchester, Manchester University Press.

Pimlott, B. (1985) *Hugh Dalton*, London, Jonathan Cape.

Plant, R. (1974) *Community and Ideology*, London, Routledge and Kegan Paul.

Poole, K.P. (1978) *The Local Government Service in England and Wales*, London, George Allen and Unwin.

Pratchett, L. and Wilson, D. (eds) (1996) *Local Government and Local Democracy*, Basingstoke, Macmillan.

Prior, D. (1995) 'Citizen's Charters', in Stewart, J. and Stoker, G. (eds) *Local Government in the 1990s*, Basingstoke, Macmillan.

Rallings, C. and Thrasher, M. (1994) *Local Elections in England and Wales*, Plymouth, Local Government Chronicle Elections Centre.

Rallings, C. and Thrasher, M. (1996) *Participation in Local Election*, in Pratchett, L. and Wilson, D. (eds) *Local Government and Local Democracy*, Basingstoke, Macmillan.

Rallings, C. and Thrasher, M. (2000) *Local Elections Handbook*, Plymouth, Local Government Chronicle Elections Centre University of Plymouth.

Rawlinson, D. and Tanner, B. (1990) *Financial Management in the 1990s*, Harlow, Longman.

Redcliffe-Maud, J. (1969) *Royal Commission on Local Government in England 1966–1969*, Cmnd. 4040, Vol. I and Vol. III, London, HMSO.

Redlich, J. and Hirst, F.W. (1970) *The History of Local Government in England*, 2nd edn, Keith-Lucas, B., London, Macmillan.

Regan, D.E. (1977) *Local Government and Education*, London, George Allen and Unwin.

Rhodes, R.A.W. (1981) *Control and Power in Central–Local Government*, Farnborough, Gower.

Rhodes, R.A.W. (1986a) *The National World of Local Government*, London, Allen and Unwin.

Rhodes, R.A.W. (1986b) 'Power Dependence: Theories of Central–Local Relations: A Critical Assessment', in Goldsmith, M. (ed.) *New Research in Central–Local Relations*, Farnborough, Gower.

Rhodes, R.A.W. (1988) *Beyond Westminster and Whitehall*, London, Allen and Unwin.

Rhodes, R.A.W. (1991) 'Theory and Methods in British Public Administration: The View from Political Science', *Political Studies*, 39, 3, 533–54.

Rhodes, R.A.W. (1999) *Control and Power in Central–Local Government Relations*, 2nd edn, Aldershot, Ashgate.

Rhodes, R.A.W. and Marsh, D. (1992) 'Policy Networks in British Politics: A Critique of Existing Approaches', in Marsh, D. and Rhodes, R.A.W. (eds) *Policy Networks in British Politics*, Oxford, Oxford University Press.

Ridley, N. (1988) *The Local Right: Enabling not Providing*, London, Centre for Policy Studies.

Robson, W.A. (1954) *The Development of Local Government*, 3rd edn, London, George Allen and Unwin.

Salmon, C.B. (1976) *Royal Commission on Standards in Public Life*, Cmnd. 6524, London, HMSO.

Sandford, M. (2005) *The New Governance of the English Regions*, Basingstoke, Palgrave.

Saunders, P. (1979) *Urban Politics: A Sociological Interpretation*, London, Hutchinson.

Saunders, P. (1981) *Social Theory and the Urban Question*, London, Hutchinson.

Saunders, P. (1984) 'Rethinking Local Politics', in Boddy, M. and Fudge C. (eds), *Local Socialism?*, London, Macmillan.

Seebohm, F. (Chair) (1968) *Report of the Committee on Local Authority and Allied Personal Services*, Cmnd. 3703, London, HMSO.

Sharpe, L.J. (1970) 'Theories and Values in Local Government', *Political Studies*, 18, 2, 153–74.

Sharpe, L.J. and Newton, K. (1984) *Does Politics Matter?*, Oxford, Oxford University Press.

Sheldrake, J. (1992) *Modern Local Government*, Aldershot, Dartmouth.

Smitham, K. (1991) 'The New Urban Right: A Study of Bradford City Council 1988–1990', BA Public Administration, Sheffield, Sheffield City Polytechnic.

Snape, S. (2004) 'Liberated or Lost Souls: Is there a Role for Non-Executive Councillors?', in Stoker, G. and Wilson, D. (eds) *British Local Government into the 21st Century*, Basingstoke, Palgrave.

Stanyer, J. (1976) *Understanding Local Government*, Oxford, Martin Robertson.

Stewart, J. (1971) *Management in Local Government*, London, Charles Knight.

Stewart, J. (1974) *The Responsive Local Authority*, London, Charles Knight.

Stewart, J. (1986) *The New Management of Local Government*, London, Allen and Unwin.

Stewart, J. (2000) *The Nature of British Local Government*, Basingstoke, Macmillan.

Stewart, J. (2003) *Modernising British Local Government*, Basingstoke, Palgrave, Macmillan.

Stoker, G. (1991) *The Politics of Local Government*, 2nd edn, Basingstoke, Macmillan.

Stoker, G. (1994) *The Role and Purpose of Local Government*, London, Commission for Local Democracy.

Stoker, G. (1995) 'Intergovernmental Relations', *Public Administration*, 73, 101–22.

Stoker, G. (ed.) (1999) *The New Management of British Local Governance*, Basingstoke, Macmillan.

Stoker, G. (ed.) (2000) *The New Politics of English Local Governance*, Basingstoke, Macmillan.

Stoker, G. (2004) *Transforming Local Governance: From Thatcherism to New Labour*, Basingstoke, Palgrave.

Stoker, G. and Wilson, D. (eds) (2004) *British Local Government into the 21st Century*, Basingstoke, Palgrave.

Stone, C. (1989) *Regime Politics: Governing Atlanta*, Lawrence, University of Kansas Press.

Sullivan, H. and Skeltcher, C. (2002) *Working Across Boundaries: Collaboration in Public Services*, Basingstoke, Palgrave.

Taaffe, P. and Mulhearn, T. (1988) *Liverpool: A City that Dared to Fight*, London, Fortress.

Thomas, R. (1978) *The British Philosophy of Administration*, London, Longman.

Toqueville de, A. (1946) *Democracy in America*, tr. Henry Reeve, ed. H.S. Commager, Oxford, Oxford University Press.

Travers, T. (1986) *The Politics of Local Government Finance*, London, George Allen and Unwin.

Travers, T. (1995) 'Finance', in Stewart, J. and Stoker, G. (eds) *Local Government in the 1990s*, Basingstoke, Macmillan.

Travers, T. (2004) *The Politics of London*, Basingstoke, Macmillan.

Tullock, G. (1975) *The Vote Motive*, London, Institute for Economic Affairs.

Walker, D. (1983) *Municipal Empire: The Town Halls and their Beneficiaries*, London, Temple-Smith.

Walsh, K. (1995) *Public Services and Market Mechanisms*, Basingstoke, Macmillan.

Webb, S. and Webb, B. (1920) *A Constitution for the Socialist Commonwealth of Great Britain*, Cambridge, Cambridge University Press.

Widdicombe, D. (1986) *The Conduct of Local Authority Business*, Cmnd. 9797, London, HMSO.

Williams, P. (1979) *Hugh Gaitskell*, London, Jonathan Cape.

Wilson, D. and Game, C. (2006) *Local Government in the United Kingdom*, 4th edn, Basingstoke, Macmillan.

Wollmann, H. and Schröter, E. (2000) *Comparing Public Sector Reform in Britain and Germany*, Aldershot, Ashgate.

Wood, B. (1976) *The Process of Local Government Reform 1966–1974*, London, George Allen and Unwin.

Young, K. and Rao, N. (1997) *Local Government since 1945*, Oxford, Blackwell.

# Index